THE ACQUISITION OF LANGUAGE

THE ACQUISITION OF LANGUAGE
The Study of Developmental Psycholinguistics

DAVID McNEILL
University of Chicago

HARPER & ROW, PUBLISHERS
NEW YORK, EVANSTON, AND LONDON

For Nobuko

CONTENTS

PREFACE

The problem of writing a book about the acquisition of language is somewhat like the problem of reconstructing a dinosaur while the bones are still being excavated. It can happen that after you have connected what you earnestly believe are the hind legs you find that they are jaw bones; the equivalent of this has taken place several times during the course of my writing. Rather than start over, I have decided that a third or fourth hind leg would not look too absurd. More serious than the difficulty of incorporating new findings of fact is the problem of incorporating new developments in theory. I am thinking especially of the work of Fillmore (1968) and others on the semantic basis of syntax. Revisions at this level correspond to being told that the bones do not make a dinosaur, but a whale instead. Inasmuch as the linguistic issues are themselves unsettled (cf. Chomsky, 1967), and especially inasmuch as the implications of these issues are still unknown for language acquisition, I have not attempted to treat them.

In writing I have made no distinction between beginners at the study of developmental psycholinguistics and practitioners of it. In a deep sense there is no distinction, and I hope the book will be useful to both types of readers. One possible basis for confusion lies in the relation of my past work to the present study. I have made no consistent effort to point out changes in point of view, of which there have been several, assuming that student readers have no need to be distracted by such details and colleague readers will notice such changes whether I point them out or not, in no case does it strike me as particularly important to make these convolutions obvious.

The organization of the book is rational rather than didactic, by which I mean that the order of chapters and the flow of discussion within each mounts to form a particular argument. This argument is outlined in Chapter 1. While such an approach gives a book a certain coherence it would not otherwise have, it also means that the book must be read more or less in sequence for this coherence to become apparent. Some readers will not care to do that. To such readers I urge that facts are not necessarily what they seem and that the context in which facts appear is important; the entire argument should be read. Nonetheless there is a table of contents, and of course an index.

The book was written during 1968 and 1969 while I was a visitor at the Center for Cognitive Studies at Harvard University, and its roots go back to an earlier visit there in 1964 and 1965. It was then that my interest in the topic of language acquisition was aroused by first-hand contact with the work of R. Brown and his students. No one remains at the Center for Cognitive Studies without experiencing its extraordinary atmosphere of stimulation and challenge. A number of discussions with J. S. Bruner and R. Jakobson in particular have left their mark.

I have benefited from the comments of various people who have kindly read parts of the manuscript: U. Bellugi of the Salk Institute, K. Kelley of the University of California at Los Angeles, and D. Slobin of the University of California at Berkeley. T. G. Bever of Columbia University read the entire manuscript, making a number of excellent suggestions as to exposition, many of which I have incorporated.

Mrs. M. Kimball of the University of Michigan was helpful in the preparation of bibliographic information and Mr. J. W. MacDonald of Harvard University was helpful on phonological matters. Mrs. B. Gardner at Harvard drew most of the figures, including the difficult spectrographic tracings in Chapter 4. The rendition of scrabbled manuscript into neat typescript, a process repeated innumerable times, was the labor of Mrs. M. Atamian; Mrs. C. McLey prepared the final draft for the publisher.

Most crucial for this book, but most difficult to acknowledge because their contributions are not the kind that fall into lists, have been my wife and daughter; they accorded the writing of this book an importance that I can only hope, in the end, it at least half possesses.

D. M.

University of Chicago
February, 1970

1

INTRODUCTION

Every book should have a theme. In the present case it is the concept of a sentence. How do sentences develop in the language of children and how do they influence the course of language acquisition? My purpose is to integrate a quantity of material. It so happens that the concept of a sentence provides a point around which much else in language acquisition revolves. Such "sentence-centrism" is in part a historical accident—a renewed interest in child language has coincided with the development of transformational generative grammar. The emphasis in transformational grammar on sentence structure inevitably has influenced the psychological investigation of children.

But there is a second and deeper reason why the concept of a sentence should occupy a central place. Not only do children acquire knowledge of sentence structure—itself an important fact—but virtually everything that occurs in language acquisition depends on *prior* knowledge of the basic aspects of sentence structure. The concept of a sentence may be part of man's innate mental capacity. The argument of the book is designed to justify this assertion.

In brief, the argument is as follows. The facts of language acquisition could not be as they are unless the concept of a sentence is available to children at the start of their learning. The concept of a sentence is the main guiding principle in a child's attempt to organize and interpret the linguistic evidence that fluent speakers make available to him. What outside observers see as distorted or "telegraphic" speech is actually a consistent effort by a child to discover how a more or less fixed concept of a sentence is expressed in the language to which he has, by accident, been exposed.

This effort can be viewed as a succession of hypotheses that a child adopts concerning the form sentences take in the language around him. Children everywhere begin with exactly the same initial hypothesis: sentences consist of single words. The entire structure of a sentence must be squeezed through this tiny space. This simplest of hypotheses leads to the most peripheral of differences between children learning different languages. Only the words differ. A child exposed to English might use *hot* as a comment and a Japanese child would use *atsui,* but the difference is merely in sound, not in conceptual or linguistic structure. Not only are words sentences at the beginning, they are the same sentences in different languages.

As a child adopts additional linguistic hypotheses, and thus enlarges

2

the space through which the structure of a sentence passes, more important differences appear between languages. There is a natural order in the emergence of grammar which depends on the scope of the rules being learned. The most comprehensive rules paradoxically require the least time and experience with language, and therefore appear in development first. The striking fact, central to language acquisition, is that these rules of wide scope within each language are also shared by different languages. My assumption is that they are linguistic universals and are a result of children's capacities for language. It is for this reason that they appear early in development, and are the same regardless of the language being acquired.

In many ways the acquisition of a language resembles the formation of a percept. In both language acquisition and perception there is a preliminary analytic phase, during which general properties are worked out, followed by a constructive phase, during which details are elaborated. For language, the first phase results in deep structure and the second in transformational structure. Perhaps the structure of a language is perceived through a process not fundamentally different from the perception of a line drawing, with the exception that perceiving a language takes over 300 million times longer — two or three years compared to two or three deciseconds. The analogy with perception is not pursued in this book. If there is anything to it, our thinking about language acquisition (not to mention perception) will have to be changed in basic ways.

The book is organized around the argument summarized above. After a chapter on methodological problems, I describe in Chapter 3 the structures that appear in child speech; such structures suggest biological preparation. The fourth chapter places child language in the context of animal communication and considers the evolution of linguistic capacity. Chapter 5 contains the major theoretical arguments of the book; it explains the facts of development presented in Chapter 3 and can be regarded as a further description, in linguistic and psychological terms, of the biological specialization discussed in Chapter 4. The sixth chapter, on transformations, extends this argument from the universal aspects of language to the idiosyncratic aspects. The acquisition of transformations raises the question of linguistic experience; the seventh chapter is a symptomatically brief discussion of that question. Chapter 8 includes a variety of topics loosely connected with semantic development, and the final chapter treats sound development. At the end of the book is a Linguistic Appendix that contains an introduction to the main ideas of transformational generative grammar; it assumes no prior knowledge of the subject and covers the points that are essential to the disucssion of language acquisition. Readers unfamiliar with transformational grammar are urged to pass over the book and begin with this Appendix. Others may want to refer to it from time to time.

2

**METHODOLOGY AND
METHODOLOGICAL ISSUES**

There is little in the study of language acquisition that can be called Methodology, with a capital "M." The very speed of linguistic development constrains the methods used in studying it. Massive changes in the grammatical status of children take place between one-and-a-half and three years. The age at which studies can be conducted is thereby fixed, and it is no one's fault that this is an age for which there is, in general, no well-developed methodology. In such circumstances, the simplest methods — e.g., turning on a tape recorder — are as good as any, and the bulk of recent observations has been collected in this way.

Studies of the development of syntax can be organized in terms of three contrasting strategies.

1. Observers have examined either the production or comprehension of speech.

2. They have attempted to trace either general linguistic advancement or the emergence of particular grammatical systems.

3. They either have conducted experimental studies or made observations of spontaneous linguistic behavior.

Of the eight possible categories of methods formed in this way, only four have been used at all, and most studies have used just two. There have been no studies, for example, of general comprehension. Most have worked with spontaneous linguistic production, following either the development of general linguistic competence or of particular linguistic systems. Certain strategies naturally go together — comprehension, for example, has almost always been studied experimentally. There has been one study, Sinclair-de Zwart (1967), relating linguistic development to intellectual development — which is, perhaps, a fourth strategy, as well as a substantive issue.

Rather than make a list of existing research methods, a list that may change tomorrow, it seems more profitable to discuss those broader categories of research that present certain methodological issues. Of these, there are two.

General vs. Particular Description
The richest details and the deepest insights so far have come from longitudinal collections of speech samples. Such studies have followed

general linguistic development as well as the emergence of particular grammatical systems. Very often the same project lends itself to both strategies, so their proper relationship must be understood. But first a word on the studies themselves.

Almost without exception, observational studies have been engaged with the production and not the comprehension of speech. All are descendants of the early diary studies conducted by linguists who found themselves to be new parents (Stern and Stern, 1907; Leopold, 1939, 1947, 1949a, 1949b). Contemporary longitudinal studies differ from the earlier works mainly in using other people's children and in making tape-recorded protocols. Weir (1962), Braine (1963a), Brown and Bellugi (1964), Miller and Ervin (1964), McNeill (1966b), Gruber (1967), and Bloom (1968) have all contributed in varying amounts to this literature.

Typically, a small group of children is visited at home once or twice a month, and everything the child says, and everything said to him, is tape recorded. The recordings are usually supplemented by running commentaries on the general situation in which the speech was uttered. The ultimate step in such extra-linguistic record-keeping is the placing of everything on film or TV tape, a step taken by Bullowa, Jones, and Bever (1964). Bloom (1968) was able to make exceptionally detailed on-the-spot commentaries without the use of video recording. The customary interval between visits has been two to four weeks, but longer intervals are possible; Bloom dropped by every six weeks, for example.

The sole reason for these visits is to collect a sizeable corpus of spontaneous utterances from a child. The significant part of the study lies in the analyses made of this corpus. For many purposes it does not matter if one accumulates a child's speech over several samples and combines it into a larger corpus, or collects a larger corpus at less frequent intervals and performs an analysis of it. It is in the analysis of the corpus that the two strategies – general or particular description – differ; the decision to conduct one or the other analysis rests in part on certain methodological issues.

In a general description one tries to write a grammar that covers a child's complete corpus. The hope is to capture his total linguistic system at the time the corpus is collected, without distortion from adult grammar. It is often done by performing a distributional analysis of the child's speech. The procedure followed is clearly described in Brown and Fraser (1964); Braine (1963a) also provides some helpful comments. In a distributional analysis an investigator searches for words that appear in the same contexts, the assumption being that such words are members of the same grammatical class in the child's grammatical system. Words with different privileges of occurrence are assumed to belong to different grammatical classes.

Suppose, for example, that a corpus collected from a 2-year-old includes the following utterances:

7

My cap
that cap
a shoe
that horsie
other dog
a daddy
big shoe
red sweater

One could conclude that the words on the left all belong to a single grammatical class, that the words on the right all belong to a different grammatical class, and that the child's grammar at this point considers a "sentence" to be any word from the first class followed by any word from the second class. The wisdom of these conclusions will be called into question below.

Words are placed into the same categories in a distributional analysis when there are no systematic differences in their usage relative to other words — they then have identical privileges of occurrence. *My* and *that* belong together because they both appear with *cap. Horsie* and *cap* go together because they both follow *that. Cap* and *shoe* are semantically similar, or so one assumes, so words that they follow — *my, that, a,* and *big* — are placed together in the first class, and words that in turn follow these words — *cap, shoe, horsie,* and *daddy* — go together into the second class. *Other* can be added to the first class because of the similarity of *horsie* and *dog,* as can *red* because of the similarity of *sweater, cap,* and *shoe.*

As these examples make clear, the independence of distributional analysis from the analyst's own knowledge of language is limited. A distributional analysis does not insist on the co-occurrence of words in completely identical contexts — such co-occurrences are too few in number — but also counts as co-occurrence appearances in the context of "meaningfully related" words. Moreover, one assumes that non-occurring combinations — for example, *that sweater* or *big daddy* — are allowed by the child's grammar but are not observed because of sampling limitations.

Having established what seem to be a child's grammatical classes, the rules of grammar are written so as to describe the manner in which classes are combined — in this case, Class 1 + Class 2. More complex categories demand more complex rules, but the rules always summarize the patterns of categories observed in a child's corpus. Studies that have prepared distributional analyses in this manner are Braine (1963a), Brown and Fraser (1964), and Miller and Ervin (1964).

An important methodological question is raised by such investigations. One combines individual utterances (*my cap, my shoe*) into categories according to certain principles (shared privileges of occurrence), and then states the regularities observed among the categories so formed (Class 1 + Class 2 is a sentence). But none of this necessarily leads to a statement of a child's linguistic competence. It is a summary of his *performance,* whereas a statement of competence is a theory about what he *knows.* Moreover, there is a serious question whether a theory of competence can ever be developed from manipulations of a corpus. Many linguists deny that it can be done (cf. Chomsky, 1964b, and Lees, 1964, for a discussion in the context of child language). A corpus is incomplete, unsystematic, and (in the case of adults, at least) insensitive to a number of important grammatical distinctions. Insofar as utterances from children are limited in the same way, a distributional analysis will not lead to a correct description of competence; and there is no way, of course, to tell when a corpus is so limited. A distributional analysis at best provides a description of a child's grammatical classes, plus some hints as to his grammatical rules. But a theory of competence that explains these classes and rules may well take an entirely different form, a phenomenon we shall see repeatedly in the chapters that follow. The most elaborate general analyses of child grammar go far beyond the distributional evidence of a corpus (e.g., Brown, Cazden, and Bellugi, 1968).

As a description of performance, distributional analysis is but one source of information among many. Other observations, dealing with other aspects of performance, are often of equal importance and in some cases are more easily justified.

Among such other sources of information are observations made under the second strategy mentioned above, particular description. Rather than attempt to describe the total corpus collected from a child at some point in time, one examines the emergence of a particular grammatical system as it is manifested at different times. One might study the development of negation (Bellugi, 1964), or questions (Klima and Bellugi, 1966), or a number of other grammatical systems. The advantage of this strategy lies in the limited demands it places on observation, and arises from the fact that it does what a distributional analysis typically strives to avoid doing—it exploits the fact that adult grammar is the end-point of linguistic development. A distributional analysis attempts to discover parts of a grammar from a corpus. The second strategy begins with a part of adult grammar and judges if there is sufficient evidence in the corpus to justify ascribing it to a child. The demands on the second strategy are weaker than the demands on the first, for it must only recognize the applicability of a known theory—it does not have to discover an unknown theory.

When an adult analysis cannot be ascribed to a child, one can still describe the sequence a child follows in reaching the adult system. Thus, for example, children first negate by saying *not want,* then *don't want some,* then *don't want none,* and finally, *don't want any* (Bellugi, 1964). At each point, one can say what a child lacks with respect to the adult system—he does not have auxiliary verbs, he does not have negative pronouns, he does not have indeterminate pronouns, respectively. But one cannot merely say that the child's grammatical system is the adult system minus, say, auxiliary verbs. These observations are data. Finding the grammar that explains them is a matter of theory construction, and the distinction between theory and data is as important in language acquisition as anywhere else.

It is possible to carry the second strategy to the level of true experimentation. Instead of observing the spontaneous occurrences of particular grammatical features, one tries to evoke them. Ervin (1964), working with W. Miller, tested children's knowledge of English plurals by naming free-form figures made of wood with nonsense syllables: for example, a child is first shown a figure shaped like a salt cellar and called a *bunge,* and then is presented with a second figure exactly like the first. What does he call the two figures together, *bunge* or *bunges?* The latter would indicate mastery of the rule for the pluralization of English nouns ending in sibilants. The age at which a child demonstrates such mastery can be compared to the age at which he correctly uses such genuine plurals as *oranges.*

A similar method can be used to elicit the past-tense inflection of verbs. The procedure suffers some uncertainty in this case. A failure to elicit a past-tense inflection may result from a failure of the experimenter to present the appropriate conditions as much as from a failure of the child to add past-tense inflections. Nonetheless, one can approach the problem by demonstrating a novel gesture, saying at the same time *I'll sib it,* and then asking a child what had been done.

A child's ability to change sentences into transformationally related sentences—to change, for example, active sentences into passives— has been studied by Brown (1968), working with A. Olds, by means of the "alligator test." Two adults, each with a puppet, engage in the following dialogue:

Bear	The cat chased the dog.
Alligator	The dog was chased by the cat.
Bear	The zebra pushes the hippo.
Alligator	The hippo is pushed by the zebra.

And so on. The alligator speaks only in passive sentences. After a child has watched such an exchange for a while, he is given the alligator and asked to play its part. The method can be extended to many kinds of sentences and to many kinds of relations among sentences. Bellugi (1967) suggests studying negation in this way; questions could be approached through the alligator, also.

Bellugi (1967) has described a number of tests of negation, some for comprehension, others for production. All are suitable for use with young children. The variety of syntactic forms covered is quite large and only a sampling will be given here.

To test a child's comprehension of negatives affixed to auxiliary verbs, a child is shown a doll with movable arms. One arm is up and one is down. The child is told to make the doll fit the sentences, "The boy can put his arms down" and "The boy can't put his arms down."

To test a child's comprehension of negation used in Wh-questions, a child is shown an array of objects—a boy doll, an orange, an apple, a ball, a toy, a tomato, and an ashtray—and is asked "what can the little boy eat?" and "what can't the little boy eat?"

To test a child's comprehension of affirmative pronouns (such as *some*) and negative pronouns (such as *none*), a child is shown a doll and a few blocks, and is told to make the doll fit the sentences, "The doll can push some of the blocks," and "The doll can push none of the blocks."

To elicit negative indefinite forms, i.e., pronouns based on *any*, a child is first shown a doll with a hat on its head, being told "Here is John. He has something on his head," and then is shown a second, hatless doll, being told "Here is Bill. What does he have on his head? He doesn't have _____."

A child can be given forms systematically distorted to bear on points of syntactic interest, and then be asked to correct them. For example "he not touching it," which violates a rule in English that negatives must be attached to auxiliaries.

Perhaps the best known test of children's productive abilities is the one devised by Berko (1958). A comparable test has been developed independently by Bogoyavlenskiy (1957) for use with Russian children (cf. Slobin, 1968). Berko investigated the development of the morphological inflections of English: plural marking of nouns, past-tense marking of verbs, comparative marking of adjectives, and some others. The test uses a set of drawings of exotic creatures doing ordinary things and ordinary creatures doing exotic things. Berko used it with children four to six years old, although it has been used with children as young as two (Lovell, 1968). One drawing, for example, shows a shmoo-like creature. It is introduced as a *wug*—"Here is a wug." Then two more are shown, the experimenter saying, "Here are two others, there are two . . . ," his voice trailing off, trying to elicit a plural inflection. The test includes items presenting each of the conditioning phonemic environments of the plural and past-tense inflections of English; thus, by the end, one has collected a complete sample of a child's morphological inflections.

Studies of Comprehension

A second methodological issue involves the comprehension of grammatical forms—how it is to be investigated, and why. Unlike the first methodological issue, which involves the clarification of an existing method, this methodological issue involves the clarification of the requirements of a method that does not yet exist.

There are several reasons for studying comprehension. As one of the linguists at The Fourth Conference on Intellective Processes pointed out (Bellugi and Brown, 1964), in comprehension the investigator knows what the input to the process is—it is the sentence comprehended. Thus, when comprehension fails, the source of trouble can be located. The same cannot be said for production.

Even though the results of production are easy to observe, it is not always obvious what the observations mean. Does the fact that a child systematically excludes auxiliary verbs from his speech signify the absence of Aux from his grammar, or does it, on the contrary, indicate censorship of Aux from his speech in order to meet the constraints of an abbreviated memory span? Although these are matters of production, it is through the testing of comprehension that such questions can be settled.

In what follows, the few studies that have attempted to investigate comprehension are described, their limitations pointed out, and some promising new techniques presented.

Brown (1957) demonstrated that certain of the major grammatical classes have semantic correlates for children. To study comprehension he used an ingenious test that apparently has not been employed since. A child is shown a drawing of someone performing a strange action with a peculiar substance contained in an odd bowl. The picture thus presents an action, a mass, and a container—three states that would be described in English by a verb, a mass noun, and a count noun, respectively. As the picture is shown, the experimenter says what it is; either it shows *how to wug,* or *some wug,* or *a wug.* Whatever the child is told, he is next shown three drawings—one of the action alone, one of the mass alone, and one of the container alone—and is asked to select the one that portrays what was labeled in the first picture. To the degree that a child is sensitive to the referential implications of verbs, mass nouns, and count nouns, he will be able to make appropriate choices (but see Braine, 1970, for a different interpretation). Brown used this test with nursery-school children, finding them to be sensitive to the implications of each grammatical class. In view of the claim sometimes made (e.g., Slobin, 1966a), that children first construct grammatical classes on a semantic basis, it would be useful to repeat the experiment with younger children, say 2-year-olds.

A second test of the comprehension (as well as the production) of speech appears in an experiment by Fraser, Bellugi, and Brown (1963). Their method is called the ICP Test, standing for Imitation, Comprehension, and Production. Again, a set of drawings is shown to a child, this time in pairs. Each pair presents a referential correlate of some syntactic contrast—e.g., subject versus direct object (a boy pushing a girl and a girl pushing a boy). In all, 10 different contrasts are represented. Comprehension is tested by saying to a child, "Here are two pictures, one of a boy pushing a girl, and the other of a girl pushing a boy," care being taken not to show which picture goes with which sentence. The child is then asked to point to the picture that illustrates one of the sentences: "Show me the picture of the girl pushing the boy." The test of production begins in the same way, but instead of asking the child to point to the picture for a sentence, he is asked to give a sentence for a picture. Fraser et al. conducted their study with 3-year-olds. Lovell and Dixon (1965) have done it successfully with 2-year-olds.

Shipley, Smith, and Gleitman (n.d.) have studied comprehension in children as young as 18 months by giving them commands and observing whether or not the command is followed. Bever, Mehler, and Valian (1967) have used a similar method. In the case of Shipley et al.,

12

the commands are either well-formed by adult standards (e.g., *throw me the ball*) or are typical child-forms (e.g., *ball; throw ball; Please, Johnnie, throw ball*). In addition, a command might contain only words known to a child (as in the examples above) or it might contain one or more words novel to him (e.g., *gor ball; throw ronta ball; gor ronta ball*). A major difficulty with the method resides in the identification of comprehension. Except when a child performs exactly as instructed, there is no way to tell if he has successfully analyzed a command or merely has responded to a part of it, e.g., the noun. In commands using novel verbs, it is obviously impossible for a child to perform exactly as instructed.

Such studies of comprehension, clever though they often are, suffer a common limitation. All use portrayable correlates of various grammatical contrasts and classes. But not every aspect of syntax has a portrayable correlate: indeed, most of syntax cannot be so represented. It is always possible, of course, that further ingenuity will discover more grammatical forms that can be tested in this way. However, this hope has little significance. As the method is extended further, it must use more and dubious connections between language and portrayable events. The methodological problem is to devise tests of comprehension that make use of the linguistic materials themselves, not the fortuitous correlations between language and the external world.

Two studies that point in this direction are Bellugi (1965) and Brown (1966). They searched their longitudinal records for spontaneous dialogues between children and adults, looking at the children's answers to the adults' questions. The aptness of the answer was used as an index of comprehension. If an adult asks, for example, *what did you hit?* and a child answers *arm,* we can assume that the question was understood. But if the answer is *hit,* we can conclude that the child does not yet know the transformation relating Wh-forms to the underlying objects of sentences. Some caution must be exercised in accepting appropriate answers at face value, as it is always possible that extralinguistic factors evoke an utterance that happens to be appropriate. Nonetheless, the method applies to any Wh-question and involves spontaneous linguistic performance. But only Wh-questions are within its reach, so it is hardly general, even though it is not limited by language–environment correlations.

A third study escapes some of these shortcomings. Slobin and Welsh (1967) have used the simplest of methods for studying linguistic development — imitation. For reasons discussed below (Chapter 7), it is evident that children usually reformulate adult sentences when they imitate. Adult sentences too long to be retained in immediate memory are altered to fit the child's grammar. A child produces in imitation only what he produces in spontaneous speech, which means that imitation can be used to study children's productive capacities, a fact known and utilized for some time (Menyuk, 1963; Lenneberg, Nichols and Rosenberger, 1964). Slobin and Welsh use imitation to study comprehension as well. They exploit the fact that a successful reformulation in imitation depends on a successful comprehension of the sentence imitated. In contrast to the use of imitation to study production, where the focus is on verbatim repetition, the focus in comprehension is on nonverbatim repetition combined with the preservation of meaning. The method can be (and has been) used with very young children. Children can be induced to repeat what adults say, particularly if (as in Slobin and Welsh's study) they are highly familiar with the investigator. The sentences to be imitated are entirely a matter of the investigator's choice, so the method can be used across a large range of sentence types.

The following are a few of the examples given by Slobin and Welsh. The child was two-and-a-half. The first two imitations are meaning-preserving, the last two meaning-changing:

Adult   Here is a brown brush and here is a comb
Child   *Here's a brown brush an' a comb*
Adult   John who cried came to my party
Child   *John cried and he came to my party*
Adult   The batman got burned and the big shoe is there
Child   *Big shoe is here and big shoe is here*
Adult   The boy the book hit was crying
Child   *Boy the book was crying*

The first two imitations indicate an ability to comprehend but not produce certain grammatical forms, whereas the last two indicate a failure to comprehend. The second example is particularly striking: The child decomposes an embedded sentence into the matrix and constituent sentences underlying it. Slobin and Welsh's method deserves exploration, for it appears to have the virtues of generality and naturalness that the other methods for testing comprehension lack.

The Berkeley Cross-Cultural Project
Although not a method itself, except insofar as a program for investigating language acquisition in other cultures may be called a method, a group at the University of California (Berkeley) has compiled a manual of procedures (Slobin, 1967) for use in field studies of children and their language. Several reports have recently been issued covering such languages as Luo (Blount, 1969), Maya (Stross, 1969), Samoan (Kernan, 1969) and Black English (Mitchell-Kernan, 1969).

3
THE PATTERN OF
EARLY SPEECH

Let us start with a description of the speech of a 2-year-old. The following examples from records collected by Brown and Bellugi (1964) will set the stage. There are three samples. The first is from a child at 28 months, the second from the same child at 35 months, and third from him at 38 months. Major changes take place from sample to sample, a number of which will be discussed below.

CHILD—28 MONTHS	ADULT
What dat . . . somebody pencil	Whose pencils are they?
Floor	Floor?
Where birdie go? Birdie Birdie up dere Birdie Read dat?	
Read dat?	Will you read it to me?
What innere?	Is that a hammer, Adam?
Hammer Hit hammer, mommy No Cromer _____, mommy? Hurt	Poor Adam. Did you hurt yourself? What happened, Adam?
Screw (did) happen	Screw happened? You didn't even have a screw.
have screw _____ no down there . . . table . . . get broom	Does that one fit?
Yep, it fit Yep, it fit	Does it fit?
No . . . fit Put suitcase . . . for?	What did you put it in the suitcase for?

16

CHILD—28 MONTHS (Continued)	ADULT (Continued)
What dat?	That's tape. We'll use that one tomorrow.
All right 'morrow	Shall we use it tomorrow?
Yep Use morrow, yep Sure, use 'morrow	

CHILD—35 MONTHS	ADULT
What his name?	His name
His name, Ursla?	I know his name
No . . . I don't know his name I don't know Can't come up, fellah (to a yo-yo) Going pick pick up Lemme do again Don't . . . don't hold with me Turning round It's stop	 Yes, it is turning around It stopped?
What dat . . . feeled . . . like? What dat feeled like?	It feels like rubber, I guess
I . . . going . . . drop my books (drops one book) An' what happens? I going drop it . . . inne dump truck	
No . . . please cry, cracker	What?
Cracker	Please what?
Please cry, cracker	Please cry?
Yes	How can a cracker cry? Crackers can't talk.
Why not . . . cracker can't talk? Romper domper tell me boo Romper domper tell me boo I got someping show you What's dat . . . you have? Why me go? Why me going?	

CHILD—35 MONTHS (Continued)	ADULT (Continued)
D'you want brush him? D'you want he walk? Where's it? Why you rolling up? Hey, why . . . why you waking me up? What you doing . . . taking out? Why you knocking me off?	I'm not knocking you off.
Why not? I can't . . . couldn't . . . show it . . . to her	You're going to show it to her?
No I too big Those are mines Dat's mines	

CHILD—38 MONTHS	ADULT
I like a racing car D'you like some? I broke my racing car	Oh, did you used to have one?
Yes Look at dat one	
Like dis part broke Dis part broke, like that It's got a flat tire What is dat? It's a what? He . . . his mouth is open What shall we shall have? Why he going to have some seeds?	What part broke?
Why it's not working?	
You got some beads?	Yes
Just like me? I got bead 'round myself Hit my knee	Hit *my* knee
Hit your knee What dat teacher will do?	
Why you pull out?	

CHILD—38 MONTHS (Continued)	ADULT (Continued)
Who put dust on my hair?	Dust in your hair
	Can you tell Ursula what the lesson is . . . on the blackboard?
On the black which board? We going see another one We can read 'bout dis You wanto read? What is dat? What is dat got? It's got a flat tire When it's got flat tire, it's needs to go to the . . . to the station. The station will fix it. Tank come out through what? Really . . . tank come out through . . . here Mommy don't let me buy some	
What is dis?	That's a marble bag
A marble bag for what?	For marbles. It would be good to carry tiny cars.
What is dat? Can I keep dem? Why I can keep dem? Now can I keep dem? We don' do some games It's broked?	

At 28 months, the combinations of words may often seem random and the meanings bizarre, but this is not the case. Even the first word combinations are organized according to definite principles, and the content is never bizarre, though it can be banal. The following sections of the chapter review the evidence for these claims.

Telegraphic Speech

Brown and Fraser (1963) called the patterned speech of very young children "telegraphic." The word aptly captures one characteristic feature of children's first multiple-word utterances. As in telegrams, certain words are systematically eliminated. Looking at the sample collected at 28 months, for example, we see that articles, auxiliary verbs, copular verbs, and inflections of every sort are missing—*put suitcase . . . for?, where birdie go?, what innere?,* and *yep, it fit.*

This telegraphic analogy is provocative and worth considering. Perhaps child speech is telegraphic for the same reason that real telegrams are—to save on costs. Just as a telegram-writer deletes the least informative words of a message to save currency, a child may do the same to save space in memory. The fact that identical words, by and large, are eliminated in both situations adds some credence to the argument. But there are two difficulties, one conceptual and one factual, which make it clear that economization cannot be the explanation of telegraphic speech.

The factual problem is that children learning Russian also omit inflections from their early speech (Slobin, 1966b). Russian is a case-inflected language, and so conveys a good deal of structural information through inflections. Indeed, some of the information conveyed by word order in English is conveyed by inflections in Russian. In terms of informational importance, therefore, Russian children eliminate what American children retain, though both eliminate inflections. Clearly, it is not informativeness that counts in these cases.

The conceptual difficulty is that, although the least informative words of English tend not to appear in child speech, the lack of informativeness is itself a highly implausible explanation of this fact (Weksel, 1965). The only way a child could know whether a word is informative without knowing its syntactic role is by keeping records of the speech he has heard from his parents. Equipped with such records he could discover the frequency with which words are used, and so estimate which ones are informative. But this is a vast actuarial undertaking, implausibly vast for a 2-year-old, whose exposure to speech is necessarily limited and whose ability to keep unedited records must be small indeed.

Telegraphic speech is the outcome of the process of language acquisition. It is not the process itself. To understand it, we must penetrate more deeply into what children do.

Holophrastic Speech

It is essential to begin the description of language acquisition even before the period of telegraphic speech. "Holophrastic speech" refers to the possibility that the single-word utterances of young children express complex ideas, that *ball* means not simply a spherical object of appropriate size, but that a child wants such an object, for example, or that he believes he has created such an object, or that someone is expected to look at such an object.

Many investigators of children's language (e.g., Stern and Stern, 1907; de Laguna, 1927; Leopold, 1949a; McCarthy, 1954) have said that the single words of holophrastic speech are equivalent to the full sentences of adults. It is true, of course, that adults often require a full sentence to paraphrase the content of children's holophrastic speech, but this is not what is meant by the term "holophrastic." Rather, holophrastic speech means that while children are limited to uttering single words at the beginning of language acquisition, they are capable of conceiving of something like full sentences. Let us look into this possibility, for it is central to understanding the course of events in the later stages of language acquisition.

In what sense do children have in mind the content of a full sentence while uttering a single word? There are several aspects of holophrastic speech to which we will pay attention in considering this question. No one believes that children have detailed and differentiated ideas in the adult manner. As Leopold (1949a) puts it, ". . . the word has at first an ill-defined meaning and an ill-defined value: it refers to a nebulous complex, factually and emotionally; only gradually do its factual and emotional components become clearer, resulting in lexical and syntactic discriminations" (p. 5). A degree of semantic imprecision in holophrastic speech is therefore taken for granted. There remains, however, a question of what it is that children are imprecise about, and several factors seem to be important.

Often children's single-word utterances are closely linked with action. Action and speech appear to be fused. Leopold's daughter, for example, said *walk* as she got out of a cart to walk, *away* as she pushed an object away, and *blow* as she blew her nose (all at 20 months); Leopold calls these utterances self-imperatives. In addition there were normal imperatives, utterances directed toward someone else. Leopold observed *mit* from *komm mit, ma* from *come on,* and *away* from *put it away,* again all at 20 months. (Leopold's daughter grew up as a German-English bilingual.) It is not clear that the two kinds of imperatives were in any way distinct for the child.

Besides imperatives children's early speech often is imbued with emotion. Leopold's daughter said [dididi], for example, in a loud voice to indicate disapproval and in a soft voice to indicate approval. Leopold believes that such examples typify the first step of linguistic development, which occurs when a child attaches emotional significance to sounds accidentally produced while babbling. Meumann (1894) held a similar view. This expressive aspect of children's speech apparently maintains a dominating role for some time. According to Stern and Stern (1907; summarized in Blumenthal, 1970), the first word combinations of children consist of one part interjection and one part statement, the interjection part continuing from the earliest stages of development 6 to 12 months before.

There is a third characteristic of holophrastic speech. Holophrastic speech refers to things. It includes the capacity to name. A child expresses his feelings or evokes an action toward some object referred to by his utterance. The utterance [mam:a], for example, meant for Leopold's daughter both "delicious!" and "food." It had both an expressive and referential component. (It did not mean "mama" until six months later.)

There are three main characteristics of holophrastic speech. We can call them conative, expressive, and referential, after Jakobson (1960), and find examples of all three in Table 1. Table 1 lists the first seven "words" Leopold observed in the development of his daughter (the symbolism and glosses are Leopold's). The "words" are typical of the

Table 1   **The First Seven "Words" in One Child's Linguistic Development** (data from Leopold, 1949b)

Utterance	Age (months)	Gloss	Function
ʔə ?	8	An interjection. Also demonstrative, "addressed" to persons, distant objects and "escaped toys"	E, R? C?
dididi	9	Disapproval (loud) Comfort (soft)	E
mamːa	10	Refers vaguely to food. Also means "tastes good" and "hungry"	R, E
nenene	10	Scolding	E? C?
tt!	10	Used to call squirrels	C
pIti	10	Always used with a gesture, and always whispered. Seems to mean "Interest(ed) (-ing)"	E, R
dɛː	10	An interjection. Also demonstrative. Used with the same gesture as above.	E, R

utterances recorded by others (Stern and Stern, 1907). The presumed function served by each has been indicated by a code — "C" for conative, "E" for expressive, and "R" for referential. As this coding makes clear, most utterances serve several functions, and among the three functions the referential function is unique in never appearing alone.

Holophrastic Speech as Predication   The expressive and conative aspects of holophrastic speech are best understood on nonlinguistic grounds. Expressiveness is an example of the exclamatory function of primate communication in general. The fusion of speech with action is probably an inevitable consequence of sensory-motor intelligence (Piaget, 1952), and, like expressiveness, is an example of general primate communicativeness. Both the expressive and conative aspects of child speech are considered in the next chapter. Here we consider a more particular question, the referential function of holophrastic speech. It is because of this function and the way it is used that holophrastic speech corresponds to the full sentences of adults.

De Laguna (1927) viewed the single-word utterances of children as predicates, as comments, made on the situation in which a child finds himself. The holophrastic word is the comment; together with the extralinguistic context, the topic of the comment, it forms a rudimentary kind of proposition and thus amounts to a full sentence conceptually.

22

It is worth quoting de Laguna in full on this:

It is precisely because the words of the child are so indefinite in meaning, that they can serve such a variety of uses; and it is also— although this sounds paradoxical—for the same reason, that they are fit to function as complete rudimentary sentences. A child's word does not . . . designate an object or *a property* or *an act; rather it signifies loosely and vaguely the object together with its interesting properties and the acts with which it is commonly associated in the life of the child. The emphasis may be now on one, now on another, of these aspects, according to the exigencies of the occasion on which it is used. Just because the terms of the child's language are in themselves so indefinite, it is left* to the particular setting and context to determine the specific meaning for each occasion. *In order to understand what the baby is saying you must see what the baby is doing.* (1927, pp. 90–91, emphasis in original)

We can return to Table 1, where [mamːa] is listed as having two meanings, "food" and "delicious." But there are only apparently two meanings if we accept de Laguna's theory. According to that theory [mamːa] is a comment (delicious) on an extralinguistic topic (food). There is one meaning (delicious) used predicatively. Three other "words" in Table 1 can be interpreted the same way: [ʔə ʔ], [d ɛː], and [pɪti]. On the other hand, [dididi] was not a comment (except in the trivial sense that "ouch!," for example, is a comment on a pin prick), and [nenene] and [tt!] probably were not comments either. We can now see why purely referential utterances never occur. The referential function is always used for predication. Children never utter mere labels, while they do utter purely expressive or conative sounds. This is a remarkable fact of human communication, and we shall see its effects at every stage of linguistic development.

Holophrastic Speech as Grammatical Speech Leopold's observations cover the beginning of linguistic development. There is already an indication that holophrastic speech is in a limited way grammatical, that is, relational, speech. During the following 6 to 12 months there is a constant emergence of new grammatical relations, even though no utterance is ever longer than one word. Very young children develop a concept of a sentence as a set of grammatical relations before they develop a concept of how these relations are expressed.

P. Greenfield (personal communication) was the first to note this significant phenomenon, so far as I know. She kept a diary of her daughter's speech, from what seemed to be the first meaningful utterances to the beginning of patterned speech, and noted different grammatical relations appearing during the holophrastic period. Of course, seeing a single word in a grammatical relation is a fact we can know for certain only on the part of the observer of the relation; we have to assume the child has the same relation in mind. The reason for making this assumption, in the case of Greenfield's observations, is that she found an orderly *progression* of new relations during the holophrastic period. In the early months, therefore, many opportunities were missed for perceiving relations that appeared in later months. There had been some change in the way the child used words.

The child first used *dada* at 11 months in the sense of "caretaker." It was applied indiscriminantly to her mother, father, and a third person also living in the house (Greenfield, 1967). The next step was the assertion of properties. At 12 months 20 days (12;20) the child said *ha* when something hot was before her, and at 13;20 she said *ha* to an empty coffee cup and a turned-off stove. By misusing the word the child showed that "hot" was not merely the label of hot objects but was also something said of objects that could be hot. It asserted a property. At 15 months the child used words to indicate the location of objects as well as their properties. Thus, at 14;28 she pointed to the top of the refrigerator, the usual place for finding bananas, and said *nana*. There were no bananas on top of the refrigerator at the time, so *nana* could not have been a label, and at other times the child called bananas not on the refrigerator *nana*, so she was not saying something about the refrigerator. By 15;11 the child began to use words as the objects of verbs (*door*, meaning "close the door"), as the objects of prepositions (*eye*, meaning "water is in my eye"), and as the subjects of sentences (*baby*, meaning "the baby fell down"). In no case was the verb, preposition, or sentence made explicit. With the exception of *bye bye cat* at 15;11 the child combined no words until 17 months. It is of considerable interest that most of the words noted above are "nouns"; those that are not nouns are "adjectives," i.e., attributes of nouns. "Verbs"

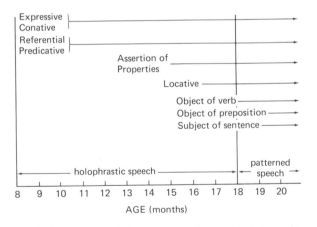

Fig. 1. A summary of the characteristics of holophrastic speech and the ages (with two children) at which they first emerge. It should be understood that the transition from holophrastic speech is gradual, not abrupt. The ages are highly approximate. Normal children may differ from those depicted here by many months.

are completely missing. As will be discussed in Chapter 5, the syntactic category of nouns is unique in that it alone appears in every grammatical relation. The richness of nouns in holophrastic speech, therefore, possesses an advantage for communication. Because all grammatical relations are implicit, nouns can be used in every available relation without endangering the comprehension of adults. Verbs do not have this property (compare a verb such as *reach* to a noun such as *banana* for conveying the locative relation).

When words are first combined, therefore, a number of grammatical relations already exist. The new development is not the appearance of grammar but the appearance of patterned speech to express grammar. How this takes place is the subject of the following sections. Figure 1 contains a diagram summarizing our observations so far, showing that patterned speech is a new phase in a child's constant effort to express grammatical relations. In a study completed too recently to be considered here in detail, Smith (1970) has found much evidence in support of this interpretation. The sequence of events pictured in Fig. 1, however, may have to be altered somewhat.

Pivot and Open Classes

The terms "pivot" and "open" are taken from Braine (1963a) and refer to the outcome of a distributional analysis of child speech. When these analyses are conducted on speech collected from children of 18 months or so, at the very beginning of patterned speech, at least two classes of words emerge. One contains a small number of words, each frequently used—the "pivot" class. The other contains many more words, each infrequently used—the "open" class. Words from the pivot class almost always appear in combination with words from the open class and never alone or with each other. Words from the open class, however, may appear alone and with each other. The two classes generally have complementary membership and take fixed positions when combined. Pivot classes may appear first or second in sentences, but no word from a single pivot class appears in both places. The open class is quick to take in new vocabulary while the pivot class is slow to do so.

Such are the characteristics of the pivot–open distinction. These characteristics can be summarized by setting down the combinations in which pivot- and open-words appear—the basic facts supporting the distinction in the first place. Using "P" and "O" for "pivot" and "open," the following occur:

$$P + O$$
$$O + P$$
$$O + O$$
$$O$$

The only possibilities that do not exist are pivot-words uttered alone or in combination with each other. Everything else is possible.

Table 2 shows the pivot and open classes of three children studied by Brown and Bellugi (1964), Braine (1963a), and Miller and Ervin (1964), respectively. The table itself is from McNeill (1966a). For want of space, only a portion of each open class is represented, but the pivot classes are included in their entirety.

Table 2 **Pivot and Open Classes from Three Studies of Child Language** (McNeill, 1966a)

Braine		Brown		Ervin	
P	O	P	O	P	O
allgone byebye big more pretty my see night- night hi	boy sock boat fan milk plane shoe vitamins hot Mommy Daddy .	my that two a the big green poor wet dirty fresh pretty	Adam Becky boot coat coffee knee man Mommy nut sock stool Tinker Toy .	this that	arm baby dolly's pretty yellow come doed .
				the a	other baby dolly's pretty yellow
				here there	arm baby dolly's pretty yellow

For the children in Table 2, sentences consisted of a word from the list on the left followed by a word from the list on the right—that is, P + O. Thus, *byebye fan, wet sock* and *that doed* all might have occurred. Not every combination allowed by Table 2 was actually observed, of course, but there are no evident differences between the combinations that did occur and those that did not and it is assumed that the gaps arise from sampling, not grammatical, limitations.

What is to be made of the pivot–open distinction? Perhaps nothing at all. It is possible that the earliest utterances of young children arise as a simplified imitation of adult speech. If so, it would be a mistake to ascribe grammatical significance to what, in this case, would be an artifact of a distributional analysis. Before proceeding, therefore, we must consider the possibility that the pivot and open classes do not coincide with the beginning of word combinations by children.

There are several reasons for rejecting this possibility. For one thing, if the sentences recorded from children are reproduced, the fact would reflect an astonishing ability to memorize verbal material. The number of *different* combinations recorded from one of Braine's (1963a) children in successive months was: 14, 24, 54, 89, 350, 1400, 2500+. It is impossible that the child echoed 2500+ different combinations already heard; at some point he began to rely on syntax. However, it is possible that the first utterances of children are only imitations. The repetition of 14 pairs of words can be done as a rote performance. Some utterances do indeed appear to be imitations. One child, for example, was able to say "I doubt that NP," the NP being any noun in her vocabulary. The sentence frame before the NP had a fixed form and differed from anything else then in the child's speech. In other cases, however, it is obvious that a child is not imitating. Braine's subject in Table 2, for example, said *allgone shoe, allgone vitamins,* and *allgone lettuce.* These utterances could not be imitations as they all are inversions of the corresponding adult models: *the shoe is allgone, the vitamins are allgone, the lettuce is allgone.* (Alternatively *allgone* is a modifier, but this usage could not be an imitation, either.) Similar observations can be made of other children. Ervin's subject said *that doed,* and Brown's *big a truck.* Children do not hear English even remotely like this from their parents, but such examples correspond to a pivot–open pattern. Their occurrence reinforces the belief that the P–O distinction reflects a genuine division of children's vocabularies into two classes.

The most compelling argument in behalf of the grammatical reality of the pivot–open distinction is that pivot-words rarely occur alone or in combination with each other. Such a development must result from a restriction on the use of words — i.e., a system of some kind for grammatical expression.

Early Phrase Structure

The distinction between P and O classes is one way of describing the beginning stages of patterned speech; we will return to it in Chapter 5. A different but closely associated way of describing these same stages is to write the rules children follow in constructing sentences. Brown and his colleagues (Brown and Fraser, 1963; Brown and Bellugi, 1964; Brown, Cazden, and Bellugi, 1968) have pursued the linguistic development of three children, beginning in each case at about two years and continuing in one case until five, describing the children's linguistic competence at different stages in the form of generative grammars.

Not amazingly, grammars written at the earliest stages of development are simple. The following three rules summarize the performance of one child in Brown's study, Adam, at 28 months (based on McNeill, 1966a):

$$
\begin{aligned}
(1) \quad & S \rightarrow (NP|VP) \\
(2) \quad & NP \rightarrow \begin{cases} (P) & N \\ N & N \end{cases} \\
(3) \quad & VP \rightarrow (V)\ NP
\end{aligned}
$$

Rules (1), (2), and (3) describe one-, two-, three-, and four-word sentences, depending on the options adopted in each rule. As usual, optional elements are enclosed with parentheses; following Fillmore (1968), linked parentheses (NP|VP) indicate that at least one element must be chosen (NP and/or VP). Rules (1) and (2) apply to such sentences as *ball, that ball,* and *Adam ball.* Rules (1), (2), and (3) apply together in *Adam want ball* and *Adam mommy pencil.* Notice that the last sentence is ambiguous in that *mommy* might originate with Rule (2) or (3)—*Adam mommy* or *mommy pencil.* Notice also that the verb of the VP in this grammar is optional, while the noun of the VP is obligatory. Other children obey the same strange rule (Bloom, 1968).

Table 3 **Sentence Patterns That Correspond to Basic Grammatical Relations**
(McNeill, 1966a)

Child's Speech

Pattern	Frequency	Corresponding Grammatical Relations
P + N	23	modifier, head noun
N + N	115	modifier, head noun, subject, predicate
V + N	162	main verb, object
N + V	49	subject, predicate
Total	349	
P + N + N	3	modifier, head noun
N + P + N	1	subject, predicate, modifier, head noun
V + P + N	3	main verb, object, modifier, head noun
V + N + N	29	main verb, object, modifier, head noun
P + N + V	1	subject, predicate, modifier, head noun
N + N + V	1	subject, predicate, modifier, head noun
N + V + N	4	main verb, object, subject, predicate
N + N + N	7	subject, predicate, modifier, head noun
Total	49	

28

The combinations allowed by Rules (1), (2), and (3) did not occur with equal frequency in Adam's speech. For example, Rule (3) was employed more often than was Rule (2), and the joint application of Rules (1), (2), and (3) occurred only 15 percent of the time. All these characteristics and more are set forth in Table 3, which shows every combination of P, V, and N in Adam's speech at the earliest point for which observations exist, along with the frequency of occurrence of each. It is possible that a larger sample would contain other combinations. There is no way to judge such a possibility; however, as will be discussed in Chapter 5, the combinations that do occur possess a consistency lacked by the combinations that do not occur.

Rule (2) defines a particular grammatical constituent. It says that Adam possessed NPs at 28 months and that NP consisted of N, PN, and NN. Rules (1) and (3) in turn contain NP as a component part. The grammars of other children include similar rules. What justification is there for ascribing to these early grammars such a constituent as NP? Why not write instead several separate rules—one each for N, PN, and NN? We would account for the same combinations of grammatical classes in Table 3. The form of Rule (2) is a hypothesis about linguistic knowledge.

There are several lines of evidence supporting Rule (2). One is that single nouns and developed noun phrases appear in the same environments (Brown and Bellugi, 1964). For example,

POSITIONS FOR SINGLE N
that (flower)
where (ball) go?
Adam write (penguin)
(horsie) stop
put (hat) on

POSITIONS FOR NP
that (a blue flower)
where (the puzzle) go?
doggie eat (the breakfast)
(a horsie) crying
put (the red hat) on

Wherever N can go, NP can go, presumably because individual Ns are actually NPs. Another fragment of evidence is that pauses in children's speech usually surround NPs, not Ns. "Put . . . the red hat . . . on" is a likely occurrence, whereas "put the red . . . hat . . . on" is not. Insofar as pauses reflect points of decision in speech (Goldman-Eisler, 1961), such utterances indicate that decisions are made in terms of NP and not N. Finally, the pronoun *it* is really a pro-NP, since it replaces NP and not N, as in the following examples from Adam's speech:

Mommy get *ladder*   Mommy get *it*
Mommy get *my ladder*   Mommy get *it*

Adam sometimes combined the pronoun and the NP the pronoun should have replaced into a single utterance, saying *Mommy get it ladder* and *Mommy get it my ladder*. That NP and N are treated alike in this case of deviation from adult English is strong evidence that NP is a genuine constituent.

Intrinsic and Extrinsic Predication

One of the sentences made possible by Rule (1) is a VP without a NP subject. Such sentences are common at two years, especially when the omitted subject refers to the child himself. Thus, for example, *hit my ball* or *read Cromer paper* were not imperatives but referred to things the child was doing. The explanation of such sentences without subjects has nothing to do with the subject, however, for it depends on the predicate.

It is in the acquisition of Japanese that a division between what we shall call extrinsic and intrinsic predicates is most clearly seen.[1] Japanese, like many languages, uses postpositions. Two of these particles, *wa* and *ga*, mark the surface subjects of sentences. While *wa* and *ga* have superficially similar distributions, their implications for the underlying structure are very different: *wa* is for intrinsic predicates and *ga* for extrinsic. Intrinsic predicates, those calling for *wa*, state a property the speaker feels to inhere in the subject. No unusual ontological insight is required. Habitual activities, for example, are regarded as intrinsic — *daddy-wa works in an office.* So is attribution — *government architecture-wa is grotesque,* membership in a hierarchy — *the collie-wa is a dog,* definition — *that-wa is a collie,* and the assertion of truisms — *all men-wa are mortal.* Sentences with *ga* have predicates that state properties the speaker feels to be extrinsic to the subject. They often form a momentary description — *there is a dog-ga in the yard* (when this is not customary) — but this is not an invariant rule. As with an intrinsic predicate the information contained in an extrinsic predicate is asserted about the subject, but unlike an intrinsic predicate the connection is thought to be adventitious.

How are *wa* and *ga* acquired? At first neither postposition appears in the speech of children. At 28 months (with the children studied by McNeill, 1966b) *ga* begins to be used, though not frequently. When used, it is used appropriately, with extrinsic predicates. About six months later *wa* appears and it too is used appropriately, with intrinsic predicates. Thus, extrinsic predicates appear to develop before intrinsic predicates. However, this is only half the story, and the second half reverses the interpretation of the first. It is possible for a native speaker of Japanese to classify utterances containing neither *wa* nor *ga* according to the postposition required. McNeill (1968b) found that approximately 90 percent of the sentences in his records were sufficiently clear to be so classified. The results of this procedure are clear: Children's early sentences contain twice as many intrinsic predicates as extrinsic predicates. Although *ga* is the postposition most often included in early child speech, *wa* is the postposition most often omitted.

We have what appears to be a contradiction. On the evidence of the postposition first acquired extrinsic predicates are dominant, whereas on the evidence provided by direct judgments of children's sentences

---

[1] Lee and Ando (n.d.) refer to this distinction as "designative" and "predicative," respectively.

intrinsic predicates are dominant. The contradiction is resolved when we observe the effect of the two predicates on the subject NPs of sentences. If we look at whether a child utters a predicate alone or a predicate with a subject, we find that subjects are usually *included* with extrinsic predicates and *excluded* with intrinsic predicates. *Wa* cannot appear without a superficial NP so it appears after *ga* even though there are twice as many contexts calling for it.

Exactly this same tendency appears in the speech of English-speaking children. English-speaking children present a situation comparable to young Japanese children (in that they also use neither *wa* nor *ga!*) and a native (but bilingual) speaker of Japanese can classify their sentences according to which postposition they "require." American children use twice as many intrinsic and extrinsic predicates as do Japanese children and also include subjects with extrinsic predicates and exclude them with intrinsic predicates (McNeill, 1968b). In Table 4 are examples of the two types of predicates from four children, two English-speaking and two Japanese-speaking.

Table 4 Intrinsic and Extrinsic Predication in the Speech of Japanese and American Children

Eve		
	(extrinsic)	Mommy sit bottom
		Fraser read Lassie
	(intrinsic)	on Wednesday (the stock answer to "When's Cromer coming?")
		on my head (said of a hairband)
Adam		
	(extrinsic)	Bunny rabbit running
		Cromer right dere
	(intrinsic)	pretty, Mommy?
		go dere, Mommy? (said of a puzzle piece)
Izanami		
	(extrinsic)	Reiko said "no"
		tape goes round and round
	(intrinsic)	the same (said of two dresses)
		office (said of her father)
Murasaki		
	(extrinsic)	the lion's mommy is seated
		a giraffe is eating grass
	(intrinsic)	can't eat the rind (said of an orange)
		delicious (said of a cracker)

We can now see why children omit mentioning themselves as the subjects of sentences. The predicates of such sentences are intrinsic to young children, perhaps because infantile egocentrism (Piaget, 1926) makes everything a child says of himself seem inherently true.

The first grammatical relation to appear in the holophrastic period is presumably the assertion of properties. Greenfield, for example, noted *hot* at 13 months. It is possible that these first relational utterances are intrinsic predicates, which assert permanent properties of objects, and not extrinsic predicates, which describe situations. The example of *hot* used with a *cold* coffee cup supports such an interpretation. Contrary to the belief of some philosophers (e.g., Quine, 1960), children may begin talking with general terms. And contrary to the beliefs of nearly everyone, they may not begin by describing things.

Elaboration of Phrase Structure

Rules (1), (2), and (3) in the grammar above describe Adam's sentences at 28 months. These sentences are a little less than two morphemes long, on the average. Nine months later length has increased only slightly—to nearly three morphemes on the average—but the grammar is much elaborated. Rather than three phrase-structural rules, there are now 14; rather than no transformational rules, there are two dozen. Table 5 presents the entire phrase-structural component and two rules from the transformational component of the grammar written for Adam's speech at 36 months. It generates sentences of the type given at the beginning of the chapter as the speech of a child at 35 and 38 months. The best way to convey an idea of how the grammar generates such sentences is to provide examples; this is done in Figs. 2–5.

First, however, it is necessary to introduce certain notational conventions. Imp and Wh are grammatical markers, representing imperative sentences in the first case, and such questions as *what, where,* and *who* in the second. Neg stands for negation, MV for main verb, and Cop for copular (e.g., *is* in *the dog is an animal*). V^c is a "catenative" verb— *wanna, gonna,* and *hafta. Adverb* is a sentence constituent, like NP, whereas Adv is the grammatical category of adverbs proper. Because Adam sometimes produced sentences of the form *that is my book* and sometimes of the form *that my book,* a distinction is drawn between *be* and β: the former leads to an expressed variant of the auxiliary verb *to be,* while the latter, although representing the same syntactic function, does not. Det stands for "determiner," a category including such words as *the, a, that, this, these,* and *those.* Prt stands for "particle"—e.g., the *up* in *look up,* and the *down* in *put down.* The symbol *some*Δ in the first transformational rule covers both *somewhere* (from phrase-structure Rule 11) and *something* (from phrase-structure Rule 13), both of which are not words but grammatical markers. The remaining symbols are defined by the grammar itself.

Figure 2 shows the deep structure of *where those dogs goed,* a well-formed question for Adam (from Brown et al. 1968). Ten of the 14 phrase-structure rules in Table 5 are used to generate this phrase marker (Rules 1, 2, 3, 4, 5, 6, 10, 11, 13, and 14); the two transforma-

---

Table 5   **Part of the Grammar of a Child 36 Months Old**
(Brown, Cazden, and Bellugi, 1968)

Complete phrase-structure rules

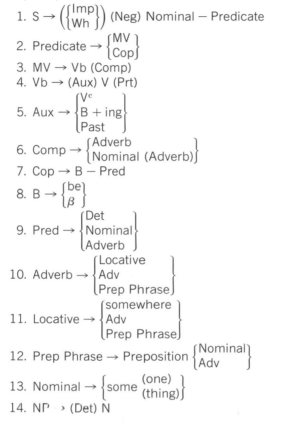

1. S → $\left(\begin{Bmatrix}\text{Imp}\\\text{Wh}\end{Bmatrix}\right)$ (Neg) Nominal − Predicate

2. Predicate → $\begin{Bmatrix}\text{MV}\\\text{Cop}\end{Bmatrix}$

3. MV → Vb (Comp)

4. Vb → (Aux) V (Prt)

5. Aux → $\begin{Bmatrix}\text{V}^c\\\text{B + ing}\\\text{Past}\end{Bmatrix}$

6. Comp → $\begin{Bmatrix}\text{Adverb}\\\text{Nominal (Adverb)}\end{Bmatrix}$

7. Cop → B − Pred

8. B → $\begin{Bmatrix}\text{be}\\\beta\end{Bmatrix}$

9. Pred → $\begin{Bmatrix}\text{Det}\\\text{Nominal}\\\text{Adverb}\end{Bmatrix}$

10. Adverb → $\begin{Bmatrix}\text{Locative}\\\text{Adv}\\\text{Prep Phrase}\end{Bmatrix}$

11. Locative → $\begin{Bmatrix}\text{somewhere}\\\text{Adv}\\\text{Prep Phrase}\end{Bmatrix}$

12. Prep Phrase → Preposition $\begin{Bmatrix}\text{Nominal}\\\text{Adv}\end{Bmatrix}$

13. Nominal → $\begin{Bmatrix}\text{some}\begin{array}{l}\text{(one)}\\\text{(thing)}\end{array}\end{Bmatrix}$

14. NP → (Det) N

Two transformation rules
   T1. *Wh* incorporation for main-verb sentences
      Wh-Nominal-Verb (Nominal) − someΔ ⇒ Wh + someΔ-Nominal-Verb (Nominal)
   T2. Affixation of *Past*
      X − Pst − V − X ⇒ X − V+Past − X

---

tions listed at the bottom of the table relate the phrase marker to the surface structure of the sentence.

Figure 3 shows the deep structure of an imperative sentence, *don't throw that ball.* Seven phrase-structure rules are involved, plus two transformations (not included in Table 5), one of which has the effect of deleting the subject of the sentence *you,* and the other of introducing

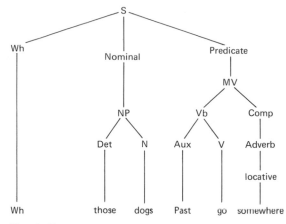

Fig. 2. Deep structure of *where those dogs goed?* (after Brown et al., 1968).

do and affixing it to *Neg*. The phrase-structure rules are 1, 2, 3, 4, 6, 13, and 14.

Who jumping on me is a Wh-question like the first sentence, but contains in addition a prepositional phrase and a verb in the progressive aspect; the auxiliary *is* has been omitted. Figure 4 is the deep structure. An affix-verb transformation parallel to T2 in Table 5 reverses the order of *ing* and *jump* and a morphological rule changes *Wh-someone* to *who*. Because β and not *be* is the form of the auxiliary, the surface structure omits *'s*.

A final example is presented in Fig. 5: *Susan is in the bath.* In this case

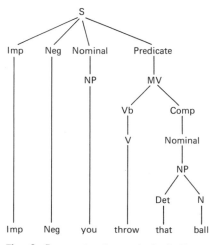

Fig. 3. Deep structure of *don't throw that ball*.

34

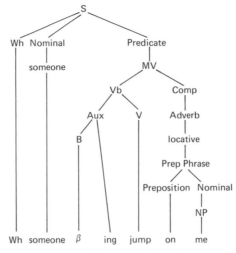

Fig. 4. Deep structure of *who jumping on me?*

be is a copular verb, not an auxiliary, so the affix-verb transformation used in deriving *who jumping on me* does not apply. Phrase-structural rules 1, 2, 7, 8, 9, 11, 12, 13, and 14 are used to generate this deep structure.

The grammar as included in Table 5 is not complete and the omissions create two distortions the reader should be warned against. One arises from the fact that only two transformations are shown. Most of

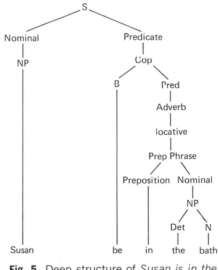

Fig. 5. Deep structure of *Susan is in the bath.*

the complexity in the phrase-structural component, especially in the development of the predicate, exists to support the transformations not in the table.

A second distortion is the manner of introducing words into the deep structure. In Figs. 2–5 words are appended to the bottom of the phrase-marker; the relation of the word to the structure of the sentence is unanalyzed. The grammar developed for Adam by Brown et al. goes further, in that words are represented as sets of syntactic features which state, for each word, the contexts the word appears in, its intrinsic characteristics, and its characteristics as the context for other words. This can be done quite compactly. For Adam at 36 months, the definition of *dog*, for example, included the following:

$$\begin{bmatrix} +\text{N} \\ +\text{Det}\underline{\quad} \\ +\text{ct} \\ \pm\text{no} \end{bmatrix}$$
dog

The +N at the top means that *dog* belongs to the category of nouns; the +ct, that *dog* belongs to the subcategory of count nouns (like *table* and unlike *sand*); the ±no, that *dog* belongs to the subcategory of nouns that can be pluralized (like *table* and unlike *pants*); and the +Det__, that *dog* can follow determiners. A rule of the grammar governs the insertion of words into phrases by requiring that the phrase-marker have the features specified in the word's lexical entry. Figure 2, for example, can receive *dog* — there is a slot of the right kind — but Fig. 4 has no place for *dog* or any other noun, since it receives only pronouns in the two nominal positions. When a lexicon is completely specified in terms of syntactic features, it is possible to play items off against each other when inserting words into phrase-markers. In this way the grammar avoids describing bizarre combinations — such nonsentences as *where is in the dog*.

Summary
In this chapter we have examined three points in the development of grammar. In time each point is nine months from the next, and in length of utterance one morpheme; but within these small increments of time and length grammar becomes highly complex. The line of development is established from the beginning. There is a continuity from the expression of grammatical relations with single words during the holophrastic period, through the use of simple word combinations, to the elaboration of grammar reflected in Table 5, in the grammatical relations each level attempts to express.

In this respect children follow a biologically unique path. No other species develops a system of communication devoted so totally to the communication of relations. Children, however, develop such a system naturally and very early. It is instructive to place human language within a larger biological context, and we turn to this in the next chapter.

THE BIOLOGICAL
BACKGROUND

Many animals exchange information in some systematic way. If one considers the variety of techniques employed, the different systems of communication that evolution has produced, a truly incredible miscellany results. Every possible sense modality is exploited somewhere — vision, hearing, olfaction, taste, touch, even sensitivity to electrical stimulation. Ants deposit chemicals to direct the aggregation and dispersion of the colony (Wilson, 1963, 1965). The Mormyridae fishes of South America emit electrical impulses (Lissman, 1951, 1958), fireflies flash lights (Lloyd, 1966), and some male spiders use semaphore signals to indicate to the huge females of their species that they are mates, not food (Bristowe, 1941). In communication, as elsewhere in nature, evolution has been fertile.

Human language is one highly specialized result of such evolution, a point carefully documented by Lenneberg (1967). It should be viewed as one of the peculiar outcomes of natural selection, related to some systems of communication elsewhere, but not exactly the same as any of them. The same, of course, is true of any system of communication, but the possibilities in nature are so various and human language uses so few of them that one cannot fail to be impressed with the sheer improbability of language.

In what follows, we consider language in relation to some of these other systems of communication. It will be convenient to divide the topic according to two criteria: how new signals are produced; and the type of information signaled. For the first, there is a traditional distinction between "grading" and "combining." Either new messages are produced by moving the signal along a physical dimension in correlation with a shift in content, or messages are produced by combining elements, each new combination standing for a new message. For content we can turn to three categories introduced by de Laguna (1927) and distinguish among expressive, nominal, and predicative messages, depending on whether the signals stand for internal states, outside events, or neither of these, but carry a meaning understood as being a comment on events of either kind. All communication systems include messages of both the expressive and nominal types, and some systems use both grading and combining, but generally there is a strong inclination toward just one method of production and one type of information. For a rough classification it is not misleading to consider communication systems as being of a piece in these respects. Table 6 shows how several systems can be classified. The table should not suggest that the members of the same cells are identical; obviously they are not. Also, the number of entries in each cell should not be taken to reflect the number of systems of that type in nature; these numbers are unknown. The empty cells, however, seem to be genuinely empty. Expressive systems are only graded and predicative systems are only combinatorial. These gaps reflect the way predicative and expressive systems of communication presumably have evolved. We will return to the question of evolution at the end of this chapter.

Table 6 **Classification of Animal Communication**

	Grading	Combining
Nominal	bees ants	finches cicadas
Expressive	wolves gulls monkeys human paralanguage	
Predicative		grammatical speech

It is noteworthy that holophrastic speech can be placed in Table 6 only with difficulty. It has expressive and graded aspects (as in Leopold's example of [dididi]) and by these criteria resembles the communications of wolves (Schenkel, 1947; Marler, 1959), gulls (Tinbergen, 1961), monkeys (Rowell and Hinde, 1962), and human paralanguage (Trager, 1958; Pittenger, Hockett, and Danehy, 1960). But the relational meanings of holophrastic speech are not conveyed through grading and they are not always expressive. If we assume that the empty cells of Table 6 reflect real affinities between types of signals and types of information, holophrastic speech contains internal contradictions that make it unstable and open to change.

To appreciate fully the biological context of language acquisition, it is necessary to consider in detail examples of the different cells of Table 6. Each section below treats one cell. We begin where there are direct influences on child language.

Primate Communication
In contrast to insects and song birds, whose communication systems are discussed later, primates exchange few signals that specifically

refer to the external environment. Alarm calls are about all they have along this line. But the repertoire of calls that relate to the internal environment is very rich; for expressive communication the primates have no equals.

Vocal Communication Among Primates The most carefully studied animal has been the rhesus monkey, and we will concentrate on him. We lose little generality focusing on one species. According to Rowell and Hinde (1962) and Rowell (1962), the rhesus possesses nine calls. All but one, the alarm call, express some aspect of an animal's inner condition. Table 7 lists the calls, gives a rough description of each, and shows the situations in which they occur.

Table 7 **Rhesus Calls**
(Marler and Hamilton, 1966, after Rowell and Hinde, 1962)

Call	Description	Situational Context
Roar	Long, fairly loud noise	Made by a very confident animal, when threatening another of inferior rank
Pant-threat	Like a roar, but divided into "syllables"	Made by a less confident animal, who wants support in making an attack
Bark	Like the single bark of a dog	Made by a threatening animal who is not aggressive enough to move forward
Growl	Like a bark, but quieter, shriller, and broken into short units	Made by a mildly alarmed animal
Shrill-bark	Not described	Alarm call
Screech	Involves an abrupt pitch change, up then down	Made when threatening a higher-ranked animal
Geckering screech	Like a screech, but broken into syllables	Made when threatened by another animal
Scream	Shorter than a screech and without a rise and fall	Made when losing a fight and being bitten
Squeak	Short, very high noise	Made by a defeated and exhausted animal at the end of a fight

Other primates have similar calls. One interesting feature of primate vocal communication is the high degree of similarity among the different species. The number of calls is the same within narrow limits— between 9 and 15—and calls with similar significance sound similar. Some kind of bark signals alarm among gorillas, chimpanzees, baboons, rhesus monkeys, and langurs. Screeching and screaming signify distress over the same range of animals. Soft low-frequency sounds are universally used in situations of confrontation. It is not without interest that these sounds have the same significance for man. We, too, shout in alarm, scream with fright, and growl with anger. Animals other than primates use altogether different signals in similar situations. The basic system of acoustic communication among primates must have evolved long ago, before the lines leading to the contemporary primate species, including man, had appeared. We should not be surprised to find these aspects of primate communication in early child speech.

The calls listed in Table 7 are completely graded into one another. Indeed, it is not clear that there are nine distinct calls. There may only be vocalization, subtly modulated along many dimensions. Rowell considers the rhesus calls to form a single system connected by a number of continuous series. Figure 6, taken from Rowell (1962) in the version given by Marler and Hamilton (1966), shows spectrographs of these calls, with arrows added to indicate the direction of grading. Marler (1965) believes the same could be shown of chimpanzee communication, and the conclusion probably can be extended to all primate communication. The basis of productivity in the acoustic communication of primates is grading, and through it, apparently, an infinite variety of messages can be created.

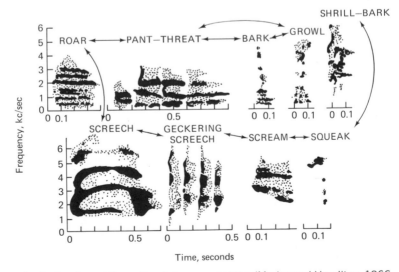

Fig. 6. Grading of the calls of rhesus monkeys (Marler and Hamilton, 1966, after Rowell, 1962).

Visual Communication Among Primates Visual and acoustic communication are aspects of unified signals as far as the animals are concerned, so it is not surprising that similar statements can be made of them with regard to function. However, the two types of communication are not yoked, or at least not tightly so, and a rich interplay is possible.

Unlike acoustic communication, the number of modal visual signals differs from species to species. All primates have some variant of "open-mouth threat," "grimace," and "lip-smacking." The first threatens other animals, the second pacifies them, and the third shows neutrality. Besides this universal core there is in one species or another yawning, tail elevation (or depression), eyelid fluttering, direct or indirect gaze, and head movements. Baboons, perhaps because they have been more extensively studied, appear to have an especially elaborate set of visual signals (De Vore, 1965). Among other things, they grind teeth, flatten ears, stand on hind legs, move shoulders forward and shrug them, and make repulsion gestures (especially toward scorpions). All such gestures serve an expressive function, insofar as one can tell from the circumstances in which they are produced. Fear, aggression, and sex are the principal motives expressed, but more subtle sentiments also find an outlet this way (some claim to see tenderness in the faces of gorilla mothers).

The expressive function of gestures probably evolved out of the protective movements naturally made by startled or threatened animals. The eyebrows are automatically lowered when the eyes are closed, for example, and eyebrow lowering is a common gesture of submission. At some point, some protective movements took on informational value, becoming gestures as well as movements, and thereafter evolved under new selection pressures. The pressures were typically associated with the development of social organization, so the gestures are typically implicated in social interactions serving functions related to their original role as protective movements. Like eyebrow lowering, grinning is a protective reaction in many primates, and as a gesture is also given by the inferior animal in an interaction. The "frozen grin" in man, appearing in subordinates, presumably has the same evolutionary origin (Andrew, 1963).

Indeed, man and other primates share a number of gestures and facial expressions. Besides grinning in submission, many primates as well as man grin in pleasure. Man, along with most monkeys and apes, protrudes his lips in threat, the "open-mouth threat." (To verify this, assume a boxer's stance, imagine yourself about to deliver a powerful blow, and note what has happened to your mouth. Also threat *words* in languages often involve lip rounding—e.g., *boo* in English, *wa* in Japanese.) We thus show our standing as primates. But other primates appear to possess considerably more elaborate systems of expressive communication than we do, especially visual expressive communication. Their secret lies in the number of gestures and the rich patterns of grading. Open-mouth threat, for example, is for us only marginally a gesture, but for monkeys and apes it is a primary signal of threat.

Evolution has apparently carried them farther down this road than it has carried us.

The influence of primate expressive communication is easy to detect in our species. An entire specialty has grown up within linguistics to study it (e.g., Trager, 1958; Duncan, 1969). We ought not be surprised, therefore, to see aspects of primate communication emerging at an early point in language development. The expressive and conative functions of holophrastic speech described in the last chapter can be understood in this way.

More surprising is a convergence between our species and the passerine birds, who are remote from us phylogenetically, in which the other primates do not participate.

Bird Song

Passerine birds, the true song birds, are human-like in a number of interesting ways. Their songs are largely categorical; in many cases novel songs are produced by combining categories; combinations enter into combinations to form hierarchical structures; individual birds add flourishes to identify themselves, like proper names; geographically separated birds of the same species sing in different but related ways, and there are bird dialects; and young birds must learn the particular combinatorial system of their locality. Song birds are thus human-like. But they are not humans. The very existence of so much similarity serves to sharpen the contrasts that remain.

Take the categorical aspect first. Figures 7a and 7b present two sound spectrographic recordings of a village weaver bird, an African finch; Fig. 7a is the bird's low-intensity alarm call and Fig. 7b its high-intensity alarm call. The calls are related in significance, marking two points on a scale of alarm, but the spectrograms are very different. Whereas the low-intensity call consists of three concentrated bands of energy, lower ones more extended in time than higher ones, the high-intensity call consists of two brief outbursts of energy, widely and identically distributed across the spectrum. Each call is a distinct acoustic category, unrelated to the other. The high- and low-intensity calls may have evolved so as to be maximally different from each other, but this does not affect the point that there is no grading. Higher intensity of alarm is not encoded by increasing (or decreasing) the intensity, frequency, or duration of the low-intensity call; it is encoded by a different call. The converse also occurs. Figure 8 shows the spectrogram of a nest call from the same weaver bird. It differs only slightly from the high-intensity alarm call, but the significance of the two calls is entirely different. The first is given by broody females, the second by males and females under attack.

Not only are bird calls categorical, but in many cases smaller units are combined into larger ones. For some birds this ability is developed to a great degree. The mistle thrush, for example, combines approximately 20 basic themes. Figure 9, taken from Marler and Hamilton (1966), shows the spectrographic record of the last four songs (40–43)

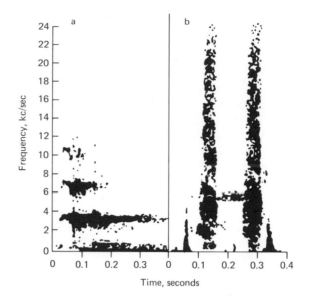

Fig. 7. Categorical bird song. Spectrographic tracings of (a) the low intensity alarm call of the village weaver bird, and (b) the high intensity alarm call of the same bird (Marler and Hamilton, 1966).

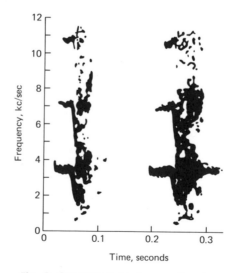

Fig. 8. Categorical bird song. Spectrograph tracing of the nest call of the village weaver bird (Marler and Hamilton, 1966).

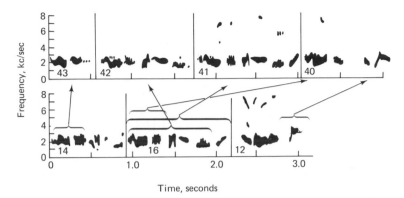

Fig. 9. Hierarchical structure in bird song (Marler and Hamilton, 1966).

in a singing bout by a mistle thrush compared to three earlier songs (12, 14, 16) in the same bout. As the arrows and brackets show, themes recur in several places and there is a hierarchical organization — parts of recurring themes themselves recurring independently. Other birds, such as the European blackbird and the song thrush, have even larger repertoires of basic themes and apparently combine them with total abandon (Marler and Hamilton, 1966).

These birds clearly possess the ability to produce songs by combining elementary parts. Moreover, some of them follow rules in forming combinations. In the sequence of themes in the mistle thrush song, for example, only five themes appear at the beginning, the same theme never both precedes and follows a given theme, most themes are never repeated, most themes can be followed by no more than one or two other themes, etc. (Isaac and Marler, 1963). It is impossible to say exactly what the rules are that summarize these regularities, but the regularities obviously exist.

What use does a mistle thrush have for upwards of 143 different songs (the largest number so far observed; Marler, 1959)? The biological function of such high productivity, and hence the pressure under which it evolved, is far from obvious. Craig (1943) believes that it reflects a primitive esthetic sense. Marler (1959) suggests that it promotes individual identification, an important function in some of these birds. It is possible, of course, that some of the productivity involved in bird songs serves no function at all, or that it is an epiphenomenal correlate of some other activity which is functional. Whatever the explanation, however, the productivity of bird song apparently serves no semantic purpose. Song birds combine sounds but they do not combine messages. If this generalization is true, productivity in bird song and productivity in human language serve fundamentally different functions and presumably evolved under very different selection pressures.

Immature male chaffinches must learn various details of the local "dialect," as must California white-crowned sparrows, European bullfinches, and mimicking birds of all sorts. Such birds do not develop

45

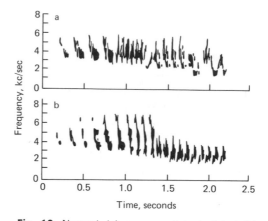

Fig. 10. Normal (a) compared to isolated (b) chaffinch songs (Thorpe, 1961).

normal songs when raised in isolation or with other species, since they must pass through a period of true acquisition. Figure 10 shows the difference between (a) a normal chaffinch song and (b) the song of a Casper Hauser chaffinch raised in isolation. The difference looks small on a spectrogram, but the major distinction is in the organization of the song and it is important to a chaffinch. The normal bird produces three distinct phrases in the song proper to which he adds a terminal flourish for purposes of individual identification. The isolated bird, on the other hand, produces just two phrases and no terminal flourish. The two songs differ in their organization; they do not differ very much in their ultimate constituents. Compare, for example, the notes in the third phrase of the normal song to some of the notes in the second phrase of the isolated song. They are the same sounds but used differently.

Thorpe (1961) has described the course of acquisition for chaffinches as "crystallization." The metaphor alludes both to the speed of development—important changes occurring within four days—and to its apparent course—elements being selected, trimmed, and rearranged to make up a full song. Chaffinches hatch in the late spring, spend the summer as juveniles, and become breeders after about nine months. A normal song first appears in the breeding period. Before this time, there is an initial phase of incoherent chirping, followed in the autumn by something called subsong. Isolated birds are identical to normal birds up to the subsong period, but isolation prevents them from passing beyond the subsong except in the most restricted ways. Thorpe lists the following differences between subsongs and full songs: the fundamental frequency of the subsong is lower; the total range of frequencies covered in the subsong is greater; the subsong is quieter; the pattern of notes is different; and phrases are longer. Some of these differences have to do with the unmotivated state of chaffinches before the breeding season. The quietness and low fundamental frequency of the subsong probably arise from this cause. The other differences, how-ever, exist because young birds have not yet discovered the locally prescribed structure of the full song. The process of acquisition consists in making these discoveries. Subsongs typically contain rattling noises, which are eliminated in the passage to full song. The frequency-spread of each note is reduced, the phraseology is sharpened, and the location of notes of particular kinds is changed. Four steps in this development, from raw subsong to full song, are shown in Fig. 11.

It is not possible to equate the crystallization of the chaffinch full song with the acquisition of language. Utterly different systems are involved. There is, nonetheless, a basis for comparison in the fact that both children and young birds develop organized structures. One way to do this is through the association of elements. First pairs are formed, then triads, and so forth, until a system of appropriate complexity has been constructed. This associative method of gluing together parts is implausible in the acquisition of language (see the Appendix), but it could conceivably be used by chaffinches. It is of some interest, there-

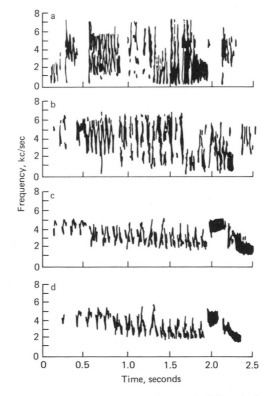

Fig. 11. Steps in the development of the chaf-finch full song. Subsong is (a), and full song is (d) (Thorpe, 1961).

fore, that chaffinches do not acquire full songs through the formation of associations. On the contrary, rather than building up large parts by associating small parts, development moves in the opposite direction, toward differentiation and rearrangement. There is convergence between man and bird where a problem of structuring exists. Language acquisition takes the form it does, perhaps, because differentiation and rearrangement are favored ways of learning any combinatorial system, regardless of the degree of complication and abstraction. It is difficult to believe that two animals as distantly related as chaffinches and man could arrive at similar solutions by chance alone.

Insect Communication

Whereas bird songs show unexpected similarities to language, insect calls show the expected dissimilarities. Even so, there are resemblances between language and some systems of insect communication. One such example is discussed directly below. But between most mammalian and insect communication there is a profound gulf. We will find little overlap between them. For this very reason, however, we gain perspective by reviewing aspects of insect communication.

Cicadas The first and simplest example is the Seventeen-Year Cicada of North America (*Cassinii*). The insect begins life as a fertilized egg inserted into the bark of a tree, soon metamorphoses into a larva and burrows underground, and there remains until attaining adult form 17 years later. Then, along with millions of contemporaries, it reemerges, congregates at some central place, courts, mates, and dies. Such is the life cycle of *Cassinii,* and at one point in it communication is crucial. It is only through the exchange of acoustic signals that these cicadas learn where to congregate and when to court. If by some calamitous turn of events cicadas lost the ability to transmit acoustic information the entire population would be eliminated in a stroke.

Cassinii gives four signals. One is clearly expressive, a raspy noise produced when the insect is seized, picked up, or eaten, which Alexander and Moore (1958) call the "disturbance squawk." If the disturbance squawk conveys information to anyone, it is to the cicada's tormentor, who might be induced to drop it. The sound apparently has no effect on other cicadas. The other three signals are all truly communicative. One is a congregation call. It consists of a series of 12 to 40 ticks delivered at a rate of some 20 per second, followed immediately by a buzz lasting one or two seconds. The congregation call is given only by males, but attracts cicadas of both sexes. Males tend to recruit one another into a chorus with the congregation call, all individuals in the same place ticking and buzzing in unison. After a large number of cicadas have gathered and the males have chorused in synchrony for a time, a ritual of courtship begins.

The other two signals available to *Cassinii* now come into play. One, the preliminary courtship call, is given by a male when he notices a female an inch or two away. The other, the advanced courtship call, is given by a male when a female is almost within grasp. The preliminary courtship call invariably occurs before the advanced courtship call, although the advanced courtship call can be given without the preliminary courtship call occurring first if a female is discovered very near by. The preliminary courtship call is a prolonged slow ticking with three to five bursts of sound per second. The advanced courtship call is a prolonged series of short buzzes also with three to five bursts of sound per second. Thus, in the typical case of a male advancing on a female, the two courtship calls together result in a ticking followed by a buzzing—that is, the pattern of signals comprising the congregation call.

Because of limitations in the mechanism for producing sound, cicadas can make ticks and buzzes but little else. Even the disturbance squawk is a tick and buzz produced simultaneously. The only avenues for change open to *Cassinii* are variations in rate and intensity, and both are exploited to distinguish congregation and courtship calls. Ticks and buzzes are themselves different for *Cassinii,* as evidenced by the fact that the two courtship calls are distinguished on this basis alone. It thus becomes clear that cicadas, for reasons of mechanical simplicity, produce a call by combining two elementary parts. Ticking at a high rate followed by buzzing also at a high rate is organized into one call, whereas ticking at a low rate followed by buzzing at a low rate is resolved into two calls.

Cassinii is not unusual in possessing a combinatorial communication system; many animals do. It is noteworthy that combinatorality appears at scattered places in the animal kingdom. As a method of producing new signals, it is not characteristic of entire orders or even entire genera, but only of species. Thus man uses a combinatorial system while other primates use a graded one. Passerine birds use combinations but Herring Gulls, for example, use grading. And, as we now see, cicadas have a combined signal while honey bees, who are discussed next, have graded ones.

Bees With respect to communication, the bee is to Insecta as man is to Mammalia. Both represent extremes of development along the evolutionary lines open to them. For insects the line has been the use of nominal signals coupled with extreme social rigidity. The Seventeen-Year Cicada shows a limited exploitation of these resources. The honey bee has carried the possibilities of nominalization and rigidity to an amazing degree of refinement.

In a famous series of experiments, von Frisch (1950, 1967) demonstrated how a worker bee, returning from a foraging expedition, communicates information about a source of food by performing a dance on the wall of the hive. Other workers, observing her dance, will fly out to the source of food. If the food source is within a radius of about 90 meters (for the bees von Frisch studied) the new workers look for it aimlessly, but always remain within the 90 meter limit. If the food source is beyond 90 meters the new bees fly directly toward it. The

49

first bee was obviously able to inform the other bees whether the source of food was near or far, and if far, how far and in what direction.

When the source of food is less than 90 meters from the hive the foraging worker performs what von Frisch called a "round dance," so called because of the circular path traced by the bee on the wall of the hive. The bee runs up, turns around and runs back over a looping course to the first turning point, then turns around again and reverses direction over the same route as before. The bee may continue in this way for some time, recruiting other bees into her dance; or she may stop and be recruited herself into the dance performed by another bee. Whether a dancer recruits or is recruited and, more generally, the degree of recruitment by any dance depends on the vigor with which the movements of the dance are executed. In the round dance, vigor means rate of progress. The dance stimulates more dancing in proportion to the number of revolutions made per unit time. Vigor in turn depends on the quality of the food source in relation to the momentary needs of the hive, something to which we return below.

When a source of food is beyond 90 meters, the dance takes a different form, becoming what von Frisch called a "waggle dance." The dancer now traces a figure-eight, the two circular parts squashed together so as to form a straight segment between them. The straight segment is the informative part. The distance of the source is reflected in the speed of the dance — the farther the slower. The quality of the source is reflected in the number of "waggles" the dancer makes with her abdomen as she traverses the straight segment — the more the better. And the direction of the source is reflected in the angle the straight segment makes with the line of gravity (the bee dancing on the vertical surface of the hive) — this angle being the same as the angle between the bee's flight path and the position of the sun. (For a different theory, that bees transmit information through vibrations, see Wenner, 1964.)

All of this is quite remarkable. To convey such facts about distance, direction, or quality, human languages use sentences. "The food is moderately far away in a northerly direction," expresses our idea. "The food" alone and out of context expresses nothing at all. Is it the same for bees? Is there any reason to suppose that bees "understand" what they communicate — understand that the rate of the waggle dance, for example, has to do with the distance of the source, or even that the dance itself has to do with food? As far as one can infer from the various experiments on bee communication, the components of the dance are like isolated names — like "food" alone and out of context for us. The crucial difference is that bees, when they receive a nominal signal, have no option as to behavior; they must react in a certain way. That is the basis of all insect communication and it is this feature that is so different from anything with which we have first-hand familiarity. Let us look at one or two specific cases.

Take the matter of distance. It is easy to deceive a forager bee as to how far she has flown. It is easy because the bee has no idea about distance, but about effort instead. If a bee is forced to walk to a source of food, her dance will report a much greater distance than that actually covered (Bisetzky, 1957; Marler and Hamilton, 1966). The same will happen if she flies uphill or into a headwind (von Frisch, 1948; Heran and Wanke, 1952). From these and many other indications, it seems clear that the rate of the waggle dance says merely "exertion, degree x." The rate of the dance refers to a certain expenditure of energy.

Take the communication of quality (Lindaur, 1961).[1] The temperature of a hive must be maintained within a narrow range or the larvae will perish. Overheating, a constant danger in the summer, is avoided by spraying water on the walls of the hive. When the temperature rises above a critical point, returning forager bees dance more vigorously in proportion to the dilution of the nectar they bring back, rather than, as usual, in proportion to its concentration. The more vigorous dance for a dilute source in turn recruits other bees, who then visit that dilute source instead of concentrated ones. The effect is to change the logistics of the hive from the intake of food to the intake of water.

The first bees to notice the rise in temperature are the newly matured ones who care for the larvae in the bowels of the hive. They discharge all their water, which causes them to beg from other nearby bees, who in turn discharge their water. Thus a line of water-deprived bees advances to the periphery of the hive. Returning foragers always attempt to unload themselves upon entering the hive and they perform their dance with a number of waggles in proportion to the ease with which they were able to do this. In the case of a temperature emergency, the bees waiting at the entrance of the hive — by now all deprived of water — greet foragers carrying dilute solutions of nectar more enthusiastically than foragers with concentrated solutions.

The crucial communicative links in this chain are the dance and the reception at the entrance of the hive. The reception is directly controlled by the need of the waiting bees for water; and the dance in turn is controlled by the reception. The entire system for adjusting the logistics of the hive remains within the bounds of nominal communication. The dancer only dances vigorously in proportion to the warmth of her welcome. The recipient of the message in turn is or is not swept up into the forager's dance. No information is exchanged about food, or water, or the relative need of the hive for the two.

The closer one looks at the mechanism of bee communication, the less room there is for anything resembling a sentence. Communication depends on the lock-step adjustment of bees to other bees. A particular signal produces a particular reaction. Every message says something about the same one or three things. The entire system is so rigid that nothing is required beyond a method of referring to biologically important states. Given nominal signals and ironclad social control, communication takes place faultlessly, but bees could never develop anything like sentences from nominal signals that so dominate action.

[1] I am grateful to Dr. Carol Feldman for drawing my attention to this example.

The Evolution of Basic Sentence Structure

Apparently man is not the only animal capable of sentence-like communication. Baboons have a two-step alarm call with something like the topic-comment structure of sentences (Marler, 1967). When the alarm is sounded the troop first looks at the animal who sounds it and then follows his line of regard to locate the predator. The call announces a "topic" (alarm) and the direction of regard is the "comment." This analogy might be mistaken, but accepting it at face value, baboons can be said to show sentence structure. However, it is a structure sharply limited in use. If baboons have a language, it is a language with only one sentence. In contrast, sentences are obligatory in human language. Whatever favored sentence structure in the evolution of language must have operated at an early point to have had such a wide scope.

It is well known that two contradictory developments occurred in the evolution of man. One was an enlargement of the skull, the other a shrinkage of the birth canal—the first occurring in response to increased brain size and the second in response to bipedalism. The problem of getting a larger infant head through a smaller maternal canal was solved by an increasing prematurity of birth. Compared to other primates, human infants are born at an earlier point in development. Table 8 shows for several primate species the ratio of the period spent in gestation to the total period of growth. Lower numbers mean relatively less intrauterine development, and, as can be seen, homo sapiens lies some distance from the other primate species.

Table 8 **Ratio of Gestation Period to Total Growth for Several Primates** (except for the ratio, from Schultz, 1956, p. 891)

	Gestation (weeks)	Total Growth (weeks)	Gestation/ Growth (×100)
Lemur	18	156	11.5
Orangutan	39	572	6.8
Macaque	24	364	6.6
Gibbon	30	468	6.4
Chimpanzee	33	572	5.6
Man	38	1040	3.6

This much is widely known, and a number of psychologists and biologists have speculated on the consequences for mental growth of such early exposure to the environment (e.g., Washburn and Hamburg, 1965). There is, however, a further implication of premature human birth, as has been pointed out by G. A. Miller (personal communication). A rela-

52

tively premature infant is a relatively helpless infant. A newborn baboon, who is not premature, can immediately change posture, locate food, and view the world. Shortly after birth it can locomote, explore, and play. These activities serve important needs, but a human infant, being more primitive, accomplishes none of these things by itself. Rather, a human baby must *indicate* to its mother what it needs and its mother must recognize the significance of what the baby indicates. There is a communication problem for newborn homo sapiens that is unique among the primates.

Following Miller, we can identify a selection pressure that almost certainly operated in the evolution of man: There was a biological advantage for mothers and infants who could communicate information about the infant's hunger, curiosity, and discomfort, inner states that other primate infants are able to adjust for themselves.

What new developments could have met this pressure? Further evolution of the primate exclamatory system would appear to have been a natural solution. All primates, including homo sapiens, can communicate information about inner states. But the primate communication system probably evolved from actual movements or from the reliable vocal correlates of actual movements (Andrew, 1963), whereas the new selection pressure arose precisely because premature infants are incapable of such controlled movements. Another possibility is a nominal system, but this too must have been blocked. Proto-man would already have been too complex socially for such a solution to succeed.

The remaining alternative is a system in which signals are arbitrarily associated with states and actions. The signals, since they are arbitrary, could be based on anything a newborn was capable of doing. Motoric helplessness is circumvented by a communication system with arbitrary signals, and natural selection would have favored mothers and infants able to use it.

There is another implication of this hypothesis. Contemporary newborns begin to babble sometime around five months. Before five months their vocalizations, while copious, are limited to a few undifferentiated sounds. The proto-human infant we are discussing must have had a gestation period longer than the one of today, but if these infants followed a similar course of development in other respects they may have been able to babble shortly after birth, not five or six months after birth as now. Good articulatory abilities would have been available at the beginning of the evolution we are describing. According to this hypothesis, then, natural selection favored an ability to pair arbitrary signals with inner states. Among the signaling possibilities, vocalization stands out as being exceptionally rich at an early age. The result would be an innate ability to produce and interpret vocal signals that do not express internal states but are arbitrarily worked out by each mother and infant. Such arbitrariness is essential for all grammatical relations. None of the relations of the holophrastic period—those of predicate, subject, object, and location—could be communicated without words being arbitrarily paired with events or objects; if the pairing is fixed, the signal is not available for communicating any grammatical relation. The emergence of grammatical relations in holophrastic speech, therefore, presupposes something like the course of evolution described above.

Can Apes Talk?

This evolution of arbitrary vocal signals assumes that the natal point for proto-humans was roughly 5 months after birth today. Birth at 5 contemporary months corresponds to a gestation/growth ratio of 5.7, which is close to the gestation/growth ratio of 5.6 for contemporary chimpanzees (Table 8). Chimpanzees may be heading toward a communication system with arbitrary signals. There have been several efforts to teach chimpanzees to talk (Kellogg and Kellogg, 1933; Hayes, 1951), but all have failed dismally. Hayes' chimpanzee, for example, could utter only a few words after many months of instruction. However, a new effort is currently underway, apparently with strikingly different results (Gardner and Gardner, 1969). The Gardners use deaf-mute signs instead of actual speech, and find at 25 months that Washoe (as the chimpanzee is called) has a vocabulary of some 30 words. Thirty words is about the vocabulary size of human children at 25 months, and is many times larger than the vocabularies acquired by the other instructed chimpanzees.

These findings are most interesting and important, and it is essential to understand what they actually show of language learning in a chimpanzee. From the description of Washoe given by Gardner and Gardner (1969) and more importantly from the films of Washoe the Gardners have been showing, I find not much room for doubt that the chimpanzee has learned to use genuine words (although this opinion is not unanimous). Moreover, she uses them spontaneously and inventively. If the words are genuine, we can ask about their properties as linguistic entities. In this regard certain peculiarities appear.

Gardner and Gardner (1969) list the first 34 words acquired by Washoe in the order of acquisition. Since all the words were at first used alone, they can be compared to holophrastic speech. Holophrastic speech consists mainly of three kinds of utterance, from an adult point of view: inventions of the child ([ʔə?]), nouns (eye), and adjectives (hot). Words that would be verbs and words that would be prepositions directly encoding relations among objects are almost completely missing; such words appear only gradually during the stage of pivot–open constructions. In all these respects Washoe's development of vocabulary is different.

Among the first 34 words she learned are 8 that would be verbs and 2 that would be prepositions, as against 16 that would be nouns and 3 that would be adjectives; no invented words are mentioned. Not only is there a relative abundance of verbs and prepositions, but these words, last to appear in human speech, are the first to appear with Washoe. Of the 10 verbs and prepositions in Washoe's vocabulary, 8 were among the first 12 words acquired. Washoe does not at first use words freely to communicate grammatical relations, as children do; she first learns specific words for relations. Children, of course, also are exposed to verbs and prepositions, but they do not include them in holophrastic speech because, presumably, if any word can appear in any relation, special relational words contain no information. With respect to vocabulary, therefore, Washoe reverses children.

Washoe also combines words and the combinations are spontaneous. Unfortunately, Gardner and Gardner provide little information about this aspect of her behavior and only about a half dozen examples are available. As will be shown in the next chapter, when children combine words they make explicit the grammatical relations that are implicit in holophrastic speech. These relations determine what gets combined with what. There seem to be no such restrictions operating on the combinations of Washoe. The few examples given include such a wide variety of relations, and some of the relations are so specialized (e.g., "in order to reach" in "open flower"), that it is difficult to believe that the words are being related at all. Also, the Gardners report, Washoe combines signs in no definite order (but the same is true of some children). It is plausible to interpret Washoe's combinations as being unintegrated sequences of words, produced perhaps in the order of their importance to Washoe, but between which there are no grammatical relations. In this respect also, Washoe reverses children.

In summary, while Washoe reveals an ability to use words to refer to events, she shows no ability to organize these words into sentences. It is, perhaps, what we should expect from an animal at the "threshold" of some kind of genuine linguistic system. Homo sapiens, having gone far beyond this threshold, is able to do far more.

**UNIVERSALS IN
CHILD LANGUAGE**

We have seen that language is unique among animal communication systems in its ability to express grammatical relations. The earliest combinations of words in child speech, which for many children result in the Pivot–Open distinction, depend on this universal ability. We will begin our discussion of linguistic universals in child language with the P–O distinction, although in the end we will dim its significance somewhat.

The P–O distinction is a natural extension of the holophrastic period. The continuity with the past is reflected, curiously, in what happens in future periods of development. In order for development to take the course it actually takes, the P–O distinction must have been established on the basis of the grammatical relations evolved in the holophrastic period. This inference brings us to our first topic.

DIFFERENTIATION AND GENERIC CLASSIFICATION

Adam, whom we discussed in Chapter 3, developed the grammatical classes of English through differentiation. The class differentiated was the P class included in Table 2, and the classes developed from it were articles, demonstrative pronouns, possessive pronouns, adjectives, and determiners. This process took place in five months. Figure 12 shows how it went. The essential aspect of differentiation is that entire adult classes are removed at once. Separate words in the same adult class do not come out of the P class at different times. Thus, a new class is formed and then removed; single words are not removed and then formed into a class. Zhenya, the son of the Russian linguist Gvozdev (1961), developed a P class like Adam's and formed adult grammatical categories through a comparable process of differentiation. It is the phenomenon of differentiation that suggests a direct relation between the P–O distinction and the grammatical relations.

Differentiation can take place only if the classes differentiated — the P class in Adam's and Zhenya's cases — are *generically appropriate* (McNeill, 1966a). A generically appropriate P class is one that ignores but potentially admits all the relevant distinctions of the adult grammar. Adam, for example, had the two articles in his P class at Time 1; he did not have one in the P class and one in the O class. Similarly, every adjective then in Adam's vocabulary was in the P class; there were none

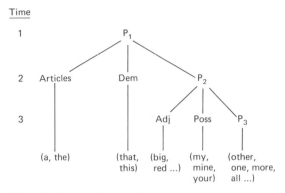

Fig. 12. The differentiation of adult grammatical classes from a single pivot class (after McNeill, 1966a).

in the O class. In fact, Adam's P class contained every member of several adult grammatical classes then available, even though none of these classes was itself distinguished in Adam's grammar. Differentiation always presupposes generic classification, a fact not usually recognized. But generic classification means that children classify words (as P and O) in a way that is consistent with the more subtle distinctions they have not yet drawn.

What guides the process of generic classification? One explanation, which will be modified later, was suggested by McNeill (1966a). The idea is to associate the telegraphic sentences of young children with the semigrammatical sentences of adults. One fact stands out in connection with semigrammaticality that makes this association plausible. Semigrammatical sentences can be placed in an order that corresponds to the distance they depart from full grammaticality. To use Chomsky's (1961) examples, while *John plays golf* is well formed, *golf plays John* and *golf plays symmetrical* are deviations, and the second is a greater deviation than the first. The order of development in child language corresponds to this order of grammaticality. McNeill gave sentences recorded from children at different ages to adults, who decided which had been uttered at an earlier age. There were no cues to age except the relative degree of grammaticalness. Vocabulary and length were matched and every sentence was grammatically deviant. An example is *a that Adam ball* versus *that a Adam ball*. The earlier sentences were picked 81 percent of the time (chance being 50 percent). Unless adults have separate standards for judging the structure of child speech (which is most unlikely, since there is no way to have developed them), this result shows a basic connection between semigrammaticality and the linguistic development of children.

Chomsky explained the rank ordering of semigrammatical sentences by reference to a hierarchy of grammatical categories in which successively higher levels divide words less and less finely. At the lowest level are all the grammatical distinctions of English; at the highest level there are no grammatical distinctions at all. A semigrammatical sentence is one represented only at some intermediate level in this hierarchy. Of two semigrammatical sentences, the one represented at a higher intermediate level is the one that deviates most. *John plays golf* is represented at all levels of the hierarchy, including the most differentiated level at the bottom, but *golf plays John* is represented only above where the distinction between animate and inanimate nouns is lost, and *golf plays symmetrical* is represented only above where the distinction between nouns and adjectives is lost.

The differentiation of grammatical classes in Fig. 12 can be taken as a record of differentiation of Chomsky's hierarchy. For this reason early sentences from children honor fewer distinctions than later sentences do, but at any point early distinctions are generically related to later ones. The later distinctions come from a lower level in this same hierarchy. The interpretation of McNeill (1966a) was that the upper levels of Chomsky's hierarchy are universal among languages and reflect children's innate linguistic abilities. There is no class of "modifiers" in English or Russian that coincides with Adam's or Zhenya's P class, but at some level in Chomsky's hierarchy articles, demonstrative and personal pronouns, adjectives, and determiners are all alike. Children at this level overlook these distinctions, but later arrive at the actual adult categories, as Adam and Zhenya did, by differentiation.

Grammatical Relations

We have not yet shown how the differentiation of grammatical categories in Fig. 12 depends on the grammatical relations of the holophrastic period. De Laguna (1927) believed that two-word sentences appear in development when children decide to announce the topics that go with their comments. We would also expect two-word sentences when children decide to mention the verbs that go with objects or the nouns that go with modifiers. Children begin to produce two-word sentences when they adopt the requirement that grammatical relations be expressed overtly in speech. Table 3, presented in Chapter 3, contained every combination of grammatical classes in Adam's speech at 28 months ("Time 1" in Fig. 12). It was remarked in Chapter 3 that the observed combinations possess a consistency lacked by the combinations not observed. We can now see that this consistency arises from the grammatical relations of subject, predicate, verb, object, modifier, and head noun.

A predicate is defined in the theory of grammar (Chomsky, 1965) as a VP directly dominated by S. For Adam, in Table 3, the following combinations are consistent with this definition: VN, NV, VNN, VPN, NVN, NNV, and NPN (the last assuming an absent V—the sentence was *Adam two boot*). A subject is an NP immediately dominated by S, a main verb is a V immediately dominated by VP, an object (of a verb) is an NP immediately dominated by VP, a modifier is a determiner immediately dominated by NP, and a head noun is an N also immediately dominated by NP. Opposite each combination of classes in Table 3 are listed the grammatical relations with which it is consistent. As the reader can see, every combination is consistent with at least one grammatical relation. More significantly, the combinations not in Table 3 are not consistent with any of these grammatical relations. With three grammatical classes, there are $(3)^2 = 9$ different patterns two words long and $(3)^3 = 27$ different patterns three words long. Five of the two-word patterns and 19 of the three-word patterns do not correspond to a grammatical relation. None of these patterns occurred in the sample of utterances collected from Adam at 28 months.[1]

An explanation of Table 3, therefore, is that Adam had organized his speech in terms of the basic grammatical relations that were already available from the holophrastic period, but he had not yet acquired any transformation of English that combines structures or adds elements — for example, conjunction or embedding. It is for this reason that such a pattern as VVN did not occur in Adam's speech, even though it corresponds to a common surface structure in the speech of adults — for example, *come and eat lunch* or *run and get the ball.* The two verbs come from *separate* underlying structures, which are combined only through transformations.

Other children also use these grammatical relations. Three children studied by Bloom (1968) and two other children followed by Brown (unpublished sources) give parallel evidence. More striking is the appearance of the same grammatical relations in the speech of children learning other languages. Evidence from the acquisition of Japanese has been discussed by McNeill (1966b). And Slobin (in press), reviewing a number of diary studies, has found evidence of grammatical relations in the speech of children separately learning more than a dozen European languages.

We can think of the process of combining words to express the grammatical relations as depending on the existence of certain syntactic features in a child's lexicon. In the case of Adam and Zhenya the function served by the P class was modification. A relation of modification holds between a determiner and a noun when both belong to the same NP. In order for this definition to hold, any word that modifies a noun must bear the features [+Det] and [+__N], and any word a determiner modifies must bear [+N] and [+Det__]. The features describe the part of a phrase-marker where the modification relation can hold. Words that appear there, according to the rules for lexical insertion, must have these features. The two features [+Det, +__N] exactly designate the pivot class of Adam and Zhenya. We can indicate in this way that their lexicons at first were organized for the purpose of modification.

This conception of word patterning can be generalized to the remaining grammatical relations defined in the previous section. If the reader will visualize a tree diagram representing the deep structure of a simple

[1] Kelley (1967) has pointed out four other patterns that might have occurred in Table 3 but did not. All, however, involve reverse English word order or transformations not yet available to Adam or both, and have therefore not been considered as being within the set of possibilities for Adam.

declarative sentence, he can derive each of the following sets of features from the definitions given before:

ORIGINATING RELATION	FEATURES
Subject	[+NP, +__VP]
Object	[+NP, +V__]
Head	[+N, +Det__]
Predicate	[+VP, +NP__]
Main verb	[+V, +__NP]
Modifier	[+Det, +__N]

(The use of +NP and +VP as features has been discussed by Chomsky, 1967.) Contextual and central features are on the same level of the phrase-marker.

It is essential to note that these features are *automatically* available whenever a child comprehends something in adult speech. A child has no other method for organizing meaning. The features have nothing to do with correct understanding, but anything that is understood, whether correctly or incorrectly, is necessarily classified according to the above list of features. If an adult sentence is *I will find it* and a child grasps the correct meaning, we can describe what he understands as follows:

Subject	I	[+NP, +__VP]
Predicate	will find it	[+VP, +NP__]
Main Verb	will find	[+V, +__NP]
Object	it	[+NP, +V__]

Grasping meaning depends on various linguistic and extralinguistic cues. Of course, it is possible, since this is not an automatic process, for a child to grasp the wrong meaning. We still can describe what he understands in terms of the syntactic features derived from the grammatical relations, but since the relations differ the features derived must differ. If the child thinks *I will find it* means "it will find me," for example, we have:

Object	I	[+NP, +V__]
Main Verb	will find	[+V, +__NP]
Predicate	I will find	[+VP, +NP__]
Subject	it	[+NP, +__VP]

Utterances like *allgone shoe,* if they are backward sentences, can be described this way. Alternatively, a word might receive the wrong central feature. In this case, *allgone shoe* could be an NP and *allgone* a modifier. The significance of the blank space in the contextual features seems to shift when there are reversals of word order, but we will see later that such shifts do not in fact occur.

Although the syntactic features that come from the grammatical relations are automatically present whenever a child understands adult speech, this information might not enter his lexicon. There is the possibility that words will appear in the lexicon with features derived from one relation but not from others, even though the words occur in several relations in adult speech. We can distinguish two cases where this situation obtains. Both in fact exist.

In one, words appear with features from a single relation because the child, for the moment, is constructing a lexicon for that relation alone. If the relation is modification, the features in the lexicon will be [+Det, +__N], and [+N, +Det__]. Zhenya and Adam presumably had a lexicon like this when their P classes were as at Time 1 in Fig. 12.

In the second case, the lexicon as a whole includes more than one relation but each word is classified only once. Especially important is the situation where two of the relations are modification and predication. Among the features will then be [+Det, +__N] and [+VP, +NP__]. Adjectives might appear under either of these features in adult speech. In *the red ball,* for example, the adjective is [+Det, +__N], while in *the ball is red* it is [+VP, +NP__]. The lexicon of a child following this second method of classifying words, if he relies on modification and predication, will contain adjectives in two places. One of Miller and Ervin's (1964) English-speaking subjects had adjectives arranged this way, as did one of McNeill's (1966c) Japanese-speaking subjects.

A complete lexicon must show that every adjective has both the predicate and modificational sets of features. The consequences of this multiple classification are different, however, depending on the initial situation in the lexicon. In a lexicon like Adam's or Zhenya's, where all adjectives have been [+Det, +__N], adjectives now gain the further feature [+VP, +NP__]. The result is differentiation of adjectives from the class of P words. If, however, some adjectives were already [+VP, +NP__], as with Miller and Ervin's or McNeill's subjects, differentiation could not take place. Some adjectives become [+VP, +NP__] while others become [+Det, +__N], the result being a convergence of adjectives from separate points. Thus, the generically appropriate classification, on which differentiation depends, itself depends on using a single grammatical relation for the classification of words. Unless this method of classification is followed, children cannot be accommodated into Chomsky's hierarchy of categories. The hierarchy is violated when a single differentiated category (adjectives) is located under separate undifferentiated categories (modifiers and predicates).

But there is no longer any reason to accommodate children into this hierarchy of categories. Indeed, we obtain a consistent theory if we assume that differentiating children, like cross-classifying children, are *not* guided by it. The change we must make in the account given earlier, therefore, is to abandon the hierarchy of categories, leaving, however, the identification of child speech with semigrammatical adult sentences. (The conception of grammatical categories as being arranged hierarchically has been replaced in recent linguistic analyses by analyses according to syntactic features; see Chomsky, 1965.)

Lexical Features as Pivots

Having established a connection between the grammatical relations and the P–O distinction via the lexicon, we can work out the remaining properties of the distinction on this new basis.

Table 9, which is taken from Slobin (in press), shows examples of P words from children learning three different languages: English, German, and Russian. The examples are from various diary studies. The chart is organized so as to reflect the semantic regularities that exist among P words. Thus some P words modify meanings (*pretty, mein,*

Table 9 **Pivot Structures in English, German, and Russian**
(Slobln, in press)

Function of Pivot	Language		
	English	German	Russian
Modify, quality	pretty__ my__ allgone__ all__ big__ other__	armer [poor]__ mein [my]__ alle [allgone]__	__bo-bo [hurt] __khoroshaya [good] __tyu-tyu [allgone]
Locate, name	there__ here__ see__ it__ that__ __on-there __up-there	__da [there] da-is [there is]__ gukuk [see]__	__tam [there]
Describe act	__away __on __off __it __do __come I__	__bah [away] __an [on] __auf [on] __aus [off]	__tprua [walk] __bay-bay [sleep] __upala [fell down] __bukh [fell down]
Demand, desire	more__ give__ want__	mehr [more]__ bitte [please]__	eshche [more]__ day [give]__
Negate	no__ don't__	nein [no]__ nicht [not]__	net [no]__ ne-nado [don't]__

bo-bo), some locate or name things (*there, da, tam*), some describe acts (*away, bah, bukh*), etc. It is impressive that each child found a need to express the concept "allgone." However, such semantic regularities are not the P–O distinction. P words, as we have seen, reflect syntactic regularities and *allgone* could just as well have been an O word. What is so interesting in Table 9 is that only certain syntactic features occur as P. With the exception of two English pronouns (*I* and *it*) the P class never contains Ns or NPs. Equivalently, the O class always contains Ns or NPs. For some reason P words express only the grammatical relations of modification, predication, and main verb.

Why are the other basic grammatical relations never a source of P words? If we take into account the fact that [N] or [NP] is involved in every grammatical relation and introduce a distinction between marked and unmarked lexical entries, we can explain this restriction. A marked lexical entry differs from an unmarked one in that it includes extra information, restricting the entry to a special use. The best choices for the unmarked entry with the features derived from the grammatical relations is N or NP. An N or NP appears in every lexical entry, and therefore has maximally general use. The best choices for the marked entries are correspondingly Det, V, and VP. In an optimal lexicon nouns will be unmarked and all other categories marked. The children whose P classes are in Table 9 evidently had optimal lexicons in this sense. If we assume that children are motivated to simplify the lexicon, no other choice of marked and unmarked entries can reduce by so much the number of different entries. Thus we have,

ORIGINATING RELATION	ENTRY	STATUS
Subject⎫ Object⎬ Head⎭	[+NP]	Unmarked
Predicate Main verb Modifier	[+VP, +NP__]⎫ [+V, +__NP]⎬ [+Det, +__N]⎭	Marked

With this division of the lexicon a child would have one class of words that appears in any context, the unmarked nouns and noun phrases, and another class of words that appears only with nouns and noun phrases, the marked verbs and determiners. The first class comprises the O words and the second the P words. P words appear only with nouns and not alone because they carry the features [+__NP] or [+__N] or the reverse. They do not appear with other P words because they lack the features [+Det__], [+__VP], and [+V__]. O words on the other hand can appear alone because they carry only [+NP] or [+N]. The distributional characteristics of the pivot–open distinction in general suggest that many children distinguish marked and unmarked categories in this way in building up a lexicon. The pivot–open distinction itself is an imperfect and superficial reflection of these basic developments.

Besides combining P words with O words children combine O words with other O words. In Brown's records O–O combinations actually outnumber P–O combinations (McNeill, 1966a). But with the exception of nouns that modify other nouns (*party shoe*), where the relation is included in the lexicon above, there is no way to explain O–O combinations with the theory given here. Even the full lexicon without marking does not provide N as a contextual feature for other Ns. In part, O–O combinations reflect grammatical relations other than the six used above to derive lexical features. The locative relation, for example, will put N together with N if there are no prepositions (*pencil table*). So will the genitive relation (*Urler suitcase*). In these cases a longer roster of grammatical relations will suffice to cover O–O patterns and no new principle is called for. According to Bloom (1968), however, many O–O combinations are related as subjects and objects. *Mommy pigtail,* for example, meant in context that Mommy should make a pigtail for the child. No addition to the list of grammatical relations can explain these combinations. Subject–object is not a grammatical relation that can be defined in the underlying structure of sentences because the two NPs are not immediate constituents of the same constituent.

Why do children omit verbs from sentences? One would suppose that the subject would be more vulnerable. To some extent verbs might be deleted to meet performance limitations in two-word sentences. Only a sample of the underlying structure would then appear in the surface structure. As we should expect from this explanation, all possible two-word combinations occur in child speech — subject–object, verb–object, and subject–verb. However, these combinations occur with unequal frequency in Bloom's records, declining in the order given. And Bowerman (1968) found that the sentences of two Finnish children almost always have animate subjects and inanimate objects. An examination of Bloom's data shows the same asymmetry. Perhaps it is connected with the deletion of verbs in child speech, since the presence of an inanimate noun in a sentence determines the syntactic character of both itself and the verb. Such a noun must be an object and the verb must be transitive. The verb, therefore, can be omitted.

The most general interpretation of verbless sentences is to regard verbs as being words that stand for grammatical relations, and that, like prepositions, they tend to appear only after combinatorial patterns with nonrelational words are established. Such an interpretation is consistent with the progression in child grammar, from the holophrastic period on, to express grammatical relations first through combinations and last through special words. Along this line, we recall that Greenfield observed the appearance of subjects and objects toward the end of the holophrastic period, but no verbs (see Chapter 3). It is interesting to recall also that Washoe, the chimpanzee, included verbs in her first "utterances," a difference which implies that the absence of verbs from child speech is the result of linguistic expression.

Word Order

The grammatical relations are logical relations. They are not relations of order. The lexical features derived from grammatical relations describe the logical connections between words, therefore, and not the order of words. The order of words in sentences comes from a different source. A child adopts the hypothesis that the abstract grammatical relations are expressed in language through word order. Schlesinger (in press) has codified this distinction between relations and order in some cases in the form of "ordering rules." Following the general policy of expressing grammatical relations through word order, lexical features such as [+Det, +__N] state where words, ones marked [+Det], must appear. However, word order is not the only method of expressing grammatical relations. Another would be that grammatical relations are expressed through the apposition of words without regard to order. In this case [+Det, +__N] signifies that words marked [+Det] must be adjacent to nouns. A third possibility, widespread in languages, is to express grammatical relations through inflections, where [+Det, +__N] shows that a morphological rule must apply to the noun.

Most children learning English at first use word order to express grammatical relations. However, not all do so. Braine (1970) cites a few examples of apposition, *see it baby* and *baby see it,* both of which were verb–object constructions and meant "see the baby." (This confusion is different from the confusion in backward sentences, where the order of words matters but the child is mistaken about the direction.) On the other hand, children learning inflected languages sometimes use word order to express grammatical relations. Finnish is a highly inflected language with flexible word order. One of Bowerman's (1969) subjects used apposition, as might be expected, but the other used fixed word order. And Zhenya learning Russian held to a fixed word order. Some children use both word order and apposition; one of Miller and Ervin's (1964) English-speaking subjects did this. Thus all combinations of ordering and apposition in child and adult language are known to occur and children might spontaneously adopt either method. Of the two, apposition is the natural prelude to inflection. English-learning children who use it may be following the erroneous hypothesis that they are learning an inflected language. The converse can be said of children learning inflected languages who use rigid word order.

With this perspective on the ordering of words, we can return to the P–O distinction. Braine (1963a) was the first to point out the distinction and was also the first to give an account of it. Pivot words were so called by Braine because in his view they are the words for which a child has learned the locations in speech. O words are used wherever P words are not, so the position of both in two-word sentences, at least, is fixed. Various characteristics of the P–O distinction follow from this simple account. Because at first a child knows the location of only a few words, P words are used in combinations with high frequency and the class itself has few members; because it is more difficult to learn the positions of words than to learn vocabulary regardless of position, the P class increases in membership slowly; because it is the location of words that a child learns, P words always appear in the same place.

The main characteristic of the P–O distinction not accounted for by this theory is the restriction of P words to combinations with O words. It is one thing to learn where to put a word in a sentence. It is something different to learn to put it nowhere else or to put it only with open words. Since the restriction on the use of pivot words carries much of the weight in justifying the grammatical relevance of the P–O distinction, an inability to account for it poses a fairly crucial problem.

Braine does not explain the actual mechanism of learning the position of words in sentences, although there has been a number of experiments purporting to demonstrate the existence of such a phenomenon (Braine, 1963b; but see also Bever, Fodor, and Weksel, 1965a). Whatever the mechanism, however, it is supposed to cause children to classify the words in the sentences they hear according to relative position. If the sentence is *will you read it to me?* a child observes *you* in the first half and *me* in the second. He could classify both words accordingly. Contextual generalization—the process by which this theory is generally known—then carries *you* and *me* into new, analogous contexts.

Two-word sentences grow to three-word sentences and beyond because a child observes the *relative* positions of words. Having learned that *you* appears in the first half of some phrases, a child can later discover that these phrases appear in the first half of sentences. More important than the increase in length gained this way is the increase in structural complexity. By learning that a word is first in a phrase and that a phrase is first in a sentence, a child learns that the sentence is hierarchically organized. Thus, positional learning, extended through contextual generalization, leads to the kind of sentence structure conventionally represented by a phrase-structural grammar (see Appendix).

The difficulty with this theory is that the order and arrangement of words in the surface structure of sentences is not necessarily the same as the arrangement of elements in the underlying structure (Bever, Fodor, and Weksel, 1965a; 1965b). It is the underlying structure that contains information represented as a phrase-structure grammar, but it is the surface structure that is available for positional learning. There is a dilemma here. Braine (1965), writing in reply to Bever et al., restricts positional learning to simple declarative sentences, where the arrangement of elements in the underlying and superficial structure is more or less the same. But syntactic learning includes among other things learning just where underlying and superficial structures *are* the same. Such a restriction begs the question it is to explain, as Bever et al. point out. The way to avoid this difficulty, equally adopted by Braine, is to construe all sentences as having the same underlying and superficial structure. But this is to avoid the problem of language acquisition and to impose instead a novel kind of linguistics, in which one asks what

68

kind of language *could* be acquired through position learning (McNeill, 1968a).

The most basic objection to Braine's theory, however, is that it does not explain how the P–O distinction is connected to the grammatical relations. By taking these relations into account, the dilemma facing Braine's theory disappears. Since a word in any position in the surface structure of a sentence can be associated with any grammatical relation in the underlying structure, it is unnecessary to restrict positional learning to simple declarative sentences or to construe all sentences as having the same underlying and surface structures. This is not to say that the theory is correct; it is only to say that a logical difficulty can be removed.

Braine and his critics have agreed that the theory of contextual generalization is an account of phrase structure; that is what they have been arguing about. We must call this agreement into question, however, The location of P words can be understood only as describing an association between grammatical relations and fixed positions in the surface structure of sentences. Such an association, if it resembles anything in grammar, is a transformation. Contextual generalization explains the appearance of this transformation, if anything.

As already noted, however, not every child uses P words. Other children associate the grammatical relations to surface structures through apposition; contextual generalization, obviously, cannot explain this form of grammatical expression. It is possible that some children invent their own inflections, though to my knowledge this has not been observed, and it also could not be explained by contextual generalization.

Summary

To summarize, the P–O distinction is a reflection in the surface structure of sentences of the grammatical relations from the holophrastic period. It occurs when children adopt word order as the means of expressing grammatical relations, but not when they adopt apposition (or inflection, if such occurs). As a learning mechanism, contextual generalization cannot be ruled out on a priori grounds, so long as it is restricted to the acquisition of word-locating transformations, but its scope is limited in this way.

GENERAL ISSUES

For the remainder of the chapter we will fit our discussion of child language into several larger and different contexts. In the section immediately below, we discuss the learning of language in relation to the theory of universal grammar. Then we consider the connection between universal grammar and the intellectual development of children. We end with a discussion of the doctrines of empiricism and of innate ideas.

Linguistic Universals

According to a traditional view, language is a systematic relation between sound and meaning. In a transformational grammar this view is embodied in the distinction between underlying and surface structures, which we have been discussing. The underlying structure is associated with meaning or content and the surface structure with sound or expression. Underlying and surface structures are in general different from each other, but they stand in specific relations described by the transformations of the language (see Appendix for further discussion). One inherent aspect of any sentence is therefore the existence of an abstract underlying structure. Fluent speakers have gained knowledge of these structures. They have done so even though they have never encountered such information in the form of examples, stimuli, or anything else. Moreover, as we have seen, children make use of the information of the underlying structure very early in the acquisition of language. From the first moment of speech, children have the ability to communicate grammatical relations in a manner understandable to adults. We can easily overlook what an astonishing fact this is, but it means that the most abstract part of language is the first to appear in development.

To develop the connection with the theory of grammar let us put the problem in a semiformal way. Consider the "Language Acquisition Device" discussed by Chomsky (1957, 1965), which we can call LAD for short (alternatively, a Language Acquisition System, or LAS—the feminine form). LAD or LAS receives a certain corpus of utterances. Many of these utterances are grammatical sentences in the language to which LAD is exposed. The corpus may be large, but it is not unlimited in size. Assume that it contains the number of utterances overheard by a typical 2-year-old child.

Given such a corpus, LAD is so constructed that it can develop a theory of the regularities that underly the speech to which it has been exposed. The theory is LAD's grammatical competence, its knowledge of the language. LAD now becomes able to go far beyond the corpus with which it began. It can distinguish the infinitely many grammatical sentences in its language from the infinitely many nongrammatical alternatives.

The situation may be diagrammed as follows:

$$\text{Corpus} \longrightarrow \boxed{\text{LAD}} \longrightarrow \text{Grammatical Competence}$$

Clearly, the problem of understanding how LAD, given a corpus, develops grammatical competence requires understanding of LAD's internal structure.

It is useful to distinguish two major components of LAD. One is a set of *procedures* for operating on a corpus—for example, conducting a distributional analysis, or using "inference rules" for finding transformations of certain kinds (Fodor, 1966). The other is a body of *linguistic information*—for example, that all sentences include noun

70

and verb phrases, or that sentences exist. It is conceivable that LAD contains only one of these components. LAD might contain a set of procedures for discovering a grammar or it might contain a set of assumptions about the form of grammar or, of course, it might contain both.

Whatever LAD contains, however, must be universally applicable. For LAD must be able to acquire any language; it will not include anything that makes some languages unlearnable. That is because no actual language, which must be acquired and is not ordinarily taught, can drift away from LAD's internal structure. Thus LAD could contain information and procedures bearing on the general form of language, but could contain nothing that is inconsistent with any particular language. The following remarks are directed to the possibility that LAD contains universal linguistic information; almost nothing has been done to examine the possibility that LAD contains universal procedures of analysis.

LAD is, of course, a fiction. The purpose in considering it is to discuss real children, not abstract ones. We can accomplish this because LAD and children present the same problem. LAD is faced with a corpus of utterances, from which it develops a grammar on the basis of some kind of internal structure. So do children. We can readily posit that children and LAD arrive at the same grammar from the same corpus, and stipulate that children and LAD therefore have the same internal structure, at least within the limits that different children may be said to have the same internal structure. Accordingly, a theory about LAD is *ipso facto* a theory about children.

The description of linguistic universals is included in the theory of universal grammar. As opposed to the grammar of a single language, the theory of grammar is a description of the general form of human language (Chomsky, 1965; Katz, 1966). The purpose is to state the universal conditions that the grammars describing individual languages must meet. Our theory of language acquisition will be that the theory of grammar and its universal constraints describe the internal structure of LAD and, thus, of children.

What are the universals mentioned in the theory of grammar, which we now presume to be a reflection of children's linguistic capacities? Some are phonological. Every language, for example, employs consonants and vowels, syllabic structure, and a handful of distinctive features (Jakobson and Halle, 1956; Halle, 1964a). In the case of syntax, every language utilizes the same basic grammatical categories, arranged in the same way—sentences, noun phrases, verb phrases, etc. Every language utilizes the same grammatical relations among these categories—subject and predicate, verb and object, etc. All of these are characteristics of the abstract underlying structure of sentences.

The transformations of a language, on the other hand, present much more idiosyncrasy. For example, in English the underlying and surface structures of auxiliary verbs are related by permuting the order of verbs and affixes (see Appendix). This transformation appears in French also

(Ruwet, 1966), and possibly elsewhere, but is not universal. Transformational idiosyncracy arises from the way a few universal transformational types are exploited. Permutation, for example, is a universal tranformational relation. It is used in a unique way in English and French. Other universal relations are deletion and addition; there are perhaps only a half dozen varieties of universal transformations.

We can collect these several considerations into a theory of language acquisition. Important aspects of the deep structure of sentences are described by universals; most transformations are idiosyncratic uses of universal transformational types. Assuming that linguistic theory describes linguistic abilities, we can say that the abstractions of the underlying structure reflect children's linguistic capacities, and are *made* abstract by children discovering the transformations of their language (McNeill, 1966b). One can say that children begin speaking underlying structure directly. The existence of abstract underlying structure, far from being problematical for this theory, is a trivial consequence of it.

The process of language acquisition we have traced in this chapter and in Chapter 3 fits the above view closely. The grammatical relations of the holophrastic period already define a basic part of the abstract underlying structure of sentences. This structure is therefore present at an early point in development. What changes is the child's method of expressing the underlying structure of sentences in speech. First single words convey underlying structures, then simple P–O or appositional combinations, then more complex combinations. There is a constant elaboration of the relation between the underlying and surface structures of sentences, i.e., a constant elaboration of the transformational structure.

The two grammars described in Chapter 3 differ greatly in complexity. The first, covering early word combinations, includes only three rules; the second, covering later combinations, contains 14. Both grammars, however, describe the underlying structure of sentences. How can this difference in complexity be reconciled with the theory that language acquisition consists of learning transformation?

The answer lies in recognizing the distinction between the structural change of a transformation and its structural index (see Appendix). All the complexity in the second grammar of Chapter 3 exists to meet the structural indices of the 24 transformations that it contains but the first grammar does not. There are few or no new grammatical relations in the second grammar (Rules 10 and 11 in Table 5 are the only ones that might include new relations). Thus we can conclude that most, if not all, of the changes in the underlying structure of sentences between the first and second grammar are induced by the transformations being acquired.

Cognition and Language

The term "language and cognition," with "language" first, describes the influence of language on thought. It is a topic with a rich history (cf. Chomsky, 1966; Whorf, 1956; Bruner, Olver, and Greenfield, 1966). Our concern in this section is with the opposite topic, with the word "cognition" first: in what manner does the structure of thought influence the structure of language?

The question is not whether the acquisition of language depends on specific abilities. We have already accepted the theory of grammar as a description of such abilities. The question concerns the origin of linguistic abilities, whether they come into language from cognition or are the result of a special linguistic capacity. It is easy to demonstrate that the content of speech is determined by intellectual development. John Stuart Mill, whose speech included the writing of a history of Rome at age six, lived in a cultured setting, had an IQ estimated to be in the 200's, and was the beneficiary (or victim) of the advanced ideas of his father about education. However, the problem of cognition and language has nothing to do with content, and Mill's precocity had nothing to do with the influence of his thought on his language. The question of cognition and language rather has to do with structure, and in this respect Mill was not unusually precocious.

Among the early arrivals in child language are the grammatical categories of noun and verb. Where do they come from? One hypothesis would be that they are the reflection, in language, of the final step in the development of sensory-motor intelligence (Piaget, 1952). During the first 18 months of life a baby develops the idea that physical objects have an independent existence. A very young baby believes that he can create and annihilate things since they are an extension of his acts. An 18-month-old child accepts the existence of things that are separate from himself. The separation implies a distinction between objects and actions, and this distinction now appears in speech as the distinction between nouns and verbs.

This argument was given by Sinclair-de Zwart (1968) in what probably is the only existing paper on cognition and language. It explains a structural arrangement in child language by reference to a universal of intellectual development. All children pass through the sensory-motor period and all therefore have nouns and verbs. Other scholars have argued that the universal features of child language can be explained along similar lines. Schlesinger (in press) has issued a strong call for such explanations and Slobin (1966a) has hinted that he would like them too. It is impressive for Sinclair-de Zwart's hypothesis that the chronology is correct. Nouns and verbs are present in child speech when words are first combined into sentences, roughly at 18 months, which also is when the sensory-motor period comes to a close. The hypothesis is plausible and appears to have empirical support, but let us look at it more closely.

In principle, one can distinguish between two different kinds of linguistic universals.

1. A *weak linguistic universal* is the reflection in language of a universal cognitive ability. The cognitive universal is a necessary *and* sufficient cause of the weak linguistic universal.

2. A *strong linguistic universal* is a reflection of a specific linguistic ability and may not be a reflection of a cognitive ability at all. The cognitive universal, if it has anything to do with the linguistic one, is a necessary but *not* a sufficient cause of the strong linguistic universal. It is not sufficient because a linguistic ability is necessary as well.

The empirical content of this distinction is purely psychological. Linguistics has nothing to do with it and linguistic theory gives no hint of the causes of linguistic universals. More surprisingly, parallels of form or function — as between action–object and verb–noun — and the synchronic development of such parallels of form or function also do not establish causation. Such observations cannot separate the two kinds of linguistic universals described above. Any parallel and synchronization are consistent equally with linguistic universals being strong or weak. We would expect that, if linguistic abilities evolved to express thought, strong linguistic universals would be parallel to cognitive universals. And if a strong universal depends on meeting two necessary conditions, one cognitive and one linguistic, the strong universal could not appear in language until both conditions were met.

Thus, neither parallel form nor developmental synchrony unambiguously bears on the weak–strong distinction. Sinclair-de Zwart's hypothesis must be evaluated on other grounds. To see how the weak–strong distinction can be approached, consider an observation reported by Braine (1970). He taught his 2-year-old daughter two new words, one the name of a kitchen appliance (*niss*) and the other the name of the act of walking with the fingers (*seb*). Neither word was used by an adult in any grammatical context. The child used both words appropriately — *niss* as a noun and *seb* as a verb — as in *more niss* and *seb Teddy*. In addition, however, she used *seb* as a noun but never used *niss* as a verb. There were sentences like *more seb* and *this seb* but none like *niss vegetables*. Braine observed a similar asymmetry in his daughter's use of newly acquired Hebrew verbs and nouns, the verbs being used as nouns but not the nouns as verbs. These observations are significant for the strong–weak distinction. Evidently the syntactic classification of a noun does not depend on an association of a word with an object. *Seb* was the name of an action but was used productively as a noun. On the other hand, the name of an object was not used as a verb. One might tentatively conclude, therefore, that the syntactic category of noun is a *strong* universal and the category of verb is *weak*. Association with action alone is necessary and sufficient to establish a verb but some further syntactic property defines a noun.

The appearance of [+NP] as the central unmarked lexical feature of the P–O distinction can be explained if nouns are strong universals and verbs weak. The specifically linguistic definition necessary for nouns would have just such an effect. The advantage noted earlier for nouns as holophrastic words (they have the widest scope of all grammatical classes since they occur in every grammatical relation) is also consistent with nouns being strong universals. The situation is not as neat as we might wish, however, for association with an object may also be sufficient for a word to become a noun. Braine's observations are ambiguous on this point. Perhaps we must further subdivide linguistic universals into weak, strong, and "erratic" types. An erratic universal has two sufficient causes and therefore no necessary ones. Either the cognitive category of an object or a linguistic ability can cause a word to become a noun.

Aside from these observations, no investigation has been carried out that bears on the causes of linguistic universals. There are not yet empirical grounds for classifying linguistic universals as strong, weak, or erratic. Such claims as Schlesinger's, that linguistic structures are ". . . determined by the innate *cognitive* capacity of the child" (Schlesinger, in press), or Sinclair-de Zwart's, that "linguistic universals exist precisely because thought structures are universal" (Sinclair-de Zwart, 1968), are premature. Also, they are unnecessarily sweeping, as there is no reason to suppose that all linguistic universals are of one kind — weak, strong, or erratic. Far more probably, language is a mixture of the three.

The question of whether thought affects language cannot therefore be answered in general or in advance. A vacuum exists precisely where speculation, which abhors a vacuum, would most like to enter — into the explanation of children's linguistic abilities. Nonetheless, the biological uniqueness of the human ability to express grammatical relations suggests that some part of this ability is specifically linguistic and results in strong or, at least, in erratic linguistic universals.

The Doctrines of Empiricism and of Innate Ideas

The proposition that language depends on an innate ability to interpret sentences carries with it certain philosophical assumptions and avoids carrying with it certain others. This last section of the chapter discusses these assumptions, both the ones carried and the ones not carried.

One of the clearest and most extreme statements of empiricism appears in George Berkeley's *New Theory of Vision,* written in 1709 (see Turbayne, 1963, for a recent reprinting). An equally clear and extreme statement in the opposite direction comes from Samuel Bailey, economist and nativist, who published in 1842 "A review of Berkeley's theory of vision, designed to show the unsoundness of that celebrated speculation." Berkeley and Bailey will be the full scope of our discussion. Since the goal is clarity, and Berkeley and Bailey are clear, the restriction does no damage.

Our concern is not with vision, of course, but with language. It is the form of the argument that matters, however, and substituting linguistic concepts for visual ones turns out not to be difficult. The structure of the argument shows through in either case. Also, we are guided by Berkeley's own use of language as a metaphor. For him vision *is* a language. In Berkeley's theory visual ideas are to tactual ideas precisely as he believes words are to meanings. We have only to reverse the analogy to reach the theory of language.

Bailey develops his argument in reaction to Berkeley. We will follow the same pattern, allowing Berkeley to lead and Bailey to attack. Berkeley's theory rests on the idea that the dimension of depth in visual experience is an illusion, for contrary to "vulgar" belief, depth is invisible. Imagine two points at different distances on a line extending from the "fund" of the eye. Both are projected as a single point onto the retina. Since this is true over the entire visual field, depth cannot be seen and our impression of it must arise from a source other than vision. Berkeley thought it came from tactual sensations — the kinesthetic and proprioceptive cues that arise as we reach out for, walk toward, or grasp objects. Through long experience these tactual impressions of depth become associated with the depthless impressions of vision. Thus we think we *see* depth but in truth we are *reminded* of it.

A number of interlocking propositions are embedded in this theory. Bailey, in reply, asserts an equal number of interlocking counter-propositions. Below is a list of the main ideas separating them, expressed in their linguistic form; the paragraphs following are numbered to correspond to these propositions.

BERKELEY	BAILEY
1. No ideas are abstract	1. Some ideas are abstract
2. Justified assertion is correct assertion	2. Justified assertion is not correct assertion
3. All ideas are derived from experience	3. Some ideas are innate
4. Meaning is arbitrary	4. Meaning is not arbitrary

1. Abstract Ideas   One difference concerns the existence of abstract ideas. Berkeley denies that they exist, by which he means that no ideas can be abstracted from perception. Berkeley cannot imagine, for example, a square without also imagining its color, size, and orientation. It is always some particular square, not an abstract or general square, that comes to mind. The meaning of the word *square,* therefore, must be some such set of perceptual ideas. Bailey's theory, in contrast, admits abstract ideas into the mind. The meaning of *square* is an abstract idea of squareness that has no essential connection to any concrete perceptual idea.

2. Justified and Correct Assertions   A little reflection shows that Berkeley and Bailey are not discussing the same concept of abstraction. Berkeley's abstract idea is a generalization of particular perceptual ideas. We might call it an *abstracted idea.* Bailey's abstract idea exists in advance of perception. We might call it an *idea in the abstract.* Berkeley denies that abstracted ideas exist, while Bailey asserts that ideas in the abstract do. Clearly, neither philosopher discussed the other's abstract idea and both could be correct. Berkeley and Bailey fail to mesh on the question of abstraction because of a further disagreement at a deeper level. To use modern terminology, Bailey distinguishes "correct" assertion from "justified" assertion, whereas

76

Berkeley does not (cf., Albritton, 1966).[2] The real division between them is this one, and they differ over abstract ideas because of it.

For Berkeley a statement is true or false according to whether it is justified by evidence. For him, justified assertion is correct assertion. If evidence justifies the use of a word, the word is correctly used. Taking this equivalence for granted, Berkeley tested the concept of squareness by looking for a perceptually abstract square, i.e., for the justification of the abstraction. However, for Bailey, correct assertion is not justified assertion. Justified assertion is about perceptual evidence, as with Berkeley, but the role of evidence is to suggest abstract ideas, which are the content of correct assertion. And a statement is true or false according to whether it refers to the correct abstract idea. Evidence will suggest that one is justified in referring to this idea. From Bailey's point of view, Berkeley's demonstration of the impossibility of an abstract idea takes for granted the controversial claim that justified assertion is correct assertion and does not reach the issue it was designed to settle—whether there are ideas in the abstract. Berkeley was quite unconscious of the circular reasoning in his argument. Neither Bailey nor Berkeley thought it was possible to disagree with their respective contradictory positions.

3. Innate Ideas   The difference between Berkeley and Bailey over correct and justified assertion coincides with the difference between them over innate ideas. If there are no innate ideas and everything in the mind is acquired from sensory experience, then justified assertion can be correct assertion. The truth value of words is fixed by the perceptual evidence that suggests them. But if there are innate ideas, a distinction must be drawn between these ideas, the abstract content of correct assertion, and the perceptual evidence that suggests or justifies them. Of course, it is possible to agree with Bailey that there are nonperceptual abstract ideas without accepting nativism, but if there are innate ideas, they must be abstract in Bailey's sense.

4. Arbitrariness of Meaning   According to Berkeley associations can be formed between any two perceptual ideas. Visual cues could have just the opposite significance from what they happen to have. So could words and sentences. Connections are established arbitrarily and depend only on long experience with the associated perceptual ideas. Bailey would agree to this. However, in Bailey's view associations between perceptual ideas and abstract ideas are more important and typical than are associations between different perceptual ideas. The difference between Bailey and Berkeley is again related to their differences elsewhere. In Berkeley's theory, where justified assertion is correct assertion, the meaning of a word is the perceptual evidence that justifies its use. Since associations are established through long

---

[2] The terminology comes from Chomsky, who used the distinction in a series of lectures on Wittgenstein in 1968.

experience between arbitrarily connected perceptual ideas, *meaning is arbitrary.* In Bailey's theory, where justified assertion suggests correct assertion, the meaning of a word is an abstract idea with which perceptual ideas are associated. These associations are arbitrary, so words and the justification of their use are arbitrary, but *meaning, the abstract idea, is not arbitrary.*

An example will clarify the implications of this difference. Bailey would find it perfectly intelligible if a concept appears in child language before it appears outside language. Words or sentences can be associated with abstract ideas without the same abstract ideas being associated with nonlinguistic perception; the opposite, of course, also can occur. Children can have the concept of causation in mind as they speak without being able to recognize physical or psychological causes. Then they would ask such questions as *why not me careful?* or *why me bend that game?,* questions about causation that simultaneously betray confusion over actual causes. For Berkeley such discrepancies are perfectly unintelligible. He would have to say that *why me bend that game?* is not about causation at all, but about some other arbitrarily established relation among events. The arbitrariness of meaning in Berkeley's theory is the principal empirical claim to which we can attach concrete significance.

It is important to see how intimately Berkeley's four propositions are interconnected. Proposition (4) follows from (1), (2), and (3) together; proposition (1) in turn follows from (2); and (2) from (3). Because all ideas are derived from experience, justified assertion is correct assertion and no ideas are abstract. Meaning, therefore, is arbitrary.

We will raise only one problem for Berkeley's empiricism; it is, however, a problem with fatal consequences. For further discussion, see McNeill (1969). Consider the child sentence, *that no fish school.* Its meaning could not be "that's not a fish school," "that's no fish school," "that's a school for nonfishes," or any other adult meaning. Each of these meanings is already associated with some other sensory ideas, namely, the sentences *that's not a fish school, that's no fish school, that's a school for nonfishes,* etc. The child sentence might have a meaning intermediate among these, but without special training it could not have one of these meanings to adults. Adults, however, are able to translate child sentences into adult sentences (whether accurately or not does not matter). Unless they confabulate a translation, or have been specially trained, translation contradicts the theorem that meaning is arbitrary. Meaning obviously is not arbitrary if *that no fish school* and *that's a school for nonfishes,* for instance, have the same meaning, for adults. Instead of an arbitrary meaning the particular meaning of *that's a school for nonfishes* converges onto *that no fish school.*

Bailey's theory explains such translations directly. Since meaning is not arbitrary, and is merely suggested by arbitrary signs, a distorted sentence can only suggest an idea already associated with an adult sentence.

78

If we place Bailey's theory alongside the theory of language acquisition described earlier in this chapter, we find a correspondence at each major point. Because the abstract structure of sentences is not arbitrary, children can both produce and comprehend speech in terms of grammatical relations; these relations are innate but must be connected to the surface structure of sentences via associations that are arbitrarily established in each language. The direction of language acquisition therefore is toward a set of unique transformational rules. As we shall see, two chapters hence, some restrictions must be placed on even this modest degree of arbitrariness. In similar fashion, a number of behaviorist theories coincide with Berkeley's theory, and they inherit from it the lethal postulate that meaning is arbitrary. Osgood (1968), in particular, seems open to this charge.

TRANSFORMATIONS

A transformation is a relation between the underlying and surface structures of sentences. If the sentence is *what do ostriches eat,* the underlying structure includes an NP object which is deleted and replaced by *what.* The transformational relation is therefore one of deletion and *what*-insertion. This transformation would be of little interest if it described only one sentence, but it occurs in all sentences with the same structure and extends to an unlimited number of other sentences with similar structures. And the relation of deletion itself appears in the derivation of many sentences with otherwise the most diverse structures (see Appendix for further examples).

How are transformations learned? The process remains one of the major mysteries in the acquisition of language. Children seem to be unable to *avoid* forming relations between underlying and surface structures. In situation after situation we find that grammatical rules are at first too general, and that a more-or-less prolonged process of learning is necessary to restrict the rule to the appropriate places. Although children obviously must have some experience with sentences in their language to arrive at the structural change of a transformation, very little experience seems necessary for it. The main contribution of experience is to limit these quickly discovered structural changes, and in some cases this process lasts for years.

The sections of this chapter present examples of this phenomenon, among others, in some detail.

Inflections

We begin with the acquisition of certain morphological details. Inflections are not usually introduced via major transformations, but they are easily traced features of the surface structure and illustrate in clear form the process mentioned above.

Table 10 lists the order of emergence of several noun and verb inflections in English (Bellugi, 1964). The data are based on observations of two children. Also shown is the relative frequency of the same inflections in the speech of the children's mothers.

There are several matters worth noting. One is that the order of emergence is the same for the two children. This order is the same even though the children's rate of development is radically different, one child taking twice as long to acquire the six inflections of Table 10 as the other. A second point is that forms employing the same phonetic

Table 10 **The Emergence of English Inflections in the Speech
of Two Children**
(Bellugi, 1964)

	Age of Appearance (in months)		Combined Rank Order in Mother's Speech
Inflection	Adam	Eve	
Present progressive, -*ing*	28	19½	2
Plural on nouns, -*s*	33	24	1
Past on regular verbs, -*ed*	39	24½	4
Possessive on nouns, -*s*	39½	25½	5
Third person on verbs, -*s*	41	26	3

variants do not appear at the same time. Three inflections have the phonemic realization -s: plural marking of nouns, genetive marking of nouns, and third person verbs. Since the last appears anywhere from two to eight months after the first, it is not phonemic development that regulates the appearance of these inflections. Finally, the order in which inflections emerge in the speech of children is only weakly correlated with the frequency of the forms in the speech of adults. The most glaring discrepancy involves third-person marking on verbs, which is the third most frequent in maternal speech but last to emerge in child speech.

Jakobson (1969) has pointed out that the order of appearance of -s in child speech corresponds to the general order of development in phrases. Plural marking of Ns precedes possessive marking of Ns, which precedes third-person marking of Vs; that is, a morphological effect within a word precedes a grammatical relation between two words within a constituent, which precedes a relation between two constituents. Jakobson concludes from this correlation that morphology precedes syntax. However, the children represented in Table 10 employed fixed word order as an expression of grammatical relations before they marked even plurality on nouns, so Jakobson's formula is not exactly correct. Rather than showing that morphology precedes syntax, Table 10 shows that when syntax is expressed morphologically it develops according to the scope of the transformation that controls the inflection. The larger this scope the later the transformation.

Now consider the equivalent phenomenon in the acquisition of Russian. Here matters are more complex; the language is highly inflected and for this reason more interesting. Slobin (in press), examining a number of reports in the Russian literature, reconstructs the following chronology: The first inflections to appear are the plural and diminutive marking of nouns and the imperative marking of verbs. This happens at 22 months or so. Second to appear are various case, tense, and person markings on verbs—a complex story to which we shortly return. Third

83

is the conditional marking of verbs, much later than the inflections of case, tense, and person, even though the conditional is structurally simple in Russian. Fourth, nouns are marked for various abstract categories of quality and action. Finally, and last by a large margin, gender is marked on nouns and adjectives.

According to Slobin, three major factors influence the point at which inflections appear in linguistic development. One is the frequency of occurrence of an inflection in adult speech; we see the effects of this factor in Table 10. The second is the superficial or transformational complexity of an inflection (e.g., the accusative emerges late in German, where it is relatively complex, and early in Hungarian, where it is simple), the effects of which also are visible in Table 10. A third factor is something Slobin calls the "semantic content" of an inflection, which probably refers both to the underlying syntactic structure of a sentence and to the intellectual content of the idea represented by an inflection. The relatively late appearance of the Russian conditional, for example, is explained by its difficult semantic content.

Gender in Russian is an ambiguous grammatical case and it is by far the most difficult aspect of Russian morphology for children to master. Errors typically continue until seven or eight years. Slobin attributes the confusion over gender to its difficult semantic content. Most nouns are arbitrarily marked, nouns with real implications of gender are marked the wrong way, etc. If there are inconsistencies with semantic gender, gender in adult Russian may have no actual semantic content. However, for children it may have definite semantic implications. If this is correct, a Russian child will *exclude* gender marking from "inappropriate" words. Gender marking will be slow to develop because a child must learn a large number of localized rules.

It is interesting to note in passing that public education in a society seems to be withheld until children have mastered morphology. English, which poses relatively few problems, is largely mastered by four or five years. Schooling begins at five or six. Russian, which poses many more problems, is not mastered until seven or eight years. Schooling begins at seven. The intellectual readiness of children for school apparently has traditionally been judged by their mastery of the peripheral morphology of language.

All parents know that children regularize strong verbs (*runned, goed, sitted*) and nouns (*foots, mouses, tooths*). However, the actual development of such forms is more complex than is usually realized. Tracing their history is instructive on a number of points. English has a number of verbs with irregular past tenses and also nouns with irregular plurals. Although children long regularize these forms by adding -*ed* to the verbs and -*s* to the nouns, this is not the way they begin (Ervin, 1964). Initially the strong verbs appear in child speech in the correct irregular form — *came* instead of *comed, ran* instead of *runned,* and *did* instead of *doed.* The development of irregular plurals shows the same phenomenon — *feet, mice,* and *teeth* appear in child speech before *foots, mouses,* and *tooths.* Regularization, when it occurs, is a step forward.

The explanation of the early appearance of such correct irregular verbs and nouns probably has to do with the frequency of these forms in adult speech. Strong verbs are by far the most common verbs and strong nouns occur frequently also. Children are thus given many opportunities to discover the association of the underlying morphemes (Past) and (Plural) to these words and they make such discoveries early.

But each irregular verb and noun is a case unto itself or nearly unto itself; no rule covers more than a few words and in many cases no more than one word. Because of this fact the weak, or regular, forms remain untouched by developments in the strong forms. A child who only knows how to say *feet, mice,* and *oxen* may have in mind plurality when he says *two box,* but he cannot express this underlying idea. Should it be *beex, bikes,* or possibly *boxen?* Obviously, it is *box.*

Ervin (1964) searched her records of child speech for the first examples of the regular past-tense and plural inflections. Correct usage of irregular forms was already present. For verbs she first found *-ed* on these same irregular forms! Overgeneralizations apparently occurred before anything existed in speech to overgeneralize from. Plural inflections on nouns first appeared with weak forms, as one would expect, but very shortly thereafter with the strong forms. The gap is usually only a matter of weeks. The appearance of *-ed* first with strong verbs, of course, is an illusion. Strong verbs are frequent in child speech, as in adult speech and Ervin accordingly had a better chance of observing *-ed* on the strong than on the weak forms. The important point is that children treat strong and weak forms alike. They encompass strong verbs within the regular past-tense rule as soon as it is formulated, and the same is true of plural inflection on nouns.

Slobin (in press) refers to such encroachments of regularity as "inflectional imperialism." There are no political connotations in the fact that inflectional imperialism is a major factor in the acquisition of Russian. It rather has to do with the language. To quote Slobin:

> *Over regularizations are rampant in the child's learning of Russian morphology — small wonder, what with the great variety of forms within each category, determined on the bases of both phonological and grammatical relations. For example, not only must the child learn an instrumental case ending for masculine, feminine, and neuter nouns and adjectives in singular and plural, but within each of these subcategories there are several different phonologically conditioned suffixes (not to mention zero-endings, morphologically conditioned suffixes, and other complications). The child's solution is to seize upon one suffix at first and use it for every instance of that particular grammatical category* (Slobin, in press).

Slobin gives as an example the evolution of the instrumental inflection in Russian. Gvozdev's son, Zhenya, first added *-om,* the suffix for masculine and neuter nouns in the singular, to all nouns, including the feminine nouns that at that time were most abundant in his speech. The corresponding feminine form, *-oy,* appeared some time later, but when it did it immediately replaced the original inflection *-om.* That was inflectional imperialism. Much later, -om reappeared in Zhenya's speech, this time appropriately. An experiment by Zakharova (1958) found the same sequence of events in a sample of 200 children.

Inflectional imperialism in Russian and English do not seem at first glance to be the same. The English -ed occurs where no general rule exists, whereas the Russian -oy invades where such a rule is already in force. One seems to fill a vacuum, the other seems truly imperialistic. We can see on closer examination, however, that the two cases are the result of a common process.

In both the Russian and English examples children begin with the most general rule possible, the one with the fewest exceptions. Instead of having several distinct ways of expressing (Past) or (Plural), English-speaking children have one way for each. Because of the complexity of Russian, the course of acquisition is more fluid than in English, but the same principles apply. As Slobin points out, Russian children first select the suffix with the fewest uses. Both -om and -oy have multiple uses in Russian, but -om has fewer noninstrumental uses (one) than does -oy (four). Instrumental -om needs to be restricted from only one noninstrumental context, therefore, whereas instrumental -oy must be restricted from four. However, when gender becomes a grammatical category, the balance between -om and -oy shifts. To mark both gender and the instrumental case, -oy becomes the inflection of greater scope, as it applies to the very large number of feminine nouns then in a child's vocabulary. The imperialism of -oy therefore results from children following the rule of greater scope. That, of course, is what they did in the first place, with -om. What changes is the criterion of scope. At first it was the number of noninstrumental contexts to be avoided. Later it is the number of feminine words to be marked. English- and Russian-speaking children thus approach morphology in a consistent way. Within the limits posed by their languages both seek rules of maximum generality.

Gvozdev remarked that the development of grammar precedes the development of morphology. The instrumental case existed before -om and -oy were used correctly. We can reconcile this observation with the fact noted earlier, that the order of development in English morphology is inversely related to the scope of the inflection. What take time and therefore appear late are rules that cover a range of structures within a single sentence. Besides the -s inflections mentioned before, which among themselves show this principle, English embeddings, tag questions, and complements develop relatively late (at four or five years) and each involves the correlation of two or more structures within a sentence. What take little time and therefore appear early, are rules that extend to a large number of different sentences without exception. Rules that cover several structures within a single sentence are typically rules of restriction—e.g., concord. Rules that cover different sentences are typically rules of generality—e.g., all sentences must have subjects and predicates. We thus again have an example of generalization appearing more readily than restriction.

Menyuk (1963, 1964a, 1964b, 1964c, 1967b, in press) has pursued a number of surveys of transformational development. She covers a wide variety of sentence types, but her results are presented in terms of a kind of contrastive analysis, where the steps of development are described as a series of special reduction rules. Inevitably, therefore, little can be said about the acquisition of actual transformations.

More direct analyses of transformations are presented by Klima and Bellugi (1966), Brown, Cazden, and Bellugi (1968), and Bellugi (1967). These studies have so far been confined to the acquisition of only two transformational systems — negation and questions — by the three Biblically named children in Brown's study, Adam, Eve, and Sarah. We shall first consider the emergence of negation and then of questions.

Brown and his colleagues have organized their longitudinal records into a series of "stages." The stages are not intended to have linguistic or psychological significance, although some of them in fact coincide with true junctures in development, but are instead defined in terms of average utterance length, measured in morphemes. They provide a way of comparing children whose rates of development are different. Figure 13 on the following page, taken from Brown et al. (1968), shows the relation between chronological age and mean utterance length for the three children of Brown's study. Roman numerals indicate the stages into which the analysis has been divided; the following discussion focuses on the first three of these.

Negation
At the first stage, coinciding with the appearance of P–O constructions, children utter such negative sentences as the following (Klima and Bellugi, 1966):

No . . . wipe finger
More . . . no
No a boy bed
Not . . . fit
No singing song
No the sun shining
No play that
Wear mitten no
Not a teddy bear
No fall!

The form of these sentences is fixed, simple, and universal. They consist of a negative word (*no* or *not*) plus an otherwise affirmative sentence. The internal structure of the sentence, if any, remains undisturbed by the negation — *the sun shining, play that,* and *a teddy bear,* for example, are all possible affirmative sentences. The earliest schema for negation then is *Neg + S*. Since a negative word (*no*) sometimes appears after sentences instead of before them, there also is the alternative form *S + no*. It is impossible to say from present observations if any distinction exists between *no* and *not.*

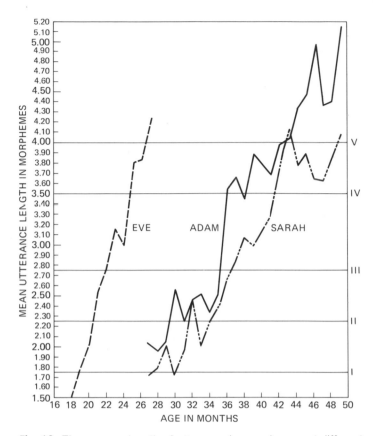

Fig. 13. The average length of utterance in morphemes at different ages for three children. Roman numerals indicate stages of development (Brown et al., 1968).

According to Slobin (1966b), Gvozdev's son Zhenya also produced negative sentences in accordance with these schemas. Whereas an adult would say *nyet nikavo* (literally, "not no-one"), Zhenya said *nyet kavo*, reducing the well-formed double negative to the single negative required by the schema *Neg + S*. French children use *non* or *pas* in an analogous fashion (Grégoire, 1937), and Japanese children do essentially the same thing with *nai* (McNeill and McNeill, 1968).

However, Bloom (1968) has called the structure of these sentences into question on the basic point of their negativity. In her records, which include much contextual information, the negative word in sentences like *no the sun shining* is anaphoric. It applies to something said previously, and the sentence with which it occurs is an affirmative contradiction. Thus *no the sun shining* might have been in response to an adult saying *it's cloudy*. Bloom believes that all instances of *Neg + S* can be explained in this way. The true negative sentences of the first stage, like the negative sentences of adult English, have a negative word woven into the structure of the sentence — *Kathryn no shoe.*

It is not clear how the conflict between Bloom's analysis and Klima and Bellugi's analysis is to be resolved. It is not certain even that there is a conflict. In Klima and Bellugi's first stage there are no sentences with internal negation. Such sentences appear, however, in Klima and Bellugi's second stage, and are mixed in with sentences of the *Neg + S* type. Bloom's first stage may therefore correspond to Klima and Bellugi's second (though Bloom matched Klima and Bellugi's stages in terms of utterance length).

In the second stage, which occurred some two to four months later depending on the child, Klima and Bellugi found a flowering of negative forms. Compared to the two simple forms of negation of the first period, there are now seven distinct types:

I can't catch you
We can't talk
I don't sit on Cromer coffee
I don't like him
No pinch me
No . . . Rusty hat
Touch the snow no
This a radiator no
Don't bite me yet
Don't leave me
That not "O," that blue
There no squirrels
He no bite you
I no want envelope

Certain of the sentences are well formed in English — *I can't catch you,* for example. Others are apparently identical to the negative sentences of the first stage — *no pinch me,* for example. The rest are intermediate, more complex than the primitive negatives of the first stage but not yet well formed — *he no bite you,* for example. The latter resemble Bloom's examples.

Although some of the sentences of the second period are apparently well formed, the grammar yielding them is not yet the grammar of adult English. In fact, *I can't catch you* and *he no bite you* have the same basic structure for children at this point in development. In adult English, sentences such as *I can't catch you* possess an underlying structure of roughly the form *Neg + NP + Aux + VP* (Klima, 1964). A transformation relates the deep structure to the surface structure of *I can't catch you* by moving *Neg* from its location at the beginning of the sentence to a position behind the modal verb *can.* The process is called "*Neg*-transportation." In other sentences, where there is no modal verb in the underlying structure, a second transformation introduces the modal *do* into the surface structure to support the negation. This process is called "*do*-support." Thus the meaning of *I don't like you* is really the meaning of *I n't like you.*

The only well-formed sentences listed among the child examples above were of these two types. If they indeed result from the processes available to adults, transformations for *Neg*-transportation and *do*-support must be involved. However, although a precursor of *Neg*-transportation might already be established in the second stage of development, there is no indication that *do*-support exists. In fact, the auxiliaries *can* and *do* appear only in the context of *Neg;* there are no affirmative sentences with auxiliaries. At this point children say *I do it, I have it?,* and *you think so?,* not *I can do it, can I have it?* and *do you think so?* Klima and Bellugi represent the fact that *do* and *can* are restricted to the context of negation by including a constituent In the children's grammar they call the negative auxiliary (Aux^{neg}). Aux^{neg} in turn leads to *don't* and *can't* as two lexical items. It can be regarded as an undifferentiated amalgam of negation and "auxiliary verbness," the two components not being distinguished until some months later.

Klima and Bellugi set down the following rules for the second stage:

$$Aux^{neg} \rightarrow \begin{Bmatrix} Neg \\ V^{neg} \end{Bmatrix}$$

$$V^{neg} \rightarrow \begin{Bmatrix} can't \\ don't \end{Bmatrix}$$

$$Neg \rightarrow \begin{Bmatrix} no \\ not \end{Bmatrix}$$

The constituent *Neg* appears in *that no fish school, he no bite you,* and other sentences of this type. The placement of Aux^{neg} is immediately after the subject-NP in the deep structure and immediately before the main verb, so *Neg*-transportation is not among the relations between deep and surface structure. Moreover, since there is no evidence that modal verbs exist outside the context of negation, a transformation for *do*-support is likewise nonexistent. In Klima and Bellugi's analysis, then, such sentences as *I don't like you* and *he no bite you* are fundamentally alike: neither includes a modal verb, both include the constituent Aux^{neg}, and in neither are the transformations for *Neg*-transportation and *do*-support involved. The well-formedness of *I don't like you* and *I can't catch you* is illusory.

There is another interpretation of sentences *like he no bite you.* One innovation occurring between the first and second stages of development may be the appearance of *Neg*-transportation. If we accept this interpretation the consequence for Klima and Bellugi's grammar is merely to reverse the order of elements assumed to underly negative sentences. Instead of $NP + Aux^{neg} + VP$, as in Klima and Bellugi, it becomes $Aux^{neg} + NP + VP$. The constituent Aux^{neg} is developed as before.

Neg-transportation now applies to every sentence, including *I can't catch you.* One advantage of this interpretation is that it leaves room for the negatives, if that is what they are, such as *no pinch me* and *no . . .*

Rusty hat, that appeared in the second stage but seem to be relics of the first. In Klima and Bellugi's analysis they are truly relics, lingering from an earlier and unintegrated system. In the alternative analysis they are identical to the underlying form of all negative sentences in the second stage.

Consider the three phrase markers below. According to the alternative analysis just given, the first is the underlying structure of *I can't catch you,* the second of *he no bite you,* and the third of *no pinch me.*

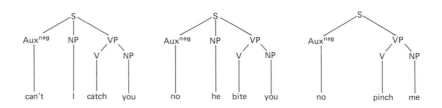

The transformation for *Neg*-transportation at the second stage is

$$Aux^{neg} + NP \implies NP + Aux^{neg}.$$

This transformation must apply to the first two phrase markers above, as they meet the condition of the transformation; *I can't catch you* and *he no bite you* result. The transformation cannot apply to the third phrase marker, however, as it has no *NP* after Aux^{neg}; the sentence remains *no pinch me.* According to the alternative interpretation, therefore, such sentences as *no pinch me* are untransformed deep structures. If children universally place negative words outside the boundaries of otherwise affirmative sentences, as this alternative analysis assumes and as the various observations already mentioned suggest, we would have a striking confirmation of the theory of language acquisition developed at the end of Chapter 5. According to that theory, the abstract underlying structure of sentences rests on the innate linguistic abilities of children; and according to Klima's (1964) analysis, as already noted, negation in the deep structure of negative sentences is external to the rest of the sentence. This deep structure is precisely as would be predicted from the abilities available to children.

Notice that the well-formedness of *I don't like you* and *I can't catch you* is illusory in the alternative analysis as well as in Klima and Bellugi's analysis. The basic kinship of these sentences to *he no bite you* remains undisturbed by assuming the existence of a transformation.

Two to six months later, again depending on the child, sentences of the following types occur:

Paul can't have one
This can't stick
I didn't did it
You don't want some supper
Donna won't let go

No, it isn't
I am not a doctor
This not ice cream
They not hot
I not crying
He not taking the walls down
Don't kick my box
Don't touch the fish
Ask me if I not make mistake
I not hurt him

There are a few new developments in the third stage, though apparently not so many as in the second. However, as is often the case, superficial changes are not valid as a guide to changes taking place in a child's grammatical system. Whereas the five new forms of the second stage resulted from changes (in Klima and Bellugi's analysis) of little scope, the negative sentences of the third stage come from a grammatical system that has been fundamentally altered: There are now auxiliary verbs; there is now a transformation for *do*-support; and, in Klima and Bellugi's analysis, there is for the first time a transformation for *Neg*-transportation.

A basic development is the English system of auxiliary verbs. Unlike the second stage, affirmative sentences with modal verbs now occur, as in *I can do it* and *can I have it?* Negation and the auxiliary are no longer tied together, as in the second stage, and the constituent Aux^{neg} has been differentiated into its negative and auxiliary components. Since *do* and *Neg* coexist in the surface structure but not in the underlying structure, a transformation for *do*-support becomes necessary to derive sentences like *I don't like you.* The continuity of surface forms between the second and third stages camouflages a basic discontinuity in the grammar. One indication of the discontinuity is that sentences based on the schema *Neg + S* no longer appear; the schema (if it is one) has been hidden by the changes of the third stage.

The development of the auxiliary system is very rapid and pervasive. It is as if the auxiliary, once freed from negation, seeped into all the available affirmative spaces in a child's grammar. As Bellugi (1967), who has studied these developments closely, puts it:

> The change suggests a carefully prepared complex system which is beginning to be set in and intricately hooked up to the children's previous language systems. If the change were not so widespread, and occurred over a long period of time in many little separate aspects, nothing would be surprising in this development . . . . It is the fact that much of the apparatus comes in in a relatively short period of time and appears in a variety of structures that surprises us (p. 90).

Table 11 gives an impression of the pace of the change. In it are shown the number of times that one child, Eve, used modal verbs in

Table 11 **The Use of Modal Verbs by One Child**
(Bellugi, 1967)

Context	Age (months)		
	26.5	27	27.5
Affirmative	8	20	27
Negative	6	12	14
Yes–No question	–	4	12

several different grammatical contexts in three successive samples of her speech; the samples were collected over a period of a month. Along with a growth in numbers is a growth in variety – more and more modal verbs appear with more and more main verbs, tenses of verbs, subjects, etc.

Negation in English is a complex system. Klima's (1964) analysis of adult grammar, for example, includes almost two dozen phrase-structural rules and an equal number of transformational rules. The sketch presented here – including as it does only three phrase-structural and two transformational rules – is clearly highly selective and incomplete. Bellugi (1967) goes somewhat further, but detailed understanding of how the entire system emerges is far from being at hand.

Two other aspects of children's negation should be mentioned. Both illustrate the autonomous and inventive character of child language, and show once again that the time-consuming step in language acquisition is the learning of restrictions on rules. One example has to do with a rather special corner of the English negative system that controls such verbs as *think, believe, anticipate, expect,* and *want.* They have the unique property that in sentences with embedded object complements either these verbs *or* the verb of the complement may be negated and meaning does not change (Lakoff, 1965). Compare, for example, the following two pairs of sentences. The first pair includes a verb open to this option and the second pair does not.

(a) I think that he won't come on time
(b) I don't think that he will come on time
(c) I know that he won't come on time
(d) I don't know that he will come on time

Sentences (a) and (b) mean the same thing, whereas (c) and (d) do not.

For the verbs open to such moveable negation, Bellugi counted the number of times the matrix and complement options were employed in the speech of the parents of Adam and Sarah. (Eve's records contained no examples of such embeddings.) The verbs used most often were *think* and *want,* and in all utterances except one negation fell on the matrix sentence. *I don't think that he will come in time* was more frequent by a large margin than was *I think that he won't come on time.* Such is the linguistic evidence Adam and Sarah obtained.

However, in the children's own speech precisely the opposite arrangement dominated, even though negation otherwise appeared in matrix sentences at this stage, as in *I don't know that.* The following examples illustrate:

He thinks he doesn't have nothing
I think it's not fulled up to the top
He thinks he doesn't have to finish it
I think we don't have a top
I think he don't like us no more
I think I can't find white
I thlnk I don't better cut it
I think I don't know what it is
I think I don't

Verbs such as *think* and *want* are exceptions to the general rules of negation in English. The general rule is to distinguish between matrix and complement negation. Children, if they have worked out this rule but not yet the exceptions to it, will treat *think* as any other verb (so that negation in the matrix is reserved for the situation where a child is *not* engaged in thought), even though this is contradicted by the evidence of parental speech. We have an indication of the inviolability of children's grammar, and the strong filtering effect it exerts on the linguistic evidence obtained from adults.

Another phenomenon in the acquisition of negation that reveals the autonomy of child grammar is the occurrence of double negation. The explanation again is that children work out general rules with ease and exceptions with difficulty. In English, adults say affirmatively, *I want some supper,* and at an early point in development children do the same (Bellugi, 1964). To negate such utterances, adults may say either *I want no supper* or *I don't want any supper.* Children at first use neither of these forms, however, but say *I don't want some supper.* Such sentences occur at the second stage of negation described above, and result from the insertion of *don't* as an Aux^{neg} into affirmative sentences by the process already described. A child receives no examples in the speech of adults that utilize this process: it is an autonomous consequence of his own grammar. A few months later double negatives appear. The pronoun *some* no longer occurs in negative sentences; the negative counterpart *none* takes its place and *I don't want no supper* is the result. The middle-class parents of these children do not use double negatives; indeed, Cazden (1965) found an indication that children exposed to double-negative dialects differ both from middle-class children and from the dialect to which they are exposed. Double negation in the speech of middle-class children is again an autonomous consequence of development.

In affirmative English sentences the sign of the verb and the sign of the pronoun are the same. There is *I want⁺ some⁺* or *I want⁺ any⁺,* and the result of the combination is also a plus. But in negative English sentences the sign of the verb and the pronoun are opposite. There is *I want⁺ none⁻* or *I don't⁻ want any⁺*, and the result is a minus. The double-negative sentences of stage 3 arise from an overgeneralization of the affirmative-sentence system to the negative-sentence system. The result is *I don't⁻ want none⁻*, the meaning of which is a minus. To discover the actual English system of matching signs in affirmative sentences and mismatching them in negative sentences a child must overturn a hypothesis of wide scope and replace it with one restricted by the sign of the predicate verb.

Let us briefly consider semantics. McNeill and McNeill (1968) found that the development of negation for two Japanese children began with the denial of the truth of statements and the existence of objects, and only later became concerned with negation on internal grounds (*I don't want*), and still later with a kind of negation that "entails" the simultaneous truth of another statement. There were thus three dimensions of negation involved, as represented in Fig. 14. "Truth" and "Existence" refer to the negation of intrinsic and extrinsic predicates respectively (see Chapter 3). "Entailment" and "Nonentailment" refer to the difference between *no, that's an apple not a pear* and *no, that's not a pear.* Both deny the truth of an intrinsic predicate (*that's a pear*) but in *no, that's an apple not a pear* the intention is to "entail" the truth of *that's an apple.* There are English examples from Bellugi (1967) that apparently are of the entailment type. "Internal" and "External" refer to denial on internal grounds (*I don't want it to happen*) and denial on external grounds (*it didn't happen*).

Before the contrast between "Internal" and "External" was established, objects and events could be refused but the expression of the refusal took a strangely solipsistic form. The Japanese have a single word for "I don't want," *iya*, but it was not used in the early stages when refusal evidently was intended (in reply to "Let's give your sister some").

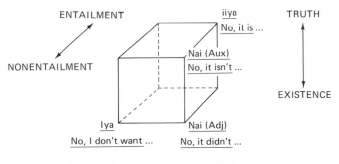

Fig. 14. A cube showing three semantic distinctions in negation. Examples from Japanese and English are located at the appropriate corners (after McNeill and McNeill, 1968).

Instead the children used a word ordinarily meaning "it doesn't exist" (*nai,* an adjective). The distinction between "Internal" and "External" did not yet matter linguistically, so they expressed a lack of willingness with a term already known to express a lack of existence.

The entire structure represented in Fig. 14 emerged within a period of four to six months, depending on the child. Although it may be true that semantic development is in general slower than syntactic development that is not the case with negation (see Chapter 8). Bloom (1968), in an independent analysis, draws conclusions for English similar to those drawn by McNeill and McNeill for Japanese. A major difference, however, exists in the order of emergence of the contrasts. Bloom found negation on internal grounds before negation of truth.

The Development of Questions

Questions at the outset are simple in the extreme, and in this respect resemble negation. Rising intonation and the use of one of a few Wh-words are the only interrogative devices. Nonetheless, even very young children distinguish between yes–no and Wh-questions — asking, for example, both *see hole?* and *what doing?*

The following account will concentrate on the development of Wh-questions and, within this limit, will concentrate on the second and third stages of development defined by Brown et al. (1968). The first stage comprises essentially the simple system just described.

During the second stage children ask such Wh-questions as the following:

Where my mitten?
What me think?
What the dollie have?
Why you smiling?
Why not he eat?
Why not . . . me can't dance?

A clue to the structure of these questions lies in the fact that, in every case except one, deleting the Wh-word (including *why not*) leaves a "grammatical" sentence as a residue. *My mitten, me think, you smiling, he eat,* and *me can't dance* are all possible declarative sentences in the second stage. The exception is *the dollie have,* which lacks an NP-object. In general, in this stage Wh-questions are formed simply by placing a Wh-word at the start of a declarative sentence, the sentence being left otherwise undisturbed.

Questions with *why* and *why not* are not different from other Wh-questions, although the distribution of the two kinds of *why*-questions is more restricted. *Why not* itself seems to be a single word possessing negative import. Both *why* and *why not* tend to occur in discourse exchanges where the declarative part of the question comes from a previous utterance of an adult and the Wh part comes from the child. Table 12 presents some examples from the speech of Adam and his mother (Brown et al., 1968). Other Wh-words in the second stage do not

Table 12 **The Restriction of "Why" and "Why Not" Questions in Discourse**
(Brown et al., 1968)

Mother	Adam
He was playing a little tune	Why he play little tune?
I see a seal	Why you see seal?
You bent that game	Why me bend that game?
Well, because she wanted to	Why she want to?
I think it's resting now	Why it's resting now?
I guess I'm not looking in the right place	Why you not looking right place?
Because you weren't careful	Why not me careful?
I don't see any	Why not you see any?
You're going to have to buy another one and give it to Ursula because you're breaking that one	Why not me break that one?

depend on such discourse exchanges. McNeill (1963) found a similar discourse restriction in children's use of personal pronouns—in its first occurrences *I* always followed adult sentences with *you.*

It seems from Table 12 that Adam's rule for deciding between *why not* and *why* is to choose *why not* when his mother's sentence is negative and *why* when it is affirmative; there is only one exception to this rule. However, it is difficult to say what further constraints there are. Adam wants to know, for example, *why you see seal?, why me bend that game?,* and *why not me careful?* Such questions suggest that although Adam seeks an explanation when he asks *why* or *why not,* his conception of an explanation is remote from an adult's. It would be surprising, of course, if it were otherwise. Piaget (1926) long ago demonstrated that children of Adam's age are unable to conceive of true explanations. All the same it seems clear that the possibility of explaining things—as opposed to what counts as an explanation—exists early in development (cf. the discussion of Berkeley and Bailey in Chapter 5).

Wh-questions in the third stage reveal a number of interesting features. Some examples from Klima and Bellugi (1966) are the following:

Where small trailer he should pull?
Where the other Joe will drive?
What he can ride in?
What did you doed?
Why he don't know how to pretend?
Why the kitty can't stand up?
How he can be a doctor?
How they can't talk?

The third stage, it will be recalled, is marked by a general emergence of the auxiliary system, and this development is much in evidence in the Wh-questions children ask. Children do not, however, use auxiliary verbs quite in the English manner. They ask, *what he can ride in?*, for example, or *why he don't know how to pretend?* An adult would put these questions differently — *what can he ride in?* and *why doesn't he know how to pretend?* Both the child and adult versions have a Wh-word in the initial position, but the child version does not invert the order of auxiliary verbs and subjects. There is no inversion in Wh-questions even though there is inversion in yes–no questions. Along with *what he can ride in?* children in the third stage also say *can he ride in it?*

Brown et al. (1968) believe that children perform just one major transformation per question, even when they have more than one available. In yes–no questions, only inversion of subject and auxiliary is required and it is performed. In Wh-questions, both inversion and a second transformation called "preposing" are required, and children perform only the latter.

"Preposing" refers to one of the transformations in Klima's (1964) and Katz and Postal's (1964) grammar for Wh-questions. In these analyses the derivation of a Wh-question begins with a deep structure that contains, in effect, a blank for the constituent being questioned. The deep structure of *what can dinosaurs eat?*, for example, is roughly *dinosaurs can eat Δ*, where Δ stands for the NP about which the question seeks information. One relation between the deep structure *dinosaurs can eat Δ* and the surface structure *what can dinosaurs eat?* is therefore preposing the Δ. A second relation is inversion of *can* and *dinosaurs*. Morphophonemic rules convert Δ to *what,* to give *what can dinosaurs eat?*

Since children say *what dinosaurs can eat?* it appears that they do not perform the inversion when they perform the preposing. *What dinosaurs can eat?* is an example of what Brown et al. call a "hypothetical intermediate" — a structure defined by the grammar of adult English only at an intermediate stage of derivation. However, children always eliminate the same transformation from Wh-questions. They never say *can he ride in what?* or *will the other Joe drive where?* If there are two generally available transformations it would seem that the reduction of either one could occur. One way to explain the presence of *what he can ride in* and the absence of *can he ride in what* is to assume that the underlying form of the Wh-questions of the third stage is not yet the adult form, in particular that the vacant constituent Δ is not yet located in the object position of sentences. Then there would be nothing to prepose. As in the second stage, *what + he can ride in* is a possible question, whereas *can he ride in + what* is not.

However, this explanation encounters a difficulty. If Wh-words are introduced at the beginning of sentences, how do children ask semantically appropriate Wh-questions? The explanation is contained in the reverse process, in the answers children give to the questions of adults. Klima and Bellugi (1966) list the following, from the second stage:

Adult   What d'you need?
Child   Need some chocolate
Adult   Who are you peeking at?
Child   Peeking at Ursula
Adult   Who were you playing with?
Child   Robin
Adult   What d'you hear?
Child   Hear a duck

Every question is answered appropriately from a semantic point of view. However, in every example except one, the child's answer is a full VP instead of the NP customary in English. A semantically appropriate reply appears in a syntactic setting that makes it clear that *what* and *who* are not associated with NP. Let us suppose that *what* has as part of its lexical entry a feature such as [+ common noun], that *who* has [+ proper noun], and that *why* has both [+ common noun] and [+ proper noun]. Whenever one of these Wh-words appears in an adult question, the reply is a sentence that includes a noun of the specified type. (The subject of the sentence is omitted in these cases.) Children with such a grammar will ask semantically appropriate Wh-questions and not prepose Wh-words while doing so. It is for this reason that subject-auxiliary inversion does not take place.

In the third stage of development children answer adult Wh-questions with NPs, as is customary in English (Brown et al., 1968). Doing so contradicts the tendency of children at the same stage to ask Wh-questions by placing a Wh-word before a sentence, according to the analysis provided here. Such contradictions, however, are not peculiar to Wh-questions. As has been widely noted, children often comprehend syntactic forms before they produce them (e.g., Fraser, Bellugi, and Brown, 1963; Lovell and Dixon, 1965). The third stage of development is transitional. Children understand Wh-words as representing particular constituents in the speech of adults, but they do not yet produce Wh-questions this way. We will return to the difference between production and comprehension below.

Exceptions to Rules
The process of discovering the restrictions placed on general rules can, in some cases, extend over many years. In contrast to the acquisition of the rules themselves, this process of learning can be slow indeed. Some speakers never discover certain exceptions.

C. S. Chomsky (1969) reports a number of important observations of these phenomena. She was interested in how children older than five understand sentences that depart from what she calls, after Rosenbaum (1967), the "Minimum Distance Principle" (MDP). The MDP is a general characteristic of English predicate complements. In *John required Mary to be an enthusiast,* for example, the subject (*Mary*) of the complement (*to be an enthusiast*) is the first NP to the left. This rule is the MDP. However, in *John promised Mary to be an enthusiast* the MDP does not apply, for the subject of the complement is *John* — i.e., the second NP to the left. *Promise* is one of a small number of exceptional English verbs where the MDP is required *not* to apply. Another such verb is *ask:* Compare *I asked Mary what to do about the enthusiast* to *I told Mary what to do about the enthusiast.* In the second the subject of *do* is *Mary,* as required by the MDP, but in the first it is *I.*

Sentences with *promise* or *ask* are more complex than sentences with *know* or *tell.* To understand them a child must not only be able to recognize that the complement has a hidden subject but also that the subject is — in contradiction to a general rule — the first NP of the main clause. Inasmuch as it takes time for children to restrict general rules in the acquisition of language, we would expect them to apply the MDP before they discover the exceptions to the MDP. When told to "ask Mary what to feed the doll" a child who knows the MDP but not that *ask* is an exception should say something like *what are you going to feed the doll?* not *what should I feed the doll?* Similarly, if asked who will do the feeding in *John promised Mary to feed the doll,* a child who knows the MDP but not that *promise* is an exception should say *Mary.* Such confusions are exactly what Chomsky found.

The course of acquisition is interesting. In the case of *promise* all children above five know about the MDP. Some as young as five also know that *promise* is an exception to the MDP while others as old as 10 do not. There seems to be no age at which all children discover that *promise* requires the MDP to be violated. A similar history exists for *ask* in that again there is no age by which all children acquire full knowledge of how to use the verb. Some as young as five never make mistakes, others as old as 10 always make mistakes. The situation with *ask,* however, is more complicated than with *promise,* because at first children interpret *ask* as *tell.* In response to the instruction "ask Mary what to put in the box" a child may tell Mary what to put in the box — a doll, for instance. In this case the MDP is applied, but because the child has interpreted *ask* as *tell* there is no reason it should not apply. Only later do children actually ask a question when instructed in this way, and then it is possible to observe incorrect applications of the MDP — "what are you going to put in the box?"

The scattered acquisition of *promise* and *ask* contrasts with the acquisition of a third grammatical feature. In sentences such as *after he got the candy Mickey left* and *Mickey thinks he knows everything,* the pronoun *he* is ambiguous — it could be "Mickey" or it could be someone else. Pronouns generally have ambiguous referents in English sentences. But when the pronoun appears in a main clause and the main clause precedes an NP there is no ambiguity, the pronoun must refer to some other NP. In *he found out that Mickey won the race,* for instance, *he* cannot be "Mickey." Chomsky looked into the acquisition of this "nonidentity" rule for pronouns. (A study of pronomial ambiguity has been carried out by Chai, 1967, who found children of 10 unable to resolve ambiguous usages.) Like *promise* and *ask* the nonidentity rule is an exception to a more general rule. Unlike these verbs, however, the

100

absence of ambiguity of the pronoun is itself the result of a grammatical rule. *Promise* and *ask* are exceptional words; pronouns in clauses before NPs are parts of exceptional structures. In contrast to the scattered acquisition of *promise* and *ask* Chomsky found a sharp discontinuity in the acquisition of the nonidentity rule. All children older than five-and-a-half and none younger than five-and-a-half possessed it. The difference in acquisition presumably has to do with the difference in the underlying grammatical situation. Rules are acquired earlier and at more uniform ages, even when they are exceptional rules, than are lexical exceptions. Exceptional information of either kind is acquired, however, later than general information. None of Chomsky's subjects failed to know the MDP or to know that English pronouns were ambiguous, though many failed to know that there are exceptions to either of these general principles.

Comprehension and Production of Speech
We reached the conclusion that children comprehend the adult structure of Wh-questions before they can produce such structures themselves. The cause of such gaps between comprehension and production is obscure. They are not, of course, a peculiarity of language. Children can recognize geometric forms before they can produce them, and they can tell melodies apart before they can sing. Olson and Pagliuso (1968) have edited a symposium devoted to this general problem.

As for language, explanations have taken four different routes. None leads to a satisfactory conclusion, however, and the problem remains unsolved.

1. There are some who believe that children acquire two grammars, one for production and one for comprehension, and that acquisition is faster for the comprehension grammar. Obviously this is merely a restatement of the problem. While it is possible that comprehension and production are separate to some degree, we do not know why one should be possible before the other.

2. Comprehension can make use of contextual information not available for production. Thus children appear to understand passive sentences before they produce them because they are helped by context; typically, only one meaning is plausible. This explanation assumes that production and comprehension do *not* differ. In an experiment by Fraser et al. (1963), however, a gap appeared between production and comprehension even when the contextual support was the same for both.

3. It has been suggested that the load on short-term memory is greater for production than for comprehension (alternatively, the units are smaller in production), so a child is likely to forget a form in production although he could remember it in comprehension (Slobin, 1964; McNeill, 1966a). While this theory explains the gap between production and comprehension, it is itself in need of explanation. What causes such a difference in the demands on memory?

4. One hypothesis is that the slowness of child speech causes the dif-

ference (McNeill, 1968c). For an adult, very slow speech leads to confusion. At a rate of one word every 3 or 4 seconds, the structure of a sentence will collapse as it is being uttered (there must be no rehearsal, of course, for this effect to occur). Doubtlessly a similar limitation exists for young children. Forms would then often be comprehended but not produced because in comprehending children typically listen to speech delivered at a rate greater than their own. Psotka (1969) tested this theory by measuring children's comprehension of speech at different rates, using the test materials of Fraser et al. (1963). He found comprehension to be poorest at 0.5 word/second, best at 1 word/second, and in-between at 3 words/second. Psotka's own normal speech rate was 3 words/second, while the children's rate (in the production test) was 1 word/second. The hypothesis mentioned above is, therefore, not correct. While comprehension deteriorates at slow speaking rates, as predicted, it is best at children's own relatively slow rate. The gap between production and comprehension evidently does not depend on children's slow rate of speech. They comprehend that rate best.

A few years ago, I wrote: "A great deal more work is necessary on the difference between comprehension and production, for it occupies an important position in studies of language acquisition" (McNeill, 1966a, p. 81). I had in mind the fact that children probably add new information to their linguistic competence mainly by comprehending speech. Production, as we will see in the next chapter, has little effect on language acquisition and to understand linguistic development, we must understand comprehension; this assessment still stands. There was, in 1966, little known of linguistic comprehension, and, regrettably, this assessment also still stands.

7

THE CONTRIBUTION
OF EXPERIENCE

The last chapter included several examples of what appears to be a general principle: Children form relationships with ease, but require time to learn the restrictions on relationships. The contribution of experience will therefore be largest in those regions of grammar where general rules apply least. The meanings of individual words are merely the most extreme form of linguistic information not covered by general rules; there are many less extreme cases and we can draw a continuum between the lexicon at one end and the most general rules at the other for each language separately. If the principle suggested by the examples of the last chapter is correct, the order of acquisition will correspond to the order of rules along this continuum, with the most general rules being learned first and dictionary entries being completed last. The observations of C. S. Chomsky (1969) show this order of acquisition.

A natural assumption is that the relationships which children form with greatest ease are the universal types of transformation. Rules that use these relationships with the fewest restrictions will be the first a child acquires. As noted in the last chapter, there are only about a half-dozen universal types of transformations; the complexity of the actual transformational rules of a language arises through the combinations of and restrictions on these universal types. It is not unreasonable to regard the universal transformational rules as being an aspect of man's capacity for language. They describe relationships for which we have a special sensitivity, and hence are maximally able to discover. One of the universal transformational relationships is permutation. It is involved, for example, in the derivation of Wh-questions, discussed in the last chapter. Young children have great difficulty in copying the left-to-right order of arrays of objects. Usually this difficulty is interpreted as showing an absence of something — a schema for order, for example. But equally it shows an ability to permute order. Languages exploit this ability in the form of a universal transformational relation. That adults are less open to such confusions, having well-established schemas for order, may be one aspect of their declining capacity for language (cf. Lenneberg, 1967, for a discussion of critical periods in language acquisition).

However, even adults show a special sensitivity to permutation in particular situations. In solving anagrams, for instance, two parallel processes of permutation can take place. One is conscious, deliberate, overt, and typical of adults; the other is unconscious, spontaneous, covert, and presumably typical of children. The following is the record of one adult solving LEKISTL, an anagram for a common kitchen utensil: ketsil, setkill, siktell, teksill, ell, sell, lel, kell, ketsill, kitsell (the subject saw the solution at this point), silklet, skillet. She tries out various combinations, following a strategy that often produces a solution. However, in this example the last of the deliberate permutations (kitsell) bears little resemblance to the answer, and the sequence from ketsil to kitsell represents almost no movement. Rather than deliberate permutation, a second covert process of permutation was taking place, and reached the solution first.

The present chapter describes what is known of the way a child's linguistic experience contributes to his acquisition of language. What is known is largely negative: learning does *not* take place through imitation; overt practice with linguistic forms does *not* play a role. More positively, we can identify "training situations" that arise during the interactions of adults and children where information about transformations is, as it were, put on display.

Since the role played by experience is greater with rules that carry more restrictions, we should focus attention on these most restricted cases, but it is not possible to do so. Ironically, most efforts to show the contribution of experience to language acquisition, which have had the goal of establishing a place for learning theory, have concentrated on the simplest cases, i.e., the ones where experience plays the least role. As a consequence, nothing much can be said about even the basic questions. What amount of exposure, for instance, and what kind of material, is necessary to learn restrictions on general rules? How does the necessary amount of experience depend on the kind of restriction being learned?

Imitation

One traditional view of language acquisition has the process advance through imitation. It has not always been clear precisely what this theory means. The word "imitation" possesses two quite different senses, and only one can be applied to language acquisition. In one sense, "imitation" refers to resemblance—one person comes to resemble another more and more closely. The trait on which the resemblance develops must necessarily be arbitrarily variable within broad limits. Resemblance in height is not the result of imitation, but etiquette and driving on the left side of the road in England are. In this sense, language also is acquired through imitation. In the second, more technical sense, "imitation" refers to a process whereby behavior is acquired by copying the behavior of a model. Such a view was applied to language acquisition by Allport (1924) and has occupied a place in psychology ever since. It is in this second technical sense that language cannot be said to result from imitation.

There is no question that children imitate the speech of adults. In fact they do it a great deal. Fully 10 percent of children's speech at 28–

35 months is imitative in the records collected by Brown (unpublished materials). There are, for example, such exchanges as the following (different adults and children are speaking):

ADULT	CHILD
Oh, that's a big one	big one
But, he was much bigger than Perro	big a Perro
Salad dressing	salad dressing
That's not a screw	dat not a screw
Are they all there?	all dere?

The fact that children imitate the speech of adults does not mean that the process of acquisition is imitation. *It runned, allgone shoe,* and *a that man* have no models in adult speech but are grammatical within a child's system. The system in which these forms are grammatical clearly could not have been derived from imitation.

It is possible, however, that adult forms are introduced into a child's speech through imitation. As long as a child's grammar is not fully developed he might produce such utterances as *a that man* but enrich his grammar through the imitation of well-formed examples. In this case, imitations will be "advanced" grammatically relative to spontaneous speech. Ervin (1964) looked into this possibility by comparing children's spontaneously occurring imitations to their spontaneously occurring free speech. The grammatical organization of the imitations was identical with the organization of the free speech. Only one child in Ervin's sample of five was an exception, and in her case imitation went in the wrong direction and was more primitive.

The result reflects a general characteristic of child speech. There is a strong tendency among children to include nothing in the surface structures of sentences that cannot be related to deep structures — i.e., nothing for which there is no transformational derivation known. The principle encompasses spontaneous speech as well as imitation. If a child does not yet include the progressive inflection *-ing* in his speech, he will not imitate *-ing* in the speech of adults, particularly if the adult model is long relative to his memory span. *Adam's nose is dripping* might be imitated *Adam nose drip* but probably not *Adam nose dripping.* It is for this reason that imitation can be used as a test of children's productive capacities, as described in Chapter 2.

The resistance of children to new forms sometimes goes to extravagant lengths. Consider, for example, the following exchange between one mother and her child (from McNeill, 1966a):

Child   *Nobody don't like me*
Mother   *No, say "nobody likes me"*
Child   *Nobody don't like me*

.
.
.

> *(eight repetitions of this*
> *dialogue)*
>
> .
>
> .
>
> .

Mother　*No, now listen carefully;*
　　　　say "nobody likes me"
Child　*Oh! Nobody don't likes me*

It is possible to instruct children to imitate, as Slobin and Welsh (1967) and Fraser, Bellugi, and Brown (1963) have done. Under these circumstances, a child's imitations may depart from his grammar. But enforced imitation is not typical of the ordinary circumstances of child speech, and phenomena observed here cannot be extended automatically to the actual acquisition of grammatical structures.

Rather than serving a didactic purpose, imitation often seems to be carried out in play. It is the opposite of instruction, therefore, if indeed it has any effect at all. A child manipulates the grammatical system already at his disposal, often in fantastic ways, but he does not go beyond it. The effect, if any, would be to reinforce the primitive structure. Take as an example one of Brown's subjects, who, starting from an ordinary imitation, went on in a fugue-like manner (mentioned by Slobin, 1964; also McNeill, 1966a):

Adult　*That's the tattooed man*
Child　*Tooman. Tattoo man. Find too tattoo man.*
　　　　Tattoo man. Who dat? Tattoo. Too man go, mommy?
　　　　Too man. Tattoo man go? Who dat? Read dat.
　　　　Tractor dere. Tattoo man.

Weir (1962) found many examples of similar grammatical play in the pre-sleep soliloquies of her two-and-a-half-year-old son. The child selected a particular paradigm—sometimes grammatical, sometimes phonological—and then elaborated on it with a stream of examples. The following uses a syntactic paradigm. It might be considered the linguistic equivalent of building up and knocking down a tower of blocks.

go for glasses
go for them
go to the top
go throw
go for blouse
pants
go for shoes

We thus arrive at a negative conclusion: The contribution of parental speech to language acquisition is not to supply specimens for children to imitate.

Overt Practice

One implication of the phenomenon of inflectional imperialism, discussed in the last chapter, is that overt practice has no influence on whether or not a form remains in a child's grammar. The regular past-tense inflection in English was so rare in the speech of Ervin's (1964) children that it appeared first on the frequent strong verbs. These verbs, in contrast, had been used for months with their correct irregular inflections. This extensive practice added nothing to the stability of the irregular inflections, which were swept away by the regular inflection, when it appeared. Obviously overt practice is not essential for developing restrictions on general rules, since it is the conflict with a general rule that in this case removes the correct and well-practiced inflection. The observations of Zhenya lead to the same negative conclusion.

Reinforcement by Approval

Behaviorist psychologists define a reinforcer as an event that increases the probability of a response. There is no arguing with such a circular definition, except to point out the circularity, but one can look at particular cases and see if they fit the definition. An event commonly alleged to be a reinforcer to young children is parental approval. Brown et al. (1968) examined all the instances of approval that appeared in the records of their three subjects, and found that its occurrence depended only on the truth value of what the child said. Grammatical form was irrelevant. A child could say *that's Popeye's* and be told "no" if it was Mickey's, but he could say under the same circumstances *that Mickey* and be told "yes." Obviously, approval, if it is a reinforcer, will increase the probability of grammatically incorrect forms as much as it does grammatically correct ones. By the usual circular definition, therefore, approval cannot be a reinforcer of grammatical form.

Training Situations

As already noted, imitation fails to affect child language because of a strong tendency in children to assimilate adult specimens to their current grammars. One way to avoid assimilation is to place the burden of introducing new forms on adults. Brown et al. (1968) discuss three situations that could conceivably have this result, "expansion," "modelling," and "prompting."

An expansion is an imitation in reverse. An adult, repeating a child's telegraphic sentence, typically adds the parts he judges to have been omitted. There is usually a number of possible adult sentences available as expansions. *That mommy hairband,* for example, could be expanded to become *that's mommy's hairband, that was mommy's hairband until you dismantled it, that looks like mommy's hairband,* etc. But often one sentence will best fit the extralinguistic situation, and that sentence becomes the expansion. (That adults can do this at all was the argument against Berkeley's theory of language discussed in Chapter 5.) If the child's meaning is correctly grasped, an expansion presents a surface structure that expresses the deep structure the child has in mind. The expansion is necessarily experienced by the child in contiguity with his intended meaning and can be effective when the child notices the way the two are related.

Cazden (1965) looked into the effectiveness of this training situation by deliberately increasing the number of expansions given to children. The children were two-and-a-half years old, spent each weekday in a nursery school, were from working-class homes, and received in the normal course of events few expansions either at school or at home. (Expansion is something middle-class parents, especially, do.) In Cazden's experiment every child spent one-half hour a day, five days a week, looking at picture books with an adult who systematically expanded everything the child said. At the beginning and at the end of the experiment, three months later, the children were given a specially devised test of linguistic performance (covering, for example, NP and VP complexity and the imitation of various syntactic forms). These children were compared to two other groups of children, in the same nursery school, who received in one case what Cazden called "models" and in the other no special treatment at all. "Modelling" is commenting—everything said by a child is commented upon, rather than improved upon, as in expansion. If a child said *doggie bite*, for example, an expansion might be *yes, he's biting*, whereas a model might be *yes, he's very mad.* Children in the modelling group also spent one-half hour a day, five days a week, looking at picture books with an adult.

The results were clear cut. Modelling was better than expanding. Relative to the group of children who received no special treatment there was a modest gain in linguistic performance among the children who received expansions but a large gain among those who received models. A greater variety of syntactic and lexical forms is required for modelling compared to expanding child speech, as Cazden pointed out. In expansion an adult is closely led by a child—he must use the child's words and something like the child's syntax—while in modelling he must avoid the child's words and often his syntax. Apparently, it is not helpful for linguistic development when a child's utterances constrain the structure and content of adult speech; however, it is this very fact that should make expansion advantageous.

Cazden apparently has shown that modelling assists linguistic development (an opposite result will be mentioned below), but it is not clear that she has shown that expansions do not. Middle-class parents expand about 30 percent of the speech of their children. One can ask why this rate is not higher, say 50 or 70 percent. One reason must be that not everything said by a child is interpretable in the extralinguistic context. In such circumstances adults would tend not to expand. In Cazden's experiment, on the other hand, the rate of expansion was by design, 100 percent. Young children might not pay attention to expansions in the face of such an avalanche (Brown et al., 1968). And even if they do pay attention some utterances in Cazden's experiment must have been inappropriately expanded (McNeill, 1966b). When an expansion goes astray a child could formulate a rule that does not exist in English. He might, for example, relate the meaning of "that's mommy's hairband" to *that looks like mommy's hairband.* The poor showing of expansion in Cazden's experiment is, therefore, to be expected even on the assumption that expansions are the only method for the acquisition of transformations. A recent study by Feldman and Rodgon (1970) compared "contingent" expansions (only clear utterances expanded) to "noncontingent" expansions (all utterances expanded) and found, as expected from the argument above, that contingent expansions helped more than noncontingent. What was surprising, however, was that *both* kinds of expansions were superior to modelling. Feldman and Rodgon's Ss were similar to Cazden's in age (two-and-a-half) and background (poor urban black families), and had had similar school experiences (day care centers). The tests of linguistic ability were not identical in the two experiments but were at least similar. It is not clear why a different result appeared with modelling. The relative effectiveness of expansion and modelling remains an open question.

Brown et al. (1968) have looked at expansion in another way. As noted before, to calibrate linguistic development they use mean length of utterance rather than, as usual, chronological age. When the calibration is carried out in this way the fastest of Brown's three subjects is Sarah, the next fastest is Adam, and the slowest is Eve. We can compare this order to the order of expansion by the children's parents, which gives Adam, Eve, and Sarah. Sarah, who is most advanced, therefore, was the one who received the fewest expansions. Let us focus on the contrast between Eve and Sarah, for they present the sharpest differences. It so happens that at any given utterance length Eve used fewer modal verbs, inflections, prepositions, articles, and other superficial sentence forms than did Sarah, while Sarah used fewer nouns, verbs, and adjectives. Thus, at any given utterance length, Sarah's speech was syntactically more like adult English, as Brown et al. point out, but Eve's was more informative. Sarah might have said *that's mommy's hairband,* a well-formed sentence five morphemes long, whereas Eve might have said, semigrammatically but with the same length, *that mommy broken hairband there.* Cazden (1967) concludes from this difference that Eve's intellectual development was greater than Sarah's. Such a difference may well exist. At any given length of utterance Eve included more information than Sarah did. But this comparison does not bear on the role of expansions, if this role is to facilitate the acquisition of transformations or the learning of restrictions on them. A child who receives more expansions has more opportunities to observe relations between underlying and well-formed surface structures. An appropriate base-line against which to measure this effect is chronological age. And on the scale of chronological age, Eve's linguistic development is far in advance of Sarah's.

The role or lack of role of expansion in linguistic development is thus open to dispute. The two experiments done on the phenomenon have contradictory outcomes. The evidence of recorded adult and child speech is interpretable in opposite ways, depending on the base-line of comparison.

"Prompting" is discussed by Brown et al. as another possible training situation, but its effectiveness is yet to be investigated. As described in the last chapter, one transformation in the derivation of English Wh-questions is the preposing of Δ. *Dinosaurs can eat* Δ becomes Δ *dinosaurs can eat.* In a "prompt" something very much like preposing is directly demonstrated to a child. A "prompt" begins with a Wh-question from an adult — *what did you eat?* If the child does not answer, the adult might repeat the question in a different form — *you ate what?* The second version differs from the first in several respects, one being that preposing has not occurred. If a child understands the second question, and so has in mind the deep structure *you eat* Δ, he is in a position to observe the relation of this deep structure to the surface structure of *what did you eat?* For a child who has not formulated the preposing transformations, a "prompt" may provide the occasion to do so. Brown et al. note that children usually answer nonpreposed questions, so "prompting" is at least potentially effective in revealing preposing to a child.

Brown et al. describe a third parent–child exchange, "echoing," which also can be mentioned, although it does not correspond to any transformation and therefore cannot demonstrate one to a child. An "echo" begins with an utterance from a child that is in part unintelligible — for example, *I ate the gowish.* An adult may then echo the child but replace the unintelligible part with a Wh-word — *you ate the what?* The form of the adult question is the same as in "prompting." However, even if a child understands the adult question, he could not discover preposing. The only relations in an "echo" exist, on the one hand, between *you ate* Δ and the surface structure of *you ate the what?,* and on the other hand between *you ate* Δ and the answer *I ate the gowish.*

"Echoing" might therefore tell a child something about answering questions but not about preposing Wh-words. It might also help him discover what in his own utterance belongs to a single sentence constituent (Brown et al., 1968); e.g., the *what* of *you ate what?* replaces an NP in the child's own sentence. It can, therefore, help in the learning of restrictions on rules.

For a child to discover a transformation (though not to discover the restrictions on transformations) a strange interpersonal contiguity must be brought about. Expansion, prompting, and imitation provide this contiguity, but echoing and modelling do not. The contiguity is this: To observe a transformational relation not yet known, an underlying structure that comes only from the child must be made contiguous with a surface structure that comes only from an adult. Diagrammatically,

CHILD	TRANSFORMATIONAL RELATION	ADULT
Underlying structure	?	Surface structure

In other words, something in the child's mind must be brought to-gether with something in the adult's speech. This contiguity must exist to understand a transformational relation as well as to produce one, so the gap between comprehension and production does not ex-plain how it is overcome.

An expansion makes an adult surface structure contiguous with a child's underlying structure when the adult correctly infers the child's meaning. A prompt does so when a child understands the revised Wh-question. Expansions and prompts therefore differ in who must do the comprehending. An imitation brings a surface structure together with the right underlying structure when a child repeats an adult sentence which he correctly understands on nonlinguistic grounds. Echoing, however, never places an adult surface structure together with a child's correct underlying structure. And modelling, by definition, avoids meeting this condition. It is obvious that contiguity is not the only factor determining the acquisition of transformations. If it were, imita-tion would help and modelling would not.

There is a disappointing inconclusiveness to what can be said con-cerning the contribution of experience to language acquisition. Even the training situations described by Brown et al., which are only four among what must be many, merely place linguistic information on dis-play. The question of how a child notices and absorbs this information is not touched. Our state of knowledge is remote from anything en-visioned in behaviorist theories of language learning (e.g., Osgood, 1968). Not only is there nothing calling for behaviorist principles of language acquisition, but when situations favorable to response learning are examined, such as imitation or overt practice, one finds no effects that behaviorist principles can explain. (See Appendix for further discussion.)

SEMANTIC
DEVELOPMENT

Semantic development is at once the most pervasive and the least understood aspect of language acquisition. It is pervasive because the introduction of semantic organization into a child's grammar has repercussions across wide areas of cognition and beyond language itself. It is little understood because there has as yet been little guidance from linguistic theory on what to expect from the introduction of semantic organization. However, theories of semantics are currently under active development and matters in this quarter may soon improve (cf. Katz and Fodor, 1963; Katz and Postal, 1964; Katz, 1966, 1967; Weinreich, 1963, 1966).

The level of sophistication in the study of semantic development is therefore not comparable to the level attained in other aspects of linguistic development. It differs from syntax, where by now several investigations of language acquisition have been carried out under the general if not the specific influence of contemporary linguistic theory, and it is diametrically opposite to the situation in phonology — in semantics there are immense quantities of data but no theory to say which, if any, of them are relevant, while in phonology there are almost no data but there is a theory to say what relevant data would be like in the event they should be collected.

The treatment of semantics in this chapter will concentrate on a few topics — the development of semantic "features," the influence of semantics on syntax, and the association of semantics with action — chosen in part because of their general interest and in part because they suggest certain theoretical issues.

Studies mainly of a statistical or normative nature have not been included. Much of this work has to do with children's word associations (e.g., di Vesta, 1964a, 1964b; Riegel, 1965b; Riegel and Feldman, 1967; Riegel and Zivian, 1967) and children's ratings on the semantic differential (e.g., di Vesta, 1966c; di Vesta and Dick, 1966; Rice and di Vesta, 1965). Extensive norms of children's free word associations have been published recently by Entwisle (1966) and of children's restricted word associations by Riegel (1965a). Di Vesta (1966a) has published norms of children's semantic differential ratings.

Also omitted are studies of children's cognitive development, including those that deal with language. Much more than a chapter is necessary to cope with this topic. Bruner, Olver, and Greenfield (1966) can be consulted for a summary of recent research. For the views of Piaget and

Inhelder one can turn to a small volume in the *Que sais-je* series (Piaget and Inhelder, 1966).

Semantic Features

It is obvious that children have some kind of semantic system at a very early point in linguistic development. Syntax and semantics are not clearly distinguished at the beginning. Indeed, one way of viewing the holophrastic period is to think of it as depending on a dictionary in which single words are paired with sentence-meanings (McNeill, 1966a). Each meaning embodies a particular grammatical relation and each word is paired with several such meanings. A holophrastic dictionary of this kind would be burdensome for memory and susceptible to ambiguity. The ambiguity can be reduced by the creation of a new dictionary in which words are paired with single sentence-meanings. But as each word must be entered several times in such a one-to-one dictionary, it would increase the burden on memory even further and it too must be abandoned. The ultimate solution is a word dictionary. It has the effect of a sentence dictionary without the bulk.

Both these hypothetical transitions require a reworking of a child's semantic system. Of the two, however, the second is by far the most significant. It is with the first construction of a word dictionary that we can date the rudiments of a semantic system basically similar to that of adults (see Katz and Fodor, 1963). In moving from a holophrastic to a sentence dictionary a child continues to record undifferentiated semantic information: The definition of one sentence is not related to the definition of any other. In moving from a sentence to a word dictionary a fundamental change is made in the format of the dictionary entries themselves. A child begins to elaborate a system of semantic features and sentences come to be interrelated by rules for using dictionary entries.

A child's first effort to compile a word dictionary presumably does not occur before his use of rules to construct sentences. It is difficult to conceive of a word dictionary without word organization, since that would result in a loss of power to encode sentence-meanings. Compilation of a word dictionary ought not to begin, therefore, before the first sign of constructions, at about 18 months. This sets a lower bound on the beginning of a true semantic component of grammar. Setting an upper bound is more difficult. Children could continue with a sentence dictionary after becoming able to construct grammatically organized sentences. Each construction would be referred to the dictionary to learn its meaning. However, such an effort must end when the variety of sentences becomes at all large. A sentence dictionary coupled with a substantial development of transformations would require keeping the same sentence-meaning in many places, once for each transformation of the same underlying structure. On the other hand, transformations lead to a large reduction in dictionary size if the dictionary is a word dictionary. A word dictionary therefore is favored in two ways by the development of transformations: without a word dictionary transformations are impossible, with one they are essential. We can set an upper bound for the first compilation of a word dictionary at the time transformations appear in large numbers, about 28–30 months.

Consider a purely hypothetical example. A dictionary entry for the word *flower* would have to include at least the following: a syntactic feature [common noun], a collection of semantic features, including perhaps (physical object) (living) (small) and (plant), plus selection restrictions that keep the word in the right semantic environment. An adult dictionary would contain more than four semantic features for *flower,* but the ones given will serve as examples. The addition of a semantic feature to a dictionary is an event with ramifying consequences. By definition, semantic features appear in more than one dictionary entry and in some cases — (small), for instance — a feature appears in a great many dictionary entries. Each new semantic feature is a distinction that separates one class of words from another.

We can distinguish two hypotheses regarding the enlargement of dictionaries. They differ in when, earlier or later, a semantic feature spreads through the dictionary.

1. Horizontal Development If the compilation of dictionary entries is sequential, so not all the semantic features associated with a word enter the dictionary when the word itself enters, words can be in a child's vocabulary but have different semantic properties from the same words in the vocabulary of an older child or an adult. Semantic development will then consist of horizontally completing the dictionary entries of words already acquired as well as the acquisition of new words.

2. Vertical Development An alternative hypothesis is that most or all of the semantic features of a word enter the dictionary when the word does, but at first dictionary entries are separated from each other so that semantic features appear at several unrelated places in the dictionary. Words could then have the same semantic properties for younger and older children, and semantic development would consist of vertically collecting these separate occurrences into unified semantic features.

Both the horizontal and vertical hypotheses might be true, of course, since they are not mutually exclusive, for the dictionary as a whole. In either case simple vocabulary counts miss entirely these internal aspects of semantic development and to this extent give a misleading picture. We will first consider evidence of horizontal development, and then (more briefly) of vertical development.

Semantic Anomaly

With the horizontal or sequential process of semantic development, sentences that adults and older children regard as anomalous younger children could regard as acceptable. With the vertical process of development there should be no such differences. Every dictionary entry contains selection restrictions setting forth the word's allowable semantic contexts (Katz and Fodor, 1963); violating them results in a semantic anomaly. The selection restrictions of a word include the semantic features that can appear as context for the word. A semantic marker in one of the senses of *crane* matches the selection restrictions of *construction;* so we can have *construction crane.* But none of the semantic markers of *construction crane* matches the selection restrictions of the predicate *laid an egg;* so we avoid as anomalous *the construction crane laid an egg* even though we accept *the crane laid an egg.*

A child who lacks knowledge of some semantic features of a word, because its entry in the dictionary is incomplete, will accept combinations that an adult, with a fuller dictionary entry, rejects as anomalous. A child would accept exactly those anomalous combinations for which the features and selection restrictions responsible for the anomaly are missing from his dictionary. If we think in terms of distribution classes — i.e., in terms of words that can appear in the same contexts — we can say that a child has distribution classes wider in scope than those of an adult. The result of horizontal semantic development is a narrowing of distribution classes and an increased tendency to reject as anomalous combinations formerly accepted.

Miller and Isard (1963) performed an experiment in which adult subjects listened to three different kinds of verbal strings through a masking noise. The strings were either fully grammatical sentences (*the academic lecture attracted a limited audience*), or anomalous sentences (*the academic liquid became an odorless audience*), or scrambled strings (*liquid the an became audience odorless academic*). A subject's task was to shadow the strings as they were heard. Since a masking noise of the right intensity randomly obliterates parts of the acoustic signal, the performance of a subject in this experiment depends on an ability to fill in the obliterated parts by guessing from what was actually heard the remaining structure of the string. At several noise levels, Miller and Isard's subjects shadowed fully grammatical strings most accurately, anomalous strings next most accurately, and scrambled strings least accurately. The difference between grammatical and anomalous strings reflects an ability to exploit the semantic restrictions on word combinations; the difference between anomalous and scrambled strings reflects an ability to exploit syntactic restrictions.

What should we expect of children in this experiment? If a child lacks some semantic features, as he would if development is horizontal, he will be less able than an adult to guess the words of a fully grammatical sentence partly obliterated by noise. If both a child and an adult heard . . . *ate the cheese,* an adult might guess that the subject of the sentence was *mouse,* but a child might guess *tiger.* What of anomalous sentences? In this case adults and children should not differ, because the presence or absence of semantic features in a dictionary is irrelevant to the reconstruction of sentences where semantic features and selection restrictions do not match. Thus, to the degree that a child lacks knowledge of semantic features, performance on fully grammatical and anomalous sentences should be the same. McNeill (1965) repeated Miller and Isard's experiment with 5-, 6-, 7-, and 8-year-olds. The procedure was identical to Miller and Isard's in all respects except that there was less exotic vocabulary and the task was immediate recall. (Children of five take so long to respond when shadowing that the test automatically becomes one of immediate recall.)

The results are summarized in Fig. 15, which shows the percent of complete strings correctly recalled by children of different ages. The conclusion to be drawn is clear: 5-year-olds are less able than 8-year-olds to take advantage of semantic consistency in sentences. The third curve in Fig. 15, for scrambled strings, is parallel to but always worse than the one for anomalous strings. The difference suggests that the ability to exploit the syntactic information contained in anomalous strings does not change between five and eight, a difference consistent with the slow completion of dictionary entries relative to the rapid development of syntax.

In general, one can conclude from this experiment that children of five find fully grammatical sentences only slightly superior to anomalous sentences. It makes little difference whether one says to a child *wild Indians shoot running buffalos* or *wild elevators shoot ticking*

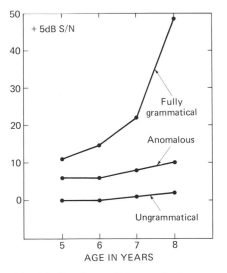

Fig. 15. The immediate recall of grammatical, anomalous, and scrambled strings of words by children of various ages. The strings were heard through a masking noise at a signal-to-noise ratio of +5 dB (after McNeill, 1965).

118

restaurants. The sentences are equally remarkable, and both have a meaning that cannot be totally grasped.

The experiment described above revealed a tendency for children to perceive and recall anomalous and fully grammatical sentences in the same (inappropriate) way. Turner and Rommetveit (1967) have in addition observed anomalous sentences in the linguistic productions of children—for instance, *the tractor drives the farmer,* and *the pony rides the girl.* These sentences were not uttered in play or fantasy; they were mistaken but serious descriptions of pictured scenes—a farmer driving a tractor, and a girl riding a pony.

The word associations of children also show effects of the horizontal development of dictionary entries. If the stimulus and response in word association are regarded as forming a grammatical unit, children's responses often make anomalous combinations with their stimuli. *Soft-wall, bright-rake,* and *fast-shout* are stimulus-response combinations given in association by 6- and 7-year-olds. Adults rarely if ever respond in this way. Word associations can be divided into two general categories according to the grammatical relation of the response to the stimulus. If the two belong to different grammatical classes the association is called "syntagmatic" (Ervin, 1961) or "heterogeneous" (Brown and Berko, 1960). If they belong to the same grammatical class the association is called "paradigmatic" (Ervin, 1961) or "homogeneous" (Brown and Berko, 1960). Both Ervin (1961) and Brown and Berko (1960) noted that young children respond mostly with syntagmatic associations, whereas older children and adults respond mostly with paradigmatic associations. The change from a predominance of the one to a predominance of the other takes place between six and eight years — the ages at which children come to distinguish anomalous and fully grammatical sentences in the experiment described above.

The coincidence of ages suggests that the shift to paradigmatic responding occurs because of semantic, not syntactic, consolidation. McNeill (1965, 1966d) offered a view of the shift in terms of the horizontal completion of dictionary entries. The argument was essentially that "syntagmatic" responses are actually often paradigmatic responses that, because of the breadth of the semantic categories available to young children, fall outside the grammatical class of the stimulus. The assumption was that paradigmatic responses match their stimuli semantically, and syntagmatic responses are grammatical continuations. Entwisle (1966) has found some support for this account in her extensive data on children's word associations.

The argument that paradigmatic responses result from vertical development has been put forward by Anderson and Beh (1968). In their experiment 6- and 7-year-olds heard word lists in which there were syntagmatic and paradigmatic associates, and tried to recognize words that were repeated in the lists. The 7-year-olds, much more than the 6-year-olds, confused paradigmatic associates, saying, for example, that *go* had appeared earlier on the list when in fact the word had been *come.* Such confusions of recognition depend on a vertical organization of the lexicon; horizontal organization cannot do it. Even one semantic marker, if it is unified vertically, can cause a recognition error; many semantic markers, if they are not unified vertically, will not cause such an error. Anderson and Beh's oldest subjects were seven. Anglin (1968) found evidence for vertical organization of the lexicon that develops through adolescence.

Why Is Semantic Development So Slow?

Semantic development stands in sharp contrast to syntactic development. Vertical organization of the lexicon may continue into adulthood. With the exception of lexical refinement, the organization of syntax appears to be complete in most respects by four or five. It is interesting that both the syntactic and semantic aspects of a lexicon are slow to develop. The crucial factor for rapid development seems to be the kind of systematic information that can be summarized in the form of a grammatical rule.

Why is there such a difference? There must be numerous reasons, and we can barely guess at them, but a few possibilities come to mind. One certainly is the complexity of the information that is encoded in a lexicon. Another is that the development of a lexicon, far more than the development of grammatical structure, depends on achieving a certain level of intellectual maturity. A child capable of saying of 20 wooden beads, 15 white and 5 green, that white beads outnumber wooden beads is also likely to say *Lassie's not an animal, she's a dog.* Presumably it is with reference to semantic development that Piaget (1967) comments, ". . . [intellectual] operations direct language acquisitions rather than vice versa." White (1965) has gathered evidence for massive changes occurring in the abilities of children at seven years, affecting cognition and language alike. Perhaps it is not surprising that a change takes place at this time, and not before, in the semantic organization of language also.

A third reason for the slow course of lexical development must be the abstractness of dictionary features. There is *nothing* in the superficial form of words that even hints at underlying semantic regularities. Phonetic symbolism is rare and specialized. Unlike syntactic abstractions, which are systematically related to surface structure by transformations, the semantic relations between words and deep structures are unsystematic. No general relation holds between the phonemic form of *school* or *uncle* or *space ship* and the meaning of these words, nor between the form of *promise* and its effect on the MDP.

One hears occasionally the hypothesis that children acquire semantic knowledge from explicit definitions. A parent may say *the zebra is an animal,* from which a child is supposed to acquire the semantic feature (animal). Perhaps the slow advance of semantic development is a result of a dependence on definitions. This argument is fallacious for a simple reason. The sentence *the zebra is an animal* may introduce the feature (animal) into the lexical entry for *zebra.* Explicit definitions can work to expand vocabulary. But they are irrelevant to the addition of semantic

120

features to a dictionary. In order for the sentence *the zebra is an animal* to influence the dictionary entry for *zebra* the feature (animal) must already be in the dictionary entry for the word *animal.* Then obviously (animal) has already been acquired and the defining sentence merely shunts it to a new lexical entry.

Not all semantic development is slow. The emergence of various semantic distinctions in negation has already been mentioned (Chapter 6). They are fully developed by children of two-and-a-half. Greenfield (1967) has carried out a similar analysis of the holophrastic word *dada,* tracing its meaning in the speech of her daughter, and found the relevant semantic distinctions (e.g., male versus female, caretaker versus noncaretaker) by the first birthday.

A Method for Discovering Semantic Features

One major obstacle faced in the study of semantic development is a sweeping ignorance on the part of psycholinguists of the semantic features of English. Very few features have been isolated and the procedures for discovering them are slow and difficult (see Katz, 1964, for an example). However, Miller (1967) has devised a method, based on word-sorting and cluster-analysis, which yields categories of words not unlike the categories defined by the semantic features of linguistics. The method requires subjects to classify written samples of words into self-imposed groups and cannot therefore be used with young children, but even so, the results obtained from adults can be used to organize and interpret observations of children. For example, Miller found that the nouns *yield, exhaust, battle, kill, deal, play, labor, joke, question, vow, counsel* and *help* fall into the clusters pictured in Fig. 16. Each node in Fig. 16 can be taken to represent a particular semantic feature — every word subordinate to it possesses that feature; every word not subordinate to it does not. It is possible to see if children honor the distinctions recovered from adults. Do children distinguish, for example, between *the clown told a joke* and *the clown told a battle?* If they do, we infer that children are acquainted at least with the seman-

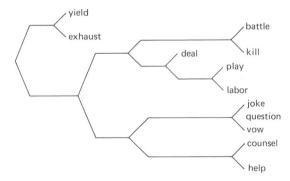

Fig. 16. A portion of an empirically derived lexicon (after Miller, 1967).

tic features defining the two large clusters containing *joke* and *battle.* What of the narrower distinction between *joke* and *help?* Do children distinguish between *jokes make everybody laugh* and *help makes everybody laugh?* The method is suggestive and deserves exploration.

Semantic Influences on Syntax

Slobin (1963, 1966c) performed an experiment with children between 5 and 11 years in which the truth of sentences had to be judged against pictured scenes. One picture showed a dog in pursuit of a cat. A true sentence with respect to this picture would be *the dog chases the cat* and a false sentence would be *the cat chases the dog.* The descriptions took several syntactic forms, variations being produced on the familiar themes of negation and passivization, to yield the following:

TRUE	FALSE
The dog is chasing the cat	The cat is chasing the dog
The cat is being chased by the dog	The dog is being chased by the cat
The cat is not chasing the dog	The dog is not chasing the cat
The dog is not being chased by the cat	The cat is not being chased by the dog

One variable in the experiment, therefore, was syntactic type — simple declarative sentences versus negative, passive, and negative-passive sentences. Another variable was the truth or falsity of the description, and a third was semantic content. Actually, two semantic factors were involved. One arises from the effects of negation and it in turn appears in two forms. Since each sentence is a description of a picture, negating it invokes negation in the sense called "Existence" by McNeill and McNeill (1968). But also, since a subject judges the truth of each sentence, a judgment of falsity invokes negation in the sense called "Truth" by McNeill and McNeill. The two varieties of negation were therefore invoked at different points in the experiment. Introducing the distinction between "Truth" and "Existence" explains an otherwise puzzling interaction that appeared in Slobin's data. He found negative *sentences* to be more difficult than affirmative *sentences,* a result also obtained by Wason (1965). In addition, he found *judgments* of falsity to be more difficult than *judgments* of truth when sentences were affirmative, but to be easier than *judgments* of truth when sentences were negative. The interaction of affirmation–negation with truth–falsity reveals a general difficulty in combining affirmation and denial. Slobin's task was relatively easy when positive judgments of "Truth" were made of sentences that were affirmative on "Existence" and when negative judgments of "Truth" were made of sentences that were negative on "Existence." The task was difficult whenever affirmation and negation had to be combined. One is reminded of the sign-matching hypothesis first adopted by children in negative sentences with indefinite pronouns (Chapter 6).

A second semantic factor is something Slobin called "reversibility."

A picture of a dog chasing a cat is reversible. Cats can chase dogs as well as vice versa. Deciding whether a sentence is true or false with respect to a reversible picture depends on deciding which word, *cat* or *dog,* is the grammatical subject and which the object and then matching this grammatical analysis to the episode shown in the picture. The difficulty of the comparison should be increased when the superficial and underlying subject and object are not the same, as in passive sentences. Thus Slobin expected and found that judgments of truth or falsity were less accurate and took longer with passive than with active sentences. The problem of verification is simplified, however, with pictures of a second "nonreversible" type. A nonreversible picture might show a girl on a pony. If a child understands that *girl* is the underlying object in *the girl is being ridden by the pony* he can correctly judge the sentence false without going through the process of matching the sentence to the picture. The semantic constraint simplifies verification by making possible a judgment on internal grounds. These grounds are the same with active and passive sentences, and Slobin found nonreversible passives to be judged as accurately and rapidly as nonreversible actives. This result held true of children at every age studied.

Thus two semantic effects, negation and reversibility, influence children's ability to verify sentences. Negation, although less complex syntactically than passivization, retards verification more. It is the semantic and not the syntactic effect of negation that dominates. Nonreversibility has even greater impact than negation, as it removes every vestige of passivization as a source of difficulty in verification.

Turner and Rommetveit (1967) report a similar result with reversible and nonreversible pictures. They required children to describe pictures as well as to judge the truth or falsity of sentences about pictures. In production, as noted above, children often reverse the order of subject and object — saying, e.g., *the pony rides the girl.* Describing a picture of a girl on a pony with the sentence *the pony rides the girl* is equivalent to saying that *the girl is being ridden by the pony* is a true sentence. In Turner and Rommetveit's experiment, children who commit the first error do not commit the second. The gains produced by nonreversibility for comprehension thus do not seem to extend to production at the ages studied (four to nine years).

A recent experiment by Bever, Mehler, and Valian (1967) helps clarify the role played by reversibility in these situations. Bever et al. used very young subjects, 2 to 4 years compared to 5 to 11 years in Slobin's experiment. The difference in age makes for an important and surprising difference in outcome. At first, reversible and nonreversible situations are treated alike when described by passive sentences. Slightly older children actually retreat from the level of performance reached by younger ones. What happens is that nonreversibility does not help or hinder performance at three years, even though children this young can comprehend some passive sentences more than half the time, but by four years comprehension of nonreversible passive sentences begins to improve and comprehension of reversible passive sentences begins to deteriorate. Children then begin to perform as in Slobin's and Turner and Rommetveit's experiments.

Bever et al. argue plausibly that children make use of semantic strategies in understanding the structure of sentences — e.g., sentences are assumed to be semantically coherent and to describe an actor, action, and recipient of the action. Strategies of this kind depend on a conviction that utterances make sense and (in the case of passives) on knowledge of what causes a situation to be reversible and nonreversible. Such information is distinct from the strictly grammatical information about the underlying relations in a sentence — subject, verb, and object. Semantic strategies apparently are acquired later than knowledge of grammatical relations, at four years instead of two, and are derived from a different source, possibly a statistical predominance of actor-action-recipient sentences. A strategy is a method, based on semantic coherence, for facilitating a syntactic analysis. It is not a syntactic analysis itself.

A statement of the strategy that apparently guides 4- and 5-year-olds (differing slightly but importantly from the version described by Bever et al.) is as follows:

1. Assume that Noun-Verb-Noun stands for Actor-Action-Recipient.

2. If this is implausible, assume that Noun-Verb-Noun stands for Recipient-Action-Actor.

Under the influence of this strategy reversible passive sentences can be construed as active sentences, even though the transformation of passivization is available. *The cat is being chased by the dog* becomes under the strategy: *cat* (actor), *chase* (action), and *dog* (recipient). The semantic coherence arising from the reversible situation leads to a reversal of grammatical subject and object. The same strategy, however, protects a child from a reversal of subject and object in nonreversible situations. *Pony* (actor), *ride* (action), and *girl* (recipient) must be rejected by a child expecting semantic coherence and *the pony is being ridden by the girl* is correctly understood as a passive sentence. Young children without a semantic strategy treat reversible and nonreversible situations alike and sentences describing both are open to the same confusions. Adults, alert to the dangers of blindly following a semantic strategy, pause to work out the grammatical structure of sentences that describe reversible situations. Older children follow a semantic strategy more or less consistently and thus are at the mercy of the reversibility of the situation.

A strategy based on nonreversibility is an example of what Jakobson (1960) has called the "metalinguistic" function of language. The expectation that sentences contain an actor, an action, and a recipient is a hypothesis about language. It is comparable to other hypotheses, for instance, that all words have a rhyme or all sentences have a middle. It is different from the linguistic hypotheses considered in Chapters 5 and 6, which comprise the syntactic competence of a child.

The Association of Semantics and Action

Children following the strategy mentioned above can use sentences to direct their own activity. But if children are required to perform an action that violates the strategy, performance becomes disrupted. Such is the conclusion that arises from experiments by Huttenlocher, Eisenberg, and Strauss (1968) and Huttenlocher and Strauss (1968).

The experiments are elegant in their simplicity. In one (Huttenlocher et al., 1968) a child sees before him a "road" consisting of a flat board divided into three spaces. The middle space already contains a toy truck. The child has in hand a second truck, which he is told to place either before or after the fixed truck. It is the way of telling that counts. Assume that the child's truck is painted green and the fixed truck is painted red. Any one of four possible instructions can then be given: (1) the green truck is pulling the red truck; (2) the red truck is pulling the green truck; (3) the red truck is pulled by the green truck; and (4) the green truck is pulled by the red truck. Another four instructions are available with the verb *push*. In every case the actor is the green truck the child is holding; it is the one to be moved. In sentences (1) and (3) therefore the actor and the underlying subject of the sentence are the same, whereas in sentences (2) and (4) the actor and the underlying object are the same. Sentences (1) and (3) should be more easily followed as instructions than sentences (2) and (4).

Sentences (1) and (2) are active sentences, whereas (3) and (4) are passive. If children treat the superficial instead of the underlying subject of a sentence as an actor then sentences (1) and (4) ought to be easiest and (2) and (3) hardest, as *green truck* is the superficial subject in the first pair and the superficial object in the second pair.

Huttenlocher et al. found that the amount of time for 9-year-old children to place the moveable truck correctly increased from sentence (1) to sentence (4). Since (1) < (2) and (3) < (4) it is clear that children associate the subject of a sentence with the actor of an action. This is the strategy discussed by Bever et al. (1967). Since (3) < (4) it is also clear that the underlying and not the superficial subject is the one associated with the actor. Finally, since (2) < (3) it is clear that passivization poses problems of its own; the situation in the experiment was reversible. Huttenlocher et al. also discovered a consistent difference between the two verbs, *push* and *pull.* For all four types of sentence children's reaction time to *push* was faster than to *pull*. In terms of comprehension, at least, a push is not a backwards pull.

An experiment by Huttenlocher and Strauss (1968) leads to similar conclusions about children following such instructions as *the red block is on top of the green block* and *the yellow block is under the brown block*. A child in this experiment was faced with a ladder, the middle step of which contained a block; he was told to place a second block above or below the block already fixed in place, the position depending on the color of the block the child had in hand. The instructions were easiest to follow when the "actor" (the child's block) was also the subject of the sentence. Since there are no passive forms of the sentences used in this experiment the association of an actor with the underlying subject of a sentence could not be demonstrated.

Bem (1967) has replicated Huttenlocher and Strauss's results in all particulars, but arrives at a rather different conclusion. In the view of Huttenlocher and Strauss sentences such as *the red block is on top of the green block,* when a child is holding a green block, are difficult because the sentence must be changed into another sentence where the child's block is the grammatical subject—*the green block is under the red block.* The extra step takes its toll in time. In Bem's view the problem facing a child is not that he must carry out a linguistic operation but that he must imagine a situation of which the sentence is a true description. Again the extra step takes its toll in time. In Huttenlocher and Strauss's view a *sentence* must be transformed, but in Bem's view a *situation* must be transformed. As a way of distinguishing the two interpretations Bem asked her subjects to describe the tower of blocks they had just made. If subjects first had to transform the sentence to make the tower the transformed sentence ought now to appear as a description. However, 90 percent of Bem's subjects used the original untransformed sentence, as if nothing had been done to alter its form.

Many psychologists have claimed that language and action in children are closely associated. Although this sometimes has meant that child language is primarily an expression of action (cf. de Laguna, 1927), the regulative function of language has been the connection more often studied. The many experiments of Luria (1959, 1961; Birch, 1966) have traced the development of verbal control, the ability of children to follow verbal instructions. The experiments of Huttenlocher et al., Huttenlocher and Strauss, and Bem bear on the same question. Verbal control may depend on the emergence of a metalinguistic hypothesis about actors, actions, and recipients. The matter deserves investigation. One would want to look into a child's knowledge of grammar in relation to his application of semantic strategies. It is clear that the two are not the same, and the problem arises of understanding how they are interrelated.

This problem arises with particular acuteness in the experiments described by Luria (1959, 1961). Working within the general framework established in the 1930s by Vygotsky (1962), Luria and his colleagues have traced the development of what they consider to be voluntary action. In the Vygotskyan scheme of things a basic continuity exists between the control of one's action by others and the voluntary control of one's action by oneself. All control is a matter of following instructions, either external or internal. Internal control depends on the development of inner speech. Inner speech in turn comes from socialized speech. Self-control is therefore preceded genetically by external control.

To very young children commands are simply occasions for action. The speech of someone else triggers an action a child is ready to perform. A child who repeatedly has been made to retrieve a coin from beneath an inverted cup will still search under the cup when told to find a coin under a nearby glass. The specific property of the instruction, that it contains the word *glass* rather than *cup,* has no effect. The same tendency appears in other situations. Told to press a ball when a light flashes, children below two-and-a-half immediately look for the light and press the ball. When the light is flashed later a child looks at it but ignores the ball. A command at this stage initiates two independent acts because children fail to react to the grammatical structure of the command.

Commands possess for young children what Luria (1961) calls an "impulsive quality." If children of three are told *not* to press a ball when a light goes on they press anyway. Moreover, if they are told to say "don't press" when a light goes on they still press even while saying "don't press." A 3-year-old child's reaction to his own speech is independent of its content. Speech is more like a metronome. If told to say "I'll press twice" when a light goes on a child of three presses once and maintains pressure for the duration of the sentence. If told to say "go! go!" when the light goes on he presses twice. It is not until four and a half or five that children react to "go! go!," "I'll press twice," and "don't press" in appropriate ways.

One wonders, in line with the remarks above, if the change at four or five results from application of a metalinguistic strategy that relates the grammatical subject, verb, and object in a sentence to the actor, action, and recipient of an action. Since this strategy is discovered relatively late in development, young children react to commands as if they had no internal structure but were, instead, merely external signals to act. However, once such a strategy is adopted ". . . the regulatory function is steadily transferred from the impulsive side of speech to the analytic system of elective significative connections which are produced by speech" (Luria, 1961, p. 92, italics omitted).

Markedness

Donaldson and Wales (1968) and Donaldson and Balfour (1968) have reported a series of investigations of children's use of such relational and antonymous terms as *less* and *more, same* and *different,* and *large* and *small.* Their results point to a very interesting aspect of semantic development, namely that unmarked forms appear before marked forms.

The clearest example is the pair *less* and *more.* Donaldson and Wales showed three-and-a-half-year-old children small cardboard apple trees from which were dangling paper apples and asked them such questions as "which tree has more apples?" and "which has less apples?" They also had children change the apples on a tree so that it would have more (or less) than the other tree. In each situation the same result appeared. Children of three-and-a-half do not distinguish *less* and *more;* for them less *is* more (Donaldson and Balfour, 1968). In one experiment, a child was shown one tree with three apples and a second with two apples. The child agreed that one of the trees did indeed have less apples and pointed to the tree with three apples to show which it was. Another child, asked to make the tree with three apples have less than the one with two apples, said "But it *is* less than that tree." In general children rarely removed apples from trees when told to make them less, and experienced confusion even when told to make them more — apples might be added to both trees, for example. At four years there was still uncertainty over the meaning of *less,* but it no longer seemed to be confused with *more.* One child, told to make a tree have less apples, asked "how can I?" Told to try, he said "take them off, you mean?," but he did not actually remove any. Told to make the tree have more, he readily added some apples.

What do these confusions over the meaning of *less* and *more* show? Clearly the words are not antonyms at three-and-a-half. Donaldson and Wales believe the meaning of *more* for their subjects was something like "larger present quantity." If this is the case the instruction to make a tree have more apples is, not surprisingly, difficult to follow — no matter which tree it is applied to, it carries no clear meaning.

For adults, as Donaldson and Wales point out, *more* has two meanings: (a) the greater member of a comparison and (b) addition. The word *less,* in contrast, has a single meaning: the lesser member of a comparison. While you can say "put more in a glass" without implying a comparison, you cannot say "take less out of a glass" without implying a comparison with having already taken out more. *Less* and *more* are antonyms in the comparative sense only; *less* does not have a subtractive sense so *more* in its additive sense does not have an antonym. One way of describing the confusion of *more* and *less* by three-and-a-half-year-old children, then, is to say that they have only the additive sense of *more* and therefore nothing to which *less* could be contrasted. Rather, *less* is absorbed into the meaning of *more.*

If this is the case, how can *more* also mean "larger present quantity," as Donaldson and Wales maintain? Of the two terms *more* is unmarked and *less* is marked. Jakobson has argued that unmarked forms appear in development before marked ones (Jakobson, 1941, 1969). The ambiguity of *more* noted above is characteristic of words that happen to be unmarked. *Man,* for instance, is unmarked and is ambiguous — it means both the species and a male member of the species. The confusion of *less* with *more* by young children is analogous to confusing *woman* with *man* in the sense of *man* the species, and the use of *more* in the comparative sense of "larger present quantity" is analogous to using *man* in the sense of male. The contrast is not between *less* and *more,* therefore, but between *more* in its two senses.

SOUND
DEVELOPMENT

If semantics is regarded as the basement of syntax, then phonology is the penthouse. It is ironic that so little can be said of the acquisition of this most visible part of language. Little can be said even though the study of sound has long been a dominant concern of linguistics and even though an explicit theory of phonemic development has existed for more than a quarter of a century (Jakobson, 1941). The problems posed by phonology have never been faced.

We must distinguish at the outset between phonemic and phonological development. The first refers to the emergence of the sound units of a language: Something can be said about phonemic development and it is here that Jakobson's theory applies. Phonological development, on the other hand, refers to the emergence of rules for combining sounds into pronounceable sequences in a language and for relating such sequences to the surface structure of sentences: Virtually nothing can be said about this aspect of development.

The Relation of Babbling to Speech

All parents know that children babble during the second six months of life. Before that time vocalization is limited and after that time speech proper begins. During the babbling period children vocalize an increasing variety of sounds in ever more complex combinations. It is possible that the babbling period is a bridge between the limited vocalization of the first six months of life and the appearance of communicative speech itself. Such a hypothesis has indeed been proposed. Allport (1924) believed that children develop a phonemic system by matching the sounds they hear to the sounds they produce in babbling. Staats and Staats (1963) and Mowrer (1954) have resurrected this view. It is a view, however, with no basis in fact; there is, on the contrary, a sharp discontinuity at both ends of the babbling period. Babbling, if it plays a part in the emergence of speech, does so far behind the scenes.

The direction of development during the first year of life is from the back of the mouth to the front for consonant-type sounds and from the front of the mouth to the back for vowel-type sounds (Irwin, 1947a, 1947b, 1947c, 1948; McCarthy, 1954; but see Bever, 1961, for some qualifications). The direction of development during the second year of life is exactly opposite. First to appear as *speech* sounds are front consonants and back vowels. The back consonants and front vowels that were the first uttered in the prespeech period are among the last organized into a linguistic system.

Children younger than three months vocalize such consonant-like sounds as *k*, *g*, and *x* and such vowel-like sounds as *i* and *u*. That is the beginning. In the babbling period many more sounds are added, sounds necessarily more forward in the case of consonants and more backward in the case of vowels. When linguistically meaningful utterances first occur, however, they consist of a front consonant, *p* or *m*, and a back vowel *a*. Front consonants and back vowels provide a starting point for speech regardless of the language to which children are exposed; children exposed to English say *tut* before *cut*, children exposed to Swedish say *tata* before *kata*, children exposed to Japanese say *ta* before *ka*, etc. (Jakobson, 1941). The early appearance of *m* and *p* as speech sounds is no doubt one reason why *mama* and *papa* are among the first words acquired by all children.

The baby-talk of adults usually corresponds to this initial phonemic organization. Ferguson (1964) found replacement of velar by dental consonants in the adult speech addressed to children among speakers of Syrian, Marathi, Comanche, English, and Spanish. An English example is *tum on* for *come on* (phonemically /kum/). The only exceptions among the languages Ferguson reviewed were Arabic and Gilyak, in both of which velar consonants play a particularly large role. Baby-talk is conventionalized speech for children. In spite of the large differences among the phonemic systems of Syrian, Marathi, Comanche, English, and Spanish the conventions for baby-talk are the same, presumably because actual child speech in each of these languages is organized in similar ways.

The front consonants and back vowels organized by children into an initial linguistic system also occur in babbling. However, many other sounds occur in children's babbling as well, including the back consonants *k* and *g* and the front vowels *i* and *u*, which are added to a child's linguistic system only after many months of further development. Instead of continuity there is discontinuity. Children quickly pass from a wealth of vocalization to concentration on a few sounds for communication. It is not a question of selecting some sounds from many; it is rather a question of why the same specific sounds occur at the beginning of every child's phonemic system. Intentional vocalization requires a structure that unintentional vocalization does not. A child who uses only *p*, *m*, and *a* in speech will at the same time use *k*, *g*, and many other sounds in nonspeech (Jakobson, 1941). As Jesperson remarked:

> It is strange that among an infant's sounds one can often detect sounds—for instance, *k*, *g*, *h*, and uvular *r*—which the child will find difficulty in producing afterwards when they occur in real words . . . . The explanation lies probably in the difference between doing a thing in play or without a plan—when it is immaterial which movement (sound) is made—and doing the same thing of fixed intention when

this sound and this sound only, is required . . . (Jesperson, 1925, p. 106).

Jakobson's theory of phonemic development is addressed to the sound structure of early speech. Before discussing this theory, however, let us look more carefully at the period of development before the emergence of speech. Doing so will make more concrete the discontinuity between speech and prespeech.

Prespeech and Neurological Maturation in the First Year of Life

There are, in fact, two discontinuities during the first year of life — one at 4 months and a second at 11 or 12 months. The two together roughly bracket the babbling period. Bever (1961) reanalyzed the extensive data reported by Irwin and his collaborators (Irwin, 1947a, 1947b, 1947c, 1948) in terms of the rate of change in sound development. Irwin transcribed children's vocalizations in the International Phonetic Alphabet, so his data consist of information on a large number of separate phonetic types. In general the data reveal a steady proliferation of phonetic types with age. Bever focused instead on the rates of change of phonetic types and found discontinuities at 4 and 11 or 12 months.

The two discontinuities mark off three periods. The first, from birth through the third month, consists of a very rapid rate of change in the frequency and variety of vowel-like sounds and a somewhat lower though still rapid rate of change in the frequency and variety of consonant-like sounds. At 4 months, the rate of change drops abruptly, ending the first period and starting the second. The second period is a succession of peaks without large intervening troughs. A peak in the rate of change in the variety of vowel-like sounds occurs between 5 and 6 months, then a peak in the rate of change in the variety of consonant-like sounds (dental and labial consonants particularly) at 7 months, and finally a large peak in the rate of change in the variety of all consonant-like sounds at 9 or 10 months. Then, total collapse at 11 or 12 months. This collapse is the beginning of true linguistic development; the events it introduces are the topic of the next section.

Bever points to similar cyclical phenomena elsewhere in development (e.g., in the amount of sleep per day) and argues that the episodic advance of vocalization reflects a series of changes in cerebral maturation, particularly of an unfolding pattern of inhibition and integration during the first year of life. The hypothesis is provocative and worth quoting:

> *The cycles observed in vocal development are produced by phases of neurological maturation. (a) The first cycle is concurrent with and presumably a manifestation of a primary level of neurological organization of vocal behavior. (b) The end of the first cycle is a result of the end of the reflex stage of behavior due to cortical inhibition. (c) The second vocal developmental cycle occurs as the cortex gradually reorganizes the activity it had inhibited.*

132

The differences in the manifest behavioral characteristics of the first and second cycles in vocal development are due to differences between the lower and higher levels of neurological organization. (a) There are two essential features of the first cycle of vocal development, and thus of the primary neurological phase, a concern with tonal activity and the primary differentiation of affective crying. (b) The second cycle and thus the second neurological phase is associated with the development of consonant-like activity, and is often referred to as the period of "preparation" for the onset of language-learning proper. The babbling stage is presumably a reflection of the process of integrating vocal activity and cortical organization (Bever, 1961, p. 47).

So much for prespeech and its alleged connection with the nervous system. We now turn to the beginnings of language.

The Differentiation of Distinctive Features

The name of Roman Jakobson is associated with what is, beyond doubt, one of the most useful concepts in contemporary linguistics, the notion of a linguistic feature. In phonemics, where Jakobson developed the idea, linguists speak of distinctive features, but essentially the same insight into language has been invaluable in semantics and syntax and previous chapters of this book have relied on it heavily.

It is Jakobson also—in a celebrated paper, *Kindersprache, Aphasie, und allgemeine Lautgesetze* (1941)—who first applied the concept of a linguistic feature to questions of language development. Moreover, in the same paper, he presented for the first time a modern conception of the relation between linguistic universals and the development of language. (The general importance of universal grammar had been realized centuries before; see Chomsky, 1966.) Developmental psycholinguistics thus owes Jakobson a considerable debt. It is fortunate that *Kindersprache* has at last been translated into English by A. Keiler (1968; see Jakobson, 1941). For a brief discussion of the theory, see Jakobson and Halle (1956); for a general discussion of distinctive features, see Jakobson, Fant, and Halle (1963).

It is remarkable that Jakobson's theory has inspired so few empirical investigations. The few studies that have been conducted, however, support the general line of argument, although not every detail (cf. Velten, 1943; Leopold, 1947). The development of a phonemic system, according to Jakobson, is the result of filling in the gap between two sounds, *a* and *p*. The process of development is differentiation. *P* is a consonant formed at the front of the mouth; it is a stop; it is unvoiced; it represents a nearly total absence of acoustic energy. *A* contrasts with *p* in each respect—it is a vowel; it is formed at the back of the mouth; it results from a complete opening of the vocal tract; it represents a maximization of acoustic energy. One might say that *a* is an optimal vowel and *p* is an optimal consonant. Each is an extreme example of its type and the contrast between them is as large as possible. With this contrast linguistic development begins on a phonemic level.

However, neither *p* nor *a* are phonemes at the outset of development. A phoneme is a meaningless sound used to distinguish meaningful messages. *P* and *a* are instead meaningful sounds that distinguish no messages. The consonant always appears with the vowel and there are only two possible utterances: *pa* and (with reduplication) *papa*. The meaning of these words may be highly diffuse, and a child may attempt to communicate more than one message with each word, but there is not yet a phonemic system.

In order to establish a phonemic system the space between *p* and *a* must be divided. The first such split occurs on the consonant side and (according to Jakobson's observations) results in a distinction between a labial stop *p* and a nasalized labial *m*. The distinction, therefore, is between nasal and oral sounds and it creates two words — *ma* and *pa* or (with reduplication) *mama* and *papa* — distinguished by what are now two phonemes, /m/ and /p/. Velten (1943) found the first consonant distinction in the speech of an English child to be slightly different: labial stops were first contrasted with continuants (/f/ and /s/) and only later with nasals. The nasal–oral distinction thus appeared second in development rather than first.

The vowel *a* at this stage merely supports the consonants /m/ and /p/ and itself has no phonemic status. It plays a crucial role of a different kind, however, for together with the consonants *a* establishes a syllable. Syllabification is present from the outset of speech. It is not obvious why such should be the case. Perhaps there is some basic rhythmicity underlying speech, as Lenneberg (1967) has argued, which takes as its earliest manifestation syllabification and reduplication. Jakobson (1941) believed that children always formed consonant-vowel (or vowel-consonant) syllables in earliest speech, but apparently this is not invariably the case. Weir (1966) observed Chinese children uttering syllables that consisted of vowels only, although Russian- and English-speaking children also included consonants, as expected. Chinese is a language in which syllabification is measured by vowels alone, whereas Russian and English are not. Weir's findings may reflect the existence of appropriate syllabification at an extremely early age.

After the consonants have been divided into nasal and oral categories there appears a division of oral consonants into labial and dental categories. /ta/ comes to be contrasted with /pa/ (Jakobson, 1941). After this there occurs the first division on the vocalic side. Narrow vowels are set off against wide vowels, as in /pi/ versus /pa/. The next step, according to Jakobson, may be in either of two directions. One alternative is to divide the narrow vowel into a narrow palatal vowel /pi/ and a narrow velar vowel /pu/. The other alternative is to create a High-Mid-Low vowel series by inserting /e/ between /i/ and /a/, as in /pi/ versus /pe/ versus /pa/.

Jakobson argues that the sequence of phonemic development is invariant and universal among children. All children pass through the same steps although children may differ from one amother in the rate of advancement. In addition the phonemic system created by the first two or three steps in phonemic development is universal among the languages of the world. "... the child possesses in the beginning only those sounds which are common to the world, while those phonemes which distinguish the mother tongue from the other languages of the world appear only later" (Jakobson, 1941, in the Keiler translation, 1968).

There is a general similarity between phonemic and syntactic development. Both begin with a primitive form that is universal, but are so organized that they may become any language through a process of differentiation.

The differentiation of the space between /p/ and /a/ is the result of successively introducing certain distinctive features. Jakobson summarizes the process of development in terms of a series of vowel and consonant triangles (Jakobson, 1941; Jakobson and Halle, 1956). The first phonemes, /p/ and /t/, together with the optimal vowel /a/, comprise what Jakobson and Halle call the "primary triangle." It defines two distinctive features—compact–diffuse on the vertical axis and grave–acute on the horizontal.

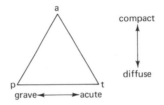

When the vowel /a/ is in turn differentiated into wide (/a/) and narrow (/i/) vowels the distinction between compact and diffuse is introduced into the vocalic category. Compact versus diffuse no longer sets vowels off from consonants and we have instead the following.

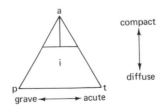

If the narrow vowel /i/, which is also palatal, is next distinguished from the velar vowel /u/, which is also narrow, the distinctive feature grave–acute is likewise introduced into the vocalic category. Grave–acute is therefore the first contrast shared by vowels and consonants. It gives rise to the following triangle.

135

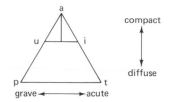

At this point, vowels embody more distinctions than consonants. Balance is restored when the front consonants /p/ and /t/ are distinguished from the back consonant /k/; /p/ and /t/ are diffuse whereas /k/ is compact. We now have two complete triangles defined by the same features.

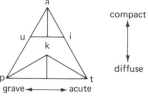

The succession of vowel and consonant triangles explains why the first phonemic contrast that children draw is between /a/ and /p/ and not between /a/ and /k/ or /i/ and /p/ or some other pair. /a/ is the most compact of all sounds, whereas /p/ (along with /t/) is the most diffuse. It is on the distinctive feature of compact–diffuse that /a/ and /p/ are the optimal vowel and consonant. To utter /a/ the mouth forms a funnel opening forward; to utter /p/ it forms a funnel opening backward. In the case of /a/ a large amount of acoustic energy is concentrated in a narrow band of frequencies; in the case of /p/ a small amount of energy is distributed over a wide band of frequencies. The sound /t/ is as diffuse as /p/ in terms of the distribution of energy, but it differs less from /a/ in the location of closure of the mouth and for this reason is not the first consonant to be set off against the vowel /a/.

The Development of a Phonemic System
and the Laws of "Irreversible Solidarity"

The laws of "irreversible solidarity" describe universal asymmetries in the phonemic systems of the languages of the world. For example, no language has back consonants without also having front consonants, but languages exist with front consonants and no back consonants. There is an "irreversible solidarity" between back and front consonants such that the former presupposes the latter, but not conversely. The laws of irreversible solidarity apply to languages (see Greenberg, 1962 and 1966, for a number of examples of universals of this kind). Jakobson's (1941) suggestion is that the same laws describe the development of language by children (as well as the loss of language by aphasics). Thus no child arrives at back consonants without first developing front consonants. /p/ and /m/ always appear before /k/ or /g/, for example. Jakobson gives many examples of such an identity between the order of acquisition and the distribution of phonemes among the languages of the world.

Phonemes that are relatively rare among the languages of the world — for example, the English /θ/ as in "*thing*"—are among the last phonemes acquired by children exposed to languages that contain them. It is as if, when children must push farther and farther from the universal core of language, fewer and fewer languages manage to force them to do so (cf. the dialect of New York speakers as described in Labov, 1964, where /θ/ is dropped in casual speech). In general, rare phonemes embody more distinctions of a more subtle type than do phonemes of wider distribution. If the acquisition of phonemes is the result of differentiation, then phonemes that embody numerous and subtle distinctions are naturally acquired after phonemes that embody less numerous and less subtle distinctions. A natural order of acquisition and distribution therefore results from the latent but universal structure of distinctive features. Jakobson (1941) argues that the structure inherent in the set of distinctive features is the result of general perceptual principles, and that the order of appearance of phonemic contrasts corresponds to the order of complication of any complex perception. This hypothesis assumes that the laws of irreversible solidarity are weak linguistic universals, although Jakobson provides no particular reason for making such an assumption.

Jakobson and Halle (1956) give the following series, presumably universal, for the successive differentiation of distinctive features. Thus 1.0 is the first contrast to be developed (/t/ versus /p/), 1.1 is the second, etc. Later contrasts rarely occur among the languages of the world. (Examples in English are given where possible.)

Consonants	dental vs. labial	
	(e.g., /t/ vs. /p/)	1.0
Vowels	narrow vs. wide	
	(e.g., /i/ vs. /a/)	1.1
Narrow vowels	palatal vs. velar	
	(e.g., /i/ vs. /u/)	1.11
Wide vowels	palatal vs. velar	1.111
Narrow palatal vowels	rounded vs. unrounded	1.112
Wide palatal vowels	rounded vs. unrounded	1.1121
Velar vowels	rounded vs unrounded	
	(e.g., /a/ vs. /u/)	1.113
Consonants	velopalatal vs. labial and dental	
	(e.g., /k/ vs. /t/)	1.12
Consonants	palatal vs. velar	
	(e.g., /s/ vs. /k/)	1.121
Consonants	rounded vs. unrounded or pharyngealized vs. non-pharyngealized	1.122
Consonants	palatalized vs. nonpalatalized	1.123

A recent study of Preston, Yeni-Komishian, and Stark (1967) nicely illustrates how one contrast, voicing, arises in development. With adults the acoustic manifestation of voicing is the relation in time between the onset of voicing and the release of the consonant. That is, all consonants, including voiceless ones, are voiced; voiced and voiceless consonants differ in when the voicing appears. To describe this situation Preston et al. speak of "Voice Onset Time" or VOT, which is the number of milliseconds by which the release of a consonant appears before voicing. VOT can range from negative values (voicing before release) through zero (release and voicing at the same instant) to positive values (release before voicing).

Consonants with smaller VOTs are perceived as voiced; consonants with higher VOTs are perceived as voiceless. As with all distinctive features, the contrast is a relative one. The VOTs of /b/, /d/, and /g/ in English, for example, are between 0 and +5 msec, whereas the VOTs of /p/, /t/, and /k/ are between +50 and +70 msec. The same voiced–voiceless contrast in Lebanese Arabic takes values of VOT of approximately −70 msec for voiced consonants and +5 to +15 msec for voiceless consonants. That is to say, the VOT of *voiced* consonants in English is the same as the VOT of *voiceless* consonants in Lebanese Arabic, but in both languages voiced consonants have smaller VOTs than do voiceless consonants.

Preston et al. measured the VOTs of the stop consonants of children just at the beginning of linguistic development, at about 12 months. The children lived either in Lebanon or the United States. It turns out that Lebanese and American children both produce consonants limited to VOTs in the region common to the two languages — between 0 and +40 msec. Are these sounds voiced or voiceless? They are neither. Ultimately Lebanese children develop a new group of sounds with VOTs in the negative range and thus make the original sounds voiceless. American children develop a new group of sounds with VOTs in the +50 to +70 range and thus make the original sounds voiced.

These observations raise an interesting question about the linguistic distinction between marked and unmarked features. A marked feature is derived from its unmarked mate through the addition of something — voicing, for example. Marked features are regarded as deviations from the corresponding unmarked features. There are reasons internal to a linguistic analysis for maintaining such a dichotomy and there are reasons (such as Jakobson's laws of universal solidarity) for supposing that the dichotomy appears in the same form in every language. But what of the development of language? Ordinarily one would say on internal grammatical grounds that voiced phonemes are marked with respect to voiceless phonemes. This could be true of Lebanese Arabic but not of English, if marking is the result of adding something. In English the additional phoneme is the voiceless member of each pair. There is a dilemma here for those who want to interpret the distinction between marked and unmarked features in a literal way. Either marking can be defined on internal linguistic grounds, in which case the concept loses contact with the notion of something being added, or marking can be defined as the result of something being added, in which case it leads to different classifications in different languages.

Lateralization of Function

Among animals man is the only one with comprehensive lateral asymmetry. Since man is also alone in possessing language, we have a sense of penetrating close to the heart of things when we discover that aspects of speech are, like handedness, laterally organized in the brain. It has been known for more than a hundred years that the left side of the brain serves a special function in language. Lesions in the left side of the brain produce more damaging aphasia than do lesions in the right side and they take longer to recover from, if indeed there is any recovery at all.

The emergence of lateralization therefore seems a promising place to look for the physiological underpinnings of language and language acquisition. Lenneberg (1967) relates it to the existence of a critical period in linguistic development: The establishment of lateral asymmetry *prevents* further linguistic development. The ability to recover from damage to the left side of the brain declines with age. A newborn with a damaged left hemisphere develops language normally with the right hemisphere; a 2- or 3-year-old with damage to the left hemisphere loses language in some degree but then quickly recovers with the right; beyond puberty, recovery is always limited or nonexistent. The degree of recovery is thus correlated with the degree of lateralization before injury.

Aside from such observations of aphasia in children the development of the lateralization of speech functions has not been studied. It is possible, nonetheless, to state some consequences of lateralization in normal adults and so to describe the terminus toward which development points. A series of studies at the Haskins Laboratories (Shankweiler and Studdert-Kennedy, 1966, 1967; Liberman, Cooper, Shankweiler, and Studdert-Kennedy, 1967; Shankweiler, 1968) has revealed a number of surprising effects on the perception of speech of left-hemisphere dominance. Their methodology, first employed by Kimura (1961), is suitable for young children and developmental studies could easily be carried out along the same lines.

Kimura observed that when an adult hears two digits simultaneously in the two ears, a different digit in each, the right ear is more accurately reported. The left hemisphere therefore dominates the right. The Haskins experiments have used this dichotic task to measure hemispheric dominance in listening separately to consonants and vowels. If one ear receives /pap/ and the other /tap/ the experiment measures sensitivity to consonants; if one ear receives /pap/ and the other /pip/ the experiment measures sensitivity to vowels. In a number of studies the right ear (left hemisphere) has been shown to be dominant in the perception of consonants, but neither ear (hemisphere) has been shown to be dominant in the perception of vowels. This difference between

139

consonants and vowels is reminiscent of the difference Kimura (1964) found between digits and melodies: Digits were best perceived by the right ear (left hemisphere) but melodies were best perceived by the left ear (right hemisphere). One consequence of lateralization therefore seems to be a migration of consonants, but not vowels, to the left side of the brain. The part of the brain involved in the perception of the melodic aspects of speech, the vowels, is different from the part involved in the perception of the nonmelodic aspects, the consonants.

Vowels and consonants have been shown to differ in another respect. If small differences in speech sounds are to be discriminated the discrimination of consonants is "categorical" but the discrimination of vowels is continuous (see Liberman et al., 1967, for a summary of the work on which this conclusion is based). "Categorical" perception means that differences among speech sounds can be detected no more accurately than the sounds can be identified. It is possible to prepare a set of artificial speech sounds (with the aid of a device called the "pattern playback") that differ from one another by a series of small steps. Each such step is of the same physical magnitude as every other, and the series as a whole ranges from a clear instance of one phoneme (say /g/) to a clear instance of another (say /b/) with a phoneme boundary somewhere in the middle. If the sounds are consonants, adjacent sounds within a single phoneme are poorly discriminated, whereas adjacent sounds separated by the same physical distance but belonging to different phonemes are well discriminated. But if the sounds are vowels discrimination depends on physical separation alone, not on category membership. One is tempted to relate the findings on categorical perception to the findings on lateral dominance by saying that the former occurs only in the left side of the brain.

In some degree this may be so, but matters are complicated by yet another set of observations. Certain kinds of epilepsy are treated by a complete surgical severance of the two cerebral hemispheres. In effect, the operation leaves a patient with two independent functioning brains within a single skull. In most circumstances the left hemisphere dominates the right, but with a certain amount of contrivance it is possible to force the right hemisphere to reveal itself in the comprehension of speech (Gazzaniga and Sperry, 1967). In one study the experimenter speaks a short phrase ("used to tell time") and then exposes to the patient's left visual field a series of written words (one of them "clock"). The spoken phrase reaches both hemispheres but the series of written words reaches only the right. Gazzaniga and Sperry's patients succeeded in matching the phrases to the words—i.e., not only does the right hemisphere understand speech but it also reads!

Unfortunately, this experiment is unclear on *what* the right hemisphere is able to understand. Although the subject was given a phrase, the correct written word could have been selected from the perception of a single spoken word ("time" in the example above), and even from the vocalic nucleus of this word. There is no evidence, therefore, that the right hemisphere can comprehend syntax, although one might plausibly

140

expect it to do so in view of the fact that language acquisition is under-way long before lateralization is complete. It is nonetheless clear that the right hemisphere has access to word meanings and possibly to the consonant structure of language. The latter observation tempers any extreme conclusions one might wish to draw from the Haskins experiments described above.

Phonological Rules

Accompanying the phonemic structure of a language are rules for using this structure. *Sporn* is not a word in English, but it could be a word (perhaps the name of an acne cure). However, *kporn* could never be a word in English, even though the individual phonemes of *kporn* are within the language just as are the phonemes of *sporn*. A phonological rule of English requires initial consonant clusters all to begin with /s/ (/l/ and /r/ follow other consonants, but /l/ and /r/ are classified as liquids, not as consonants; Halle, 1964b). Other phonological rules determine the intonation patterns of sentences. In *black board* (a kind of board) main stress falls on *board* but in *blackboard* (a writing surface) it falls on *black*. One rule for relating stress to the surface structure of sentences in English requires main stress to fall on the first vowel of an N but to fall elsewhere in constituents of other kinds (Chomsky, Halle, and Lukoff, 1956). *Blackboard* is an N and so receives main stress on *black; black board* is an NP and so receives main stress elsewhere, in this case on *board*.

There are many such rules; for examples, see Chomsky, Halle, and Lukoff (1956); Halle (1964b); Chomsky and Halle (1966, 1968). It appears from informal observation that children continue working on phonological rules for many years but there are few actual studies of this aspect of development. The entire situation is ripe theoretically and unpicked empirically.

We can mention the handful of studies that have been conducted on phonological questions. Berko's (1958) well-known work on children's morphology belongs in part in this category. Anisfeld and Tucker (1967), and Anisfeld, Barlow, and Frail (1967) have found evidence for sensitivity to the featural properties of sounds among 6-year-old children. However, Menyuk (1967a) finds that 4- and 5-year-old American children are no better at memorizing sound sequences drawn from English than they are at memorizing sequences drawn from other languages, although they are better at immediately repeating English sequences, while Messer (1967) finds even younger children able to discriminate between English and non-English sequences that differ by no more than one or two distinctive features. Clearly, work in this area has barely begun.

141

**LINGUISTIC
APPENDIX**

Take a sentence of a dozen words, and take twelve men and tell to each one word. Then stand the men in a row or jam them in a bunch, and let each think of his word as intently as he will· nowhere will there be a consciousness of the whole sentence (James, 1893, p. 199).

Thus did William James state one psycholinguistic problem. Consciousness of a whole sentence takes place in a single mind. It is something *done* with the separate words of a sentence, and this something could not be done under the conditions of James's proposed experiment. In this appendix we review what is known of the process leading to the consciousness of whole sentences.

Propelled by the same revolution of thought that led to behaviorism in psychology, American linguists of the 1920s and 1930s were concerned to describe language in absolutely neutral terms. Descriptions were to reflect data. Linguistics was engaged in the discovery of the structure inherent in samples of speech. The aim was for completely objective, automatic, and rigorous procedures that would, when correctly applied, yield a correct portrayal of these structures. This would be the grammatical analysis and it was not only to be correct but also independent of extralinguistic suppositions. Thus Bloomfield (1933) wrote: "We have learned . . . that we can pursue the study of language without reference to any psychological doctrine, and that to do so safeguards our results and makes them more significant to workers in related fields" (vii). Although one can question Bloomfield's actual independence from behaviorism, the general tenor of linguistic thought in the 1930s was that linguistics had no connection with psychology. By the same token, psychology had little direct concern with linguistics. It is not surprising, therefore, that James's problem received little attention.

However, a different approach has of late been under active development. In this alternative approach linguistics aims to describe the specialized form of knowledge that we bring to bear in the comprehension and production of sentences. Descriptions of knowledge have obvious import for psychology: Whatever we know, we know by some psychological process. Under its new development, therefore, linguistics makes strong psychological assumptions, with the result that it occupies common ground with psychology. As we shall see, the direction of traffic through this common region has been mostly one way. Discoveries in linguistics pose the challenge, psychology assimilates them. Perhaps in the future two-way traffic will become possible. If so, a full answer to James's problem will be at hand. We will understand the process that leads to the consciousness of a whole sentence. Until then, however, our discussion must be limited to describing the linguistic knowledge that is applied in this process, and it is to this better-understood question that we now turn.

No attempt will be made here to review the latest developments in linguistic theory. All have taken place too recently for their impact on the study of language acquisition to be really understood. The reader interested in following this constantly shifting frontier can turn to only a few published sources — a book edited by Bach and Harms (1968), papers by McCawley (1968), Lakoff (1968), and Ross (1967).

Linguists call the systematic characterizations of linguistic knowledge grammars. It is important to realize that these grammars are psychological theories. They strive to portray certain facts about the mind, i.e., they are supposed to be psychologically correct and they stand or fall accordingly (Katz, 1964). The psychological interest in such grammars is, therefore, straightforward. However, it is important — crucial — to understand the limitations placed on this claim to psychological validity. A grammar relates to mental phenomena of a particular kind; it is not an all-purpose psychological theory. In particular, it is not a theory about behavior — the actual encoding and decoding of speech — which brings us to a fundamental distinction.

Competence and Performance

A sharp distinction between competence and performance has been traditional in linguistics since de Saussure's *Cours de linguistique générale* (1916) and was first drawn at least as early as the eighteenth century (Chomsky, 1966). One can think about language in either of two ways. There are, first of all, actual acts of speaking and hearing, taking place in time, subject to various distractions, limited by memory and by the general weakness of human flesh. These were called *actes de parole* by de Saussure and *performance* by Chomsky (1957). Performance is linguistic behavior, either encoding or decoding speech. A theory of performance would clearly be a psychological theory, a fact that presumably needs no defense. At the present time, there are no theories of linguistic performance. Indeed, there is only the most fragmentary knowledge of the relevant parameters of such a theory, although the problem is one that now inspires considerable interest. A number of recent experimental studies can be regarded as bearing on it (e.g., Miller, 1962; Miller & Isard, 1963, 1964; Miller and McKean, 1964; Mehler, 1963; Slobin, 1966c; McMahon, 1963; Gough, 1965; Savin and Perchonock, 1965; Blumenthal, 1967; Wanner, 1968).

The second aspect of language is the knowledge of syntax, meaning, and sound that makes performance possible. De Saussure called such knowledge *langue* and Chomsky has called it *competence*. A theory of competence is also a psychological theory, although of a type not usually considered by contemporary psychologists. Piaget (1952) perhaps comes closest in his aim to characterize the structure of logical thought. Because a grammar is concerned with knowledge, not behavior, factors (such as memory limitations, time restrictions, etc.) that are important to performance can be disregarded when thinking about competence. Competence is an idealization, an abstraction away from performance (Chomsky, 1965). Theories of performance and competence, therefore, deal with different topics. A grammar is not a recipe for producing sentences. That recipe will be given by a theory of performance. Indeed, the problem for a theory of performance is to explain just how the information represented by a grammar is realized in actual acts of speaking and hearing (Miller, 1962). The linguist's solution will not answer the psychologist's problem.

Perhaps the distinction between competence and performance, and the way in which they are related, will become clearer if we consider an artificial example. In Table 13 are several strings of letters.[1] In each string there is an *a* or a *b* or both. Some of the strings have been boxed. These we shall call "sentences," by which we mean that they have a certain structure in common not shared by the other strings, the "nonsentences." Table 13 is a skeletonized version of the set of all possible strings—all possible combinations of the letters *a* and *b*—and thus is analogous to the output of that hypothetical set of one million monkeys put before one million typewriters.

Our problem is to discover the structure that makes a string a "sentence" in Table 13. This can be done by the reader if he carefully examines the "sentences" and "nonsentences" listed in the table—the problem is not a difficult one. The reader can then test his discovery by judging the status of new examples. Try, for instance, *aaaaabbbb, aaaaabbbbb, aaaab, bbbbaaaa, aaaabbbb*. The second and the last of these are "sentences," the rest are not.

The knowledge of the principle that determines which strings are "sentences" and which are not is *competence*. It is not performance. Understanding the principle does not automatically lead to a correct judgment. It would not in the case of a string that contained 10,000 *a*s followed by 10,001 *b*s. One must *count* the *a*s and *b*s and judge the result against the principle. Conversely, counting without knowledge of a principle will not tell one that *ab* is a "sentence." Counting is performance, in this instance, whereas knowledge of the principle that adjudicates the result of counting is competence. A grammar is concerned with the latter only. Some further theory is needed to explain how the principle is applied to the result of counting; this would be a theory of performance. There is, of course, competence in the counting, but that is a different domain (Klima, 1968).

The status of a grammar is the same as for any other scientific theory. It is an empirical hypothesis that deals with a mental phenomenon.

---

[1] The example is based on a lecture by G. A. Miller in 1964.

Table 13 **"Sentences" and "Nonsentences" from a Language Made Up of the Letters** *a* **and** *b* **(Many Strings Have Been Omitted). Boxed Strings are "Sentences"**

| Length 1 | a |
| | b |

Length 2	aa
	$\boxed{\text{ab}}$
	bb

Length 3	aaa
	.
	aba
	.
	bbb

Length 4	aaaa
	.
	abaa
	.
	$\boxed{\text{aabb}}$
	.
	baba
	.
	bbbb

Length 5	aaaaa
	.
	abbba
	.
	bbbab
	.
	bbbbb

Length 6	aaaaaa
	.
	aabbaa
	.
	$\boxed{\text{aaabbb}}$
	.
	bbbbbb

| Length 7 and more | . |
| | . |

Because it is an empirical hypothesis, a grammar is either true or false, and observations are made to discover its adequacy in this respect. Because it is a hypothesis about a mental phenomenon, the relevant observations have to do with knowledge of language. The possibility of describing a branch of human knowledge in an explicit way is surely one of the most exciting aspects of contemporary linguistics.

Let us now continue the example of Table 13 and consider several hypotheses that might account for the reader's understanding of the structures represented there.

Finite-State Grammars

One method of representing structure, and hence competence, is to construct a *state diagram*. Such a diagram can be thought of as portraying a machine that can be in any of several states. The machine is so restricted that when it is in one state it can move to other states only over specified legal routes. The resulting network of states and transitions will then embody a certain structure. Can such a machine, however construed, talk correctly? In particular, can it produce all and only the "sentences" in Table 13? To make the machine talk at all we must provide it with a means of recording its progress as it moves from state to state. We can do this by having the machine utter the name of the state it has just left. Since, in Table 13, the machine must produce strings of *a*s and *b*s, all the states will be labeled *a* or *b* and nothing else.

There is one further requirement to place on our machine. We want it to be superior to a mere list. One could, if patient enough, prepare a list of all the "sentences" made up from *a* and *b*—writing down *ab, aabb, aaabbb,* etc. The difficulty with this list is that it would be endless, because there is no longest grammatical sequence of *a*s and *b*s. To be an advance over a list our machine must be finite, although it may be large. It must have a finite number of states connected by a finite number of transitions, and yet be capable of producing an infinite number of correct sequences of *a* and *b*. Such a machine, if successful, would provide the *grammar* of the "sentences" in Table 13. Let us now try to construct a grammar along these lines.

The top diagram of Fig. 17 shows a machine of three states and three transitions, which is able to produce the "sentence" *ab*. It cannot, however, produce "sentences" longer than this. Running the machine twice yields a repetition, not a new "sentence," since we obtain *ab.ab*. In order to produce the next longer "sentence" we must add two new states and three new transitions, as in the second diagram of Fig. 17. This new machine produces *aabb* as well as *ab*. However, it produces nothing else, and to enrich it we must add two more states and three more transitions, as in the third diagram. However, this machine is likewise restricted—its longest "sentence" is *aaabbb*. In short, for each additional length of sentence we must add further states and transitions. Since the list of "sentences" consistent with Table 13 is endless, the number of states and transitions we must add is endless also. The machine thus fails the last requirement stated above. It is not superior

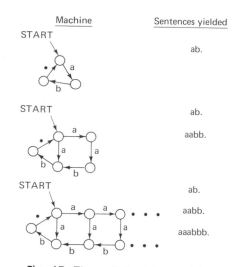

Machine	Sentences yielded
START	ab.
START	ab.
	aabb.
START	ab.
	aabb.
	aaabbb.

Fig. 17. Three finite-state machines that produce the strings in Table 13.

to a mere list, which means that a different kind of grammar is needed.

Before considering other possibilities, however, it should be noted that the "sentences" in Table 13 and the grammars in Fig. 17 are not simply empty exercises in manipulating letters of the alphabet. On the contrary, they are directly relevant to the concerns of this book. English has sentences of the kind listed in Table 13, and much psychological theorizing accounts for structures of the kind diagrammed in Fig. 17. The fact that Fig. 17 cannot represent the "sentences" in Table 13, therefore, means that much psychological theorizing cannot account for significant portions of the structure of English. Let us take up the matter of structure first.

The "sentences" in Table 13 are built like an onion. The shortest is *ab*. The next longer "sentence" consists of another *ab* sealed inside the first *ab*, and the next longer one yet results from inserting into *aabb* still another *ab*, and so on. If we use parentheses to indicate how the *a*s and *b*s are paired, a "sentence" of length six would be written as (*a*(*a*(*ab*)*b*)*b*). Such structures are called *embeddings* and, if not too long, are commonplace in English. (*The race* (*that the car* (*that the people sold*) *won*) *was held last summer*) stretches the bounds of credulity but it is a perfectly grammatical sentence (Miller, 1962).

Now let us take up psychological theory. The way to construct a finite-state device clearly is to link states by transitions. If the device is also to be a model of a learner then it must be exposed to each transition link in the chain in such a manner that states will be connected by transitions that move in the correct directions. In the case of the first diagram in Fig. 18, the device must have been exposed first to an *a* and then to a *b*. This requirement is inescapable. So long as the structure to be acquired can be presented in this steplike way, a finite-state device

149

will faithfully reproduce it. Other structures, however, lie beyond its grasp.

This limitation—faithful reproduction of transitions but nothing else—is shared by every stimulus–response theory of learning, from the simple (Skinner's) to the complex (Osgood's). It is inherent in the basic S–R paradigm. Learning occurs when one presents an appropriate stimulus together with the correct response and stamps in a connection between the two through (depending on the theory) reinforcement, repetition, drive reduction, etc. All S–R theories are variations on this basic theme, and they all lead to the development of a finite-state device. The "sentences" of Table 13 therefore could not be learned through *any* process consistent with S–R theory. The reader who understands the principle of producing these "sentences" is himself a refutation of all consistent S–R models.

This critique might be answered by observing that there is no proof that our knowledge of the "sentences" in Table 13 is anything other than what the diagrams in Fig. 17 claim. The requirement of infinite productivity might be psychologically meaningless, and an S–R analysis perhaps expresses the processes that actually take place.

There are, however, at least two things wrong with this defense. One is that the diagrams in Fig. 17 cannot account for correct judgments of "sentences" never encountered before. If a novel "sentence" goes beyond the current degree of complication of a finite-state device it must be rejected as a "nonsentence," unless there is further training. This is the point of the test the reader was asked to take. If the reader had discovered the principle underlying the "sentences" in Table 13, he could correctly judge the sentencehood of novel strings without additional instruction. And if the reader could do this, then what he had learned could not be represented by a finite-state device.

The second difficulty is the opposite side of the coin. If we assume that a speaker's knowledge of English *can* be represented by a finite-state device we are forced to make quite incredible claims about the learning ability of children. Take the following sentence: *The people who called and wanted to rent your house when you go away next year are from California* (Miller and Chomsky, 1963). It contains a grammatical connection between the second word (*people*) and the seventeenth word (*are*); changing either one but not both of these words to the corresponding singular form would produce an ungrammatical sentence. If the connection between *people* and *are* is carried by a finite-state device in our heads then each of us must have learned a unique set of transitions spanning 15 grammatical categories. Making the conservative estimate that an average of 4 grammatical categories might occur at any point in the development of an English sentence, detecting the connection between *people* and *are* signifies that we have learned at least $4^{15} = 10^9$ different transitions. This is, however, a *reductio ad absurdum*. As Miller and Chomsky point out, "We cannot seriously propose that a child learns the values of 10^9 parameters in a childhood lasting only 10^8 seconds" (p. 430). And even a highly efficient child, one who somehow *could* learn 10 transitions a second, would still miss the dependency when *people* and *are* are separated by 16 words or more.

These difficulties add up to a single flaw. There is no way for a finite-state device to express the idea of *embedding,* the insertion of one component inside another like component. However, embedding is a psychological fact. It is what the reader grasped in Table 13. It is behind the comprehension of sentences such as *the race that the car that the people sold won was held last summer* as well as *the people who called and wanted to rent your house when you go away next year are from California.* What is needed, therefore, is a hypothesis about this mental ability. One is introduced in the next section.

Embedding and Linguistic Abstraction

Finite-state devices in general and S–R models in particular can copy only those structures that consist of states and transitions among them. These models will misrepresent anything that embodies some other structure. That was the difficulty with the representation of the "sentences" in Table 13 by means of the state diagrams in Fig. 17. If the reader understands the principle underlying these "sentences" he can tell that the part missing from *aab* is a second *b* to go with the first *a*. Similarly, he can tell that the sentence *the car that the people sold was held last summer* is peculiar because there is an incorrect verb for the noun-phrase *the car*. In both cases part of what is known about the structure of the sentence is that elements separated from each other actually belong together and not with the material that separates them. What they jointly belong to is an important fact about the sentence and a correct linguistic representation must somehow portray it. It is on this hidden structural feature that a finite-state device founders.

Consider now the following two grammatical rules. Together, they will produce all and only the "sentences" consistent with Table 13.

$$X \longrightarrow aXb$$

$$X \longrightarrow ab$$

The arrow ($\longrightarrow$) means that the element on the left is rewritten as, or becomes, the elements on the right. By employing a further notational convention, that parentheses in a rule indicate optionality—the possibility of choosing or not choosing an element—the two rules above can be collapsed into one:

$$X \longrightarrow a(X)b$$

One can apply the expanded version of this rule (with the X) indefinitely. Each application lays down an *a* and a *b* with another X in between. The new X calls for application of the rule again, *ad infinitum.* This is recursive embedding. The development of a "sentence" comes to an end when the option of not including X is taken. Figure 18 shows the successive steps taken in producing a "sentence" of length six, *aaabbb*.

The constituent in these "sentences" labeled X is the part to which

151

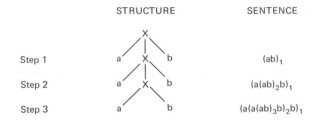

STRUCTURE   SENTENCE

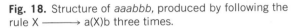

Fig. 18. Structure of *aaabbb,* produced by following the rule X ——→ a(X)b three times.

cach *ab* pair belongs even though they are separated by other *ab* pairs. The existence of X is essential to the recursiveness of the rule, since its presence on the right is the only feature that requires another application of the rule.

However, note one important thing: The constituent X is *abstract.* It never appears in the final form of a sentence, only in its derivation: *aXb* is not a "sentence" in Table 13, just as the equivalent in English, *the people Sentence are from California,* is not a sentence. Nonetheless, an abstract constituent is part of the structure of these sentences. It is such an abstraction that the reader gleaned from Table 13 and it is such an abstraction that he discovers in *the people who called and wanted to rent your house when you go away next year are from California.* On this hypothesis, therefore, speakers can grasp aspects of sentence structure that are never included in the overt form of a sentence. We touch on the question of linguistic abstractions repeatedly, since it poses a most challenging problem for psychologists. Somehow linguistic abstractions are recovered by listeners and developed by children. Just as the reader learned about X in Table 13, children learn about structural features in English that are never presented to them.

Phrase-Structure Rules

A grammar, we have said, represents linguistic knowledge. A grammatical rule, accordingly, represents a bit of linguistic knowledge. In the case of a rewriting rule such as X ——→ a(X)b the knowledge represented is that a(X)b is a species of the genus X. The rule itself is simply a means of expressing this idea.

Many aspects of language take such a form. *The frog caught a mosquito,* for example, *is* a sentence. *The frog* and *the mosquito* in turn *are* noun phrases, and *caught the mosquito is* a verb phrase. Knowledge of these elementary facts can be represented naturally by means of rewriting rules: Fig. 19 shows how it is done for *the frog caught the mosquito.* Note that each of the examples given above, where one constituent *is* an instance of something else, is represented by a separate rule. The derivation makes the genus-species relation, as it applies to the sentence, explicit.

It is easy to show that the relations established by the rules in Fig. 19

152

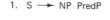

1. S ⟶ NP PredP

2. PredP ⟶ V (NP)

3. NP ⟶ Art N

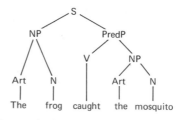

Fig. 19. Rewriting rules for producing a simple declarative sentence. The symbols have the following meanings: S = sentence; NP = noun phrase; PredP = predicate phrase; Art = article; N = noun; V = verb. Rule (2) covers both transitive and intransitive verbs, and for this reason has NP as an optional (parenthesized) element.

correspond to facts that speakers of English know about *the frog caught the mosquito.* First of all, if a speaker is asked to divide the sentence into two major parts the split will most likely be made between *the frog* and *caught the mosquito,* that is, between the NP and the PredP of the first rule. If he is now asked to divide *caught the mosquito* into two parts the line will come between *caught* and *the mosquito,* that is, between the V and NP of the second rule. It is unlikely that a speaker would divide *the frog caught the mosquito* into *the* and *frog caught the mosquito.* Speakers honor the rules because the rules reflect information speakers have about the sentence. This correspondence can be revealed in a second way.

Suppose that we take *the frog caught the mosquito* and try to derive from it another sentence in the following manner (Miller, 1962). We try to find a single word that can replace a *group* of words in the original sentence without changing the grammatical structure. Our interest lies in seeing which groups of words can be so replaced. Replacements exist only for the constituents of the sentence—English has no words that belong to no constituents. A series of these derivations is shown in Table 14, and it can be seen that the replacements obtained in this manner correspond exactly to the derivation obtained through application of the rules in Fig. 19. We have here hard-core evidence for the validity of the rules in Fig. 19.

The structures portrayed in Table 14 and Fig. 19 are a part of the phrase structure of English. Accordingly, the rules in Fig. 19 that produce this structure are called *phrase-structure rules,* and the diagram is called a *phrase-marker.* The function of the rules is to define which constituents of sentences are superordinate to which other constituents, to establish the order of constituents, to display the grammatical elements of the sentence (e.g., NP), and to define (in a way explained in Chapter 5) the basic grammatical relations—subject of a sentence, object of a verb, etc. The phrase-marker is the structure produced through application of the rules. It can be presented as a diagram, as in Fig. 19, or by means of labeled brackets:

153

$(_S$ $(_{NP}$ $(_{Art}the)$ $(_N frog))$ $(_{VP}$ $(_V caught)$ $(_{NP}$ $(_{Art}the)$ $(_N mosquito))))$

includes exactly the same information as Table 14, and both represent the structure that English speakers find in *the frog caught the mosquito*.

Note that grammatical rules *represent* linguistic structure. They describe tacit knowledge, not explicit knowledge. No one claims that the rules given in Fig. 19 are necessarily known to speakers of English *as statable rules*. If that were actually the case, linguistics could not exist. The field would be as pointless as would be a "science" to discover the rules of chess. The distinction is perhaps obvious but its importance justifies some elaboration.

One can imagine a series of interpretations of the rules in Fig. 19. At the weak end of the series phrase-structure rules might be regarded as summarizing regularities in behavior. Rules such as S → NP PredP mean that when English sentences *occur,* they consist of noun phrases followed by predicate phrases. The relevant observations for testing such a theory would be the frequency of sentences following the NP PredP format, and, no doubt, such observations would falsify the theory. Sentences like *the frog caught the mosquito* are simply not that common.

At the opposite extreme, the strong end, the claim would be that English speakers know the rules in Fig. 19 in much the form that the rules take when written. Clearly this claim is false for the vast majority of English speakers, and for all children.

The mid-point in this series of interpretations is the one intended for Fig. 19. English speakers do not know the rules in Fig. 19, but what they do know (it is claimed) is represented by these rules. Observations relevant to the intermediate interpretation do not have to do with actual speech, nor with rules that speakers can state, but with a speaker's intuitions—for instance, that *the mosquito* is a grammatical constituent in English, whereas *caught the* is not. This interpretation applies to children and adults alike. For further discussion see Fodor and Garrett (1966).

Table 14 **The Result of Replacing Groups of Words by Single Words in a Simple Declarative Sentence**
(based on Miller, 1962)

A sentence				
It		acted		
The	frog	acted		
The	frog	caught		it
The	frog	caught	the	mosquito

Phrase-structure rules, interpreted in the intermediate sense, are said to *generate* sentence structures. A term like "generate" tempts us to think that speakers actually plan sentences along the lines outlined in Fig. 19—they first decide to utter a sentence, then decide that the sentence will consist of a V and an NP and then at the end decide what vocabulary to use. Such a scheme is one possible hypothesis about linguistic performance (Yngve, 1960, 1961; Johnson, 1968). However, the theory of performance is not part of the grammatical analysis in Fig. 19. The term *generate* is used by grammarians in a logical, not a mechanical, sense. As the linguist Lees once put it, a correct grammar generates all possible sentences of a language in the same way that a correct zoology generates all possible animals. Both capture the structural relations within their subject matter.

The linguistic observations made so far serve a fairly obvious purpose. Presumably the parsing of *the frog caught the mosquito* given in Fig. 19 does not require an elaborate defense. The facts are straightforward and the principal merit in discussing them at all is that they acquaint the reader with some linguistic notation at a point where it is reasonably easy to see what the notation means. However, there are more profound and psychologically more significant insights entailed by three other linguistic concepts; it is to these concepts that we now turn.

Transformations and the Notions of Underlying (Deep) and Surface Structure

In a general way, language can be described as a system whereby sound and meaning are related to each other. That sound and meaning are separate and so need relating is evident from paraphrase, where the same meaning is expressed in different patterns of sound (*the man pursued the woman* and *the woman was pursued by the man*) and from ambiguity, where the same pattern of sound has different meanings (*outgoing tuna*). Between sound and meaning stands *syntax*. The relation between sound and meaning is therefore understood to the degree that the syntax of a language is understood. In this section we shall examine what is known of this relation.

Rationalist philosophers have argued since the seventeenth century that sentences have an inner and an outer aspect, the first connected with thought and the second with sound (Chomsky, 1966). The kind of evidence that leads to this conclusion, and hence to the phenomenon of concern here, is given in Table 15 (after Miller and McNeill, 1968). The three sentences on the left of Table 15 all have the same superficial form. They start with a pronoun *they,* followed by *are,* followed by a progressive form, followed by a plural noun. Despite this superficial identity, however, there are clear differences in structure among these three sentences. To understand the differences we will eventually need the notions of a transformation rule and of deep and surface structure.

Sentence (a) differs from sentences (b) and (c) in several fairly obvious ways. One difference is that the two kinds of sentences accept pauses

Table 15

	Sentences	Paraphrases	Nonparaphrases
(a)	They are buying glasses	————	————
(b)	They are drinking glasses	They are glasses to use for drinking	They are glasses that drink
(c)	They are drinking companions	They are companions that drink	They are companions to use for drinking

in different places. With sentence (a) one might say *they . . . are buying . . . glasses,* but probably not *they . . . are . . . buying glasses.* It is the opposite with sentences (b) and (c). One could say *they . . . are . . . drinking companions* or *they . . . are . . . drinking glasses,* but not *they . . . are drinking . . . companions* or *they . . . are drinking . . . glasses,* unless the reference was to cannibalism or suicide. A second difference is in the proper location of articles. We have *they are buying the glasses* but not *they are the buying glasses.* We have *they are the drinking companions* but not *they are drinking the companions.*

The location of pauses in a sentence is fixed by its phrase structure. Pauses tend to go around constituents, not inside them. The location of articles is likewise determined by phrase structure. They go before NPs only. We can thus summarize the differences between sentence (a) and sentences (b) and (c) by saying that they have different phrase structures. In particular, the progressive form in sentence (a) is associated with the verb *are,* whereas in (b) and (c) it has moved over to the plural noun. The essential parts of the three phrase markers are as follows: (*they*)(*are buying*)(*glasses*), (*they*)(*are*)(*drinking companions*), and (*they*)(*are*)(*drinking glasses*).

Sentence (a) and sentences (b) and (c) are distinguished in their *surface structure.* The difference, as we have seen, has to do with the distribution of pauses and the location of articles. Surface structure also is intimately connected with stress and intonation (Chomsky and Halle, 1968). In general, the surface structure of a sentence has to do with phonology — with one of the two aspects of language that need to be related by syntax.

Let us now look more carefully at sentences (b) and (c). They accept pauses in the same way, they take articles at the same places, they are accordingly bracketed in the same way, and, indeed, they have the same surface structure. But it is clear that they are not structurally identical throughout. They differ in a way that is important to meaning, the other aspect of language that is to be related by syntax. That they differ in meaning can be seen in the paraphrases and nonparaphrases of the two sentences in Table 15. Sentence (b) means "they are glasses to use for drinking" and (c) means "they are companions that drink." Exchanging the form of the paraphrase between (b) and (c) leads to a nonparaphrase. Sentence (b) does not mean "they are glasses that

156

drink" any more than sentence (c) means "they are companions to use for drinking." Despite the identity of surface form, (b) and (c) differ importantly in underlying form. We shall say that they differ in *underlying* or *deep structure*, saving until later a more precise definition of what this means. First, however, let us note two implications that follow from the fact that (b) and (c) have the same surface structure but different underlying structures.

One is that the *relation* between underlying and surface structure must be different in the two sentences. The statement of this relation is assigned a special place in a grammar. It is done by the *rules of transformation*, and it is these rules, together with the underlying and surface structure of sentences, that embody the connection between sound and meaning in a language. The reader will have realized, of course, that in a statistical sense sentences (b) and (c) are freakish. The vast majority of sentences that have different underlying structures and different transformations also have different surface structures. Sentences (b) and (c) happen not to, but for this very reason conveniently illustrate what is true of all sentences. Every sentence, however simple, has some kind of underlying structure related to some kind of surface structure by means of certain transformations. The substance of grammar consists of making explicit these three terms.

The second implication of the difference in paraphrase between sentences (b) and (c) is that the underlying and surface structures of sentences are not identical. This is evidently true of at least one of the sentences, (b) or (c). In fact it is true of all sentences. Transformations provide enormous flexibility in developing surface structures from underlying structures and this advantage has been pressed by language in even the most elementary sentence types (an example with simple declaratives is given below). Thus, the underlying structure of every sentence is abstract in the sense given above. The underlying structure, the part connected with meaning, is not present in the overt form of any sentence. The acquisition of linguistic abstractions is a universal phenomenon—it is a basic fact about the development of language and on its success rests the emergence of all adult grammar. It would be impossible to understand sentences (b) and (c) correctly if this were not so.

All these concepts—underlying structure, surface structure, linguistic abstraction, and the way transformations tie them together—can best be seen in an example. The one we shall use is borrowed from Miller and McNeill (1968) and is based on Chomsky (1957). Consider the following sentences:

He walks	(present singular)
They walk	(present plural)
He walked	(past singular)
They walked	(past plural)

These four sentences mark two distinctions: number (singular and plural) and tense (present and past). Number is marked both in the form of the pronoun and in the inflection of the present-tense verb. Tense is marked in the inflection of the verb. Let us focus on the verbs, for it is here that a transformation becomes involved.

There are three verb suffixes: -s, -ϕ (which means null, but is a suffix all the same), and -ed. They encode information of a certain type, viz., the form of the verbal auxiliary, so we might suppose that this information can be expressed by a rewriting rule of the kind already discussed. If we label the genus part of the rule C, then we can use the following context-sensitive rule:

$$C \longrightarrow \begin{cases} \text{-s in the context } NP_{sing} \\ \text{-}\phi \text{ in the context } NP_{pl} \\ \text{-}ed \end{cases}$$

and summarize all four of the sentences above by a single schema, NP + V-C.

Let us now complicate the sentences slightly by incorporating an auxiliary verb, be, and see what happens.

> He is walking
> They are walking
> He was walking
> They were walking

The first thing to note is that using a form of be adds -ing to the following main verb. C, for its part, has moved forward. It is no longer attached to the main verb but to the auxiliary, and we have be-s (pronounced is), be-ϕ (pronounced are), and be-ed (pronounced was or were, number being marked on past-tense verbs in this case, a detail we can ignore). The schema for these sentences therefore is NP + be-C + V-ing.

Next consider the effect of adding a different auxiliary verb, a form of have, to the original sentences. Doing so, we obtain:

> He has walked
> They have walked
> He had walked
> They had walked

The main verb again takes a suffix, this time -ed, and C again moves forward to the auxiliary. It is the same therefore as when be is the auxiliary, except that different pronunciation rules are involved (have-s is has, have-ϕ is have, have-ed is had) and the main-verb suffix is -ed instead of -ing. Indicating these changes, we obtain the schema NP + have-C + V-ed for the use of have as an auxiliary.

The two auxiliaries can, of course, be combined, as in these sentences:

> He has been walking
> They have been walking
> He had been walking
> They had been walking

158

Both auxiliaries have the effects already demonstrated. *Be* adds the suffix *-ing* to the following verb and *have* adds a "past" suffix to *be*. (In this case it is *be-en,* another difference in detail that we can ignore.) C also follows its usual pattern, for it is still attached to the first auxiliary verb. The schema therefore is NP + *have*-C + *be-en* + V-*ing*.

These sentences can be complicated still further by adding one of the modal auxiliaries. Modals are the words *will, can, may, shall, must.* Let us add *will:*

> *He will have been walking*
> *They will have been walking*
> *He would have been walking*
> *They would have been walking*

C has moved forward again, attached now to the modal. *Have* still adds a "past" inflection to the following *be,* and *be* still adds *-ing* to the following main verb. The schema thus is NP + M-C + *have* + *be-en* + V-*ing*, where M stands for "modal."

It is evident from these examples that C always appears with the first member of an auxiliary construction, no matter how long this construction is. The location of C is a fact known to all speakers of English — *he will had been walking* obviously is not the way to indicate past tense in an auxiliary construction. Part of an English speaker's competence thus has C at the start of a verb phrase. Another part involves the contingency between *have* as an auxiliary and a following "past" inflection, as well as the contingency between *be* as an auxiliary and the following *-ing.* Let us try to represent these facts about competence by constructing a rule that meets the following two conditions: (1) the true order of elements is maintained, and (2) elements contingent on one another are placed together. Doing so will lead to a simple solution.

Meeting the first condition requires placing C first, then M, then *have,* and finally *be.*[2] Since C appears in every sentence our rule must make it obligatory. The remaining constituents are optional, however, so we write them with parentheses. Let us call the whole construction "Auxiliary," abbreviate it "Aux," and put down the following rule:

$$\text{Aux} \longrightarrow \text{C (M) } (have) \ (be)$$

The following main verb (V) is omitted from this rule because it is introduced along with Aux by the PredP rule, which is now enlarged to read:

$$\text{PredP} \longrightarrow \text{Aux V (NP)}$$

The Aux rule is still incomplete, since it does not yet meet the second condition. The contingencies to be represented are that *have* goes

---

[2] It is not clear precisely how the connection should be developed between this ordered structure and the more abstract unordered structures described for children in Chapter 5. The whole question of ordering in the underlying structure is quite obscure and unsettled.

with -*en* (or -*ed*) and *be* goes with -*ing,* so we write these elements together and thereby produce the following:

$$\text{Aux} \longrightarrow \text{C (M)} \; (have\text{-}en) \; (be\text{-}ing)$$

after which there will always be a V.

We now have all but one of the rules necessary to generate the examples given above. The missing one, a transformation, will be provided shortly. However, in order to see the need for the transformation and to appreciate the role it plays in representing the structure of these sentences, we should first see the result of producing sentences without it. The structural relations to be expressed by the transformation will be those not expressed by the rules already developed. If we have done our job well the division between the two kinds of rules, the transformation and the phrase-structure rules, will correspond to a real division between two kinds of structural information within sentences.

Figure 20 contains a phrase-marker generated by the phrase-structure rules presented in the preceding paragraphs. Note that the order of elements at the bottom of the phrase-marker is *they* + Past + *will* + *have* + *en* + *be* + *ing* + *walk.* This string and its associated structure is the underlying structure of *they would have been walking.* The surface structure is a specific instance of the last schema given above—*they* + *will-Past* + *have* + *be-en* + *walk-ing.* The deep structure thus differs from the surface structure in the order of suffixes and verbs. It is abstract in the sense used here since the deep-structure arrangement never appears overtly. It is important to realize, nonetheless, that the deep structure in Fig. 20 reflects actual linguistic knowledge—the information summarized by C *is* always first in a predicate phrase, *have* and -*en do* always appear together, just as *be* and -*ing* always do.

The deep structure must therefore be transformed in order to obtain the surface structure. The transformation is simple: Wherever the sequence affix-verb appears in the underlying structure, change the order

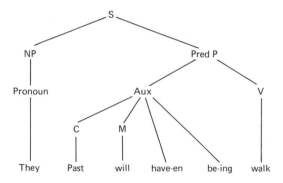

Fig. 20. Underlying structure of *they would have been walking.*

to verb-affix (Chomsky, 1957). If the reader applies this transformation he will find the surface structure of *they would have been walking* rolling out quite automatically.

There remains one important point. Note that the linguistic information expressed by the phrase-structure rules in generating *they would have been walking* is fundamentally different from the information expressed by the transformation rule. Which is to say that the distinction between the two is linguistically meaningful. The former rules define such matters as the genus-species relations within the sentence (e.g., *they* is an NP), establish the basic order of elements (e.g., C is first in the PredP), and indicate what the elements are (e.g., *have-en* is an element). Information of this kind is essential for obtaining the meaning of the sentence. The relations just mentioned, among others, are exactly what we understand of *they would have been walking.*

The transformation, in contrast, makes no contribution to meaning. It exists only because sound and meaning are not identical in English (or any language) and its sole purpose is to state the relation between them. The distinction between phrase-structure and transformation rules is thus fundamental to the analysis of language. Without it the insight that sound and meaning are separate in language would be lost; to suggest, as some have done, that transformations are methodologically unsound because they lead to arbitrary linguistic solutions, is to miss the point of transformational grammar.

The distinction between sound and meaning is a basic justification of transformational grammar, but the use of transformations in grammatical analysis is supported by other arguments as well. One is economy. If we dispense with transformations and try to generate sentences with phrase-structure rules alone the result becomes unnecessarily complex. The sentences given above, for example, require eight different and independent phrase-structure rules, one for each combination of auxiliary verb and C, instead of the single phrase-structure rule required when a transformation is allowed. Without the transformation, we would need at least the following rules: $\text{Aux}_1 \longrightarrow$ V-C, $\text{Aux}_2 \longrightarrow$ *be*-C + V-*ing*, $\text{Aux}_3 \longrightarrow$ *have*-C + V-*ed*, $\text{Aux}_4 \longrightarrow$ *have*-C + *be-en* + V-*ing*, $\text{Aux}_5 \longrightarrow$ M-C + V, $\text{Aux}_6 \longrightarrow$ M-C + *be* + V-*ing*, $\text{Aux}_7 \longrightarrow$ M-C + *have* + V-*ed*, and $\text{Aux}_8 \longrightarrow$ M-C + *have* + *be-en* + V-*ing*. Note that these rules cannot be collapsed onto one another by means of the parentheses notation used before. The changing location of C prevents it. This phrase-structure version of the auxiliary therefore not only overlooks valid linguistic generalizations — such as the fact that C always appears first in the auxiliary, or that there *is* an auxiliary, or that *-ing* depends on *be* and not on V — but it is also cumbersome. Relative economy is always an argument in support of one theoretical interpretation over another and using it in the present case inclines the balance toward a transformational solution.

The argument of economy has special significance in the context of language acquisition. We prefer to think of children doing the simpler thing, whatever that might be. In the case of linguistic development, the simpler thing is to acquire a transformational grammar instead of a phrase-structure grammar.

The suffix-transformation used in generating the English auxiliary verb is one rule within a vast and intricate network of transformations making up the language. Passive sentences, negation, questions of various kinds, conjunctions, apposition of nouns and adjectives, and many other grammatical devices all depend on transformations.

There is one set of transformations of special significance, and this appendix will conclude with a discussion of them. Recall the artificial language presented in Table 13. Its "sentences" were built like an onion —such structures as $(a(a(ab)b)b)$. The rule given to generate the "sentences" in Table 13 was X $\longrightarrow$ a(X)b, in which there is an abstract recursive element X. This much is phrase structure and it has an exact analogy in English (and all other languages).

In developing the underlying structure of any sentence it is possible to include, along with other underlying morphemes, the element S, thus calling for the insertion of *another* underlying structure at that point. That sentence, in turn, may also have an S in it, calling for the insertion of yet another underlying structure, and so forth. The result can be the same onion-like structure presented in Table 13, and it has the same effect—making infinite productivity possible through recursion. There are definite restrictions on where such embeddings may take place. Figure 21 shows a succession of underlying structures, each with another embedded within it.

Figure 21 is the result of applying phrase-structure rules alone and represents the underlying structure of (*the ostrich (that was terrified*

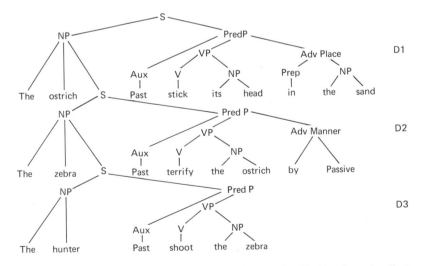

Fig. 21. Underlying structure of *the ostrich that was terrified by the zebra that the hunter shot stuck its head in the sand.*

by the zebra (*that the hunter shot*)) *stuck its head in the sand*), a sentence with two relative clauses. English employs several transformations to develop this surface structure from the deep structure in Fig. 21. In discussing them, we shall use terminology suggested by Lees (1960), and call the structure containing *S* the *matrix* and the *S* contained the *constituent.* Thus, D3 in Fig. 21 is the constituent of the matrix D2, and both are the constituent of the matrix D1. In Fig. 21, D3 is only a constituent, D1 is only a matrix, but D2 is both—a matrix for D3 and a constituent (containing D3) for D1.

These three components are complete structures unto themselves. If developed in isolation (ignoring the *S* in D1 and D2), each would result in a sentence. D1 is the deep structure of *the ostrich stuck its head in the sand;* D2 is the deep structure of a passive sentence, *the ostrich was terrified by the zebra,* and D3 is the deep structure of *the hunter shot the zebra.* It is obvious that more is required in combining these elementary structures than simply applying the transformations that each calls for alone—the auxiliary transformation in every case, and the passive transformation in D2. Doing only this much produces non-English: *the ostrich was terrified by the zebra the hunter shot the zebra stuck its head in the sand.* To avoid such a word salad, an embedding transformation must delete double occurrences of the same NP. Not every NP repeated in an English sentence need be deleted, of course. *The ostrich stuck its head in the sand and the ostrich ate the worm* is grammatical even though redundant or ambiguous. However, in the case of an embedded relative clause, deletion must occur, and the rule is that when the same NP is both a matrix subject and a constituent object the object-NP is moved to the front of its sentence structure and replaced by the word *that.* Let us call this operation the deletion transformation. In the case of Fig. 21, it produces *the ostrich that the zebra that the hunter Past + shoot Past + terrify by + Passive Past + stuck its head in the sand.* Applying the auxiliary transformation to this structure wherever called for (e.g., *Past + shoot* becomes *shot*) and the passive transformation to D2, the surface structure of which Fig. 21 is the underlying structure rolls out. (Actually, such "singulary" transformations as the affix transformation and the passive transformation are applied, when called for, to the most deeply embedded S first, then to the next most deeply embedded S, and so on up to the top, before the embedding transformations are applied. Cf. Chomsky, 1965, for a discussion of such transformational cycles.)

Again notice that a natural distinction exists between the information contained in the transformation and the information contained in the underlying structure. As before, the latter has to do with meaning and the former with the relation between sound and meaning. When one understands a relative clause he grasps the fact that there are two or more underlying structures, one inserted in the other, with the deletions described by the transformation *not* performed. Obtaining the meaning of *the ostrich that was terrified by the zebra that the hunter shot stuck its head in the sand* depends on knowing that the first *that* means

163

ostrich and the second *zebra,* which is to disregard both deletions in the semantic interpretation of the sentence.

There remains one point and we shall be done with this brief introduction to syntax. If transformations are correctly stated in a grammar they apply automatically whenever the proper conditons exist in the deep structure. In other words, transformations are obligatory (Chomsky, 1965; Katz & Postal, 1964). The specification of the "proper" condition' is done by the *structural index* of a transformation and setting it down is an important part of writing a transformational rule. Should the structural index be wrong, a transformation will relate wrong underlying and surface structures, even though the operations described in the transformation are themselves correct when the circumstances are appropriate. To supplement the rules already mentioned, then, we must add that the auxiliary transformation applies to any occurrence of affix $+ V$, the passive transformation to any occurrence of NP_1 Aux V ... NP_2 ... *by* $+$ Passive (the subscripts indicating that the two NPs must be different and the dots indicating that other unspecified material can be inserted), and the relative-clause transformation to any case where the matrix-subject and the constituent-object are the same NP. The structural index is clearly part of grammatical knowledge. Applying the relative-clause transformation to underlying structures where the subject and object-NPs are different results in a sentence that expresses the wrong meaning. If, for example, the deep structures of *the ostrich stuck its head in the sand* and *the ostrich ate the worm* are connected by the relative-clause transformation, meaning shifts and the result becomes something out of Alice in Wonderland — *the ostrich stuck its head in the sand that ate the worm.* Since violation of the structural index of a transformation leads to an inappropriate expression of meaning, it is evident that the structural index is a part of the relation between meaning and sound.

REFERENCES

Albritton, R. On Wittgenstein's use of the term "criterion." In G. Pitcher (Ed.), *Wittgenstein: The philosophical investigations.* Garden City, N.Y.: Doubleday, 1966. Pp. 231–250.

Alexander, R. D., and Moore, T. E. Studies on the acoustic behavior of Seventeen-Year Cicadas. *Ohio J. Sci.,* 1958, **58,** 107–127.

Allport, F. H. *Social psychology.* Cambridge, Mass.: Houghton-Mifflin, 1924.

Anderson, S. A., and Beh, W. The reorganization of verbal memory in childhood. *J. verb. Learn. verb. Behav.,* 1968, **7,** 1049–1053.

Andrew, R. J. Evolution of facial expression. *Science,* 1963, **142,** 1034–1041.

Anglin, J. The growth of the mental lexicon. Unpubl. paper, Dept. Social Relations, Harvard University, 1968.

Anisfeld, M., Barlow, Judith, and Frail, Catherine M. Distinctive features in the pluralization rules of English speakers. Unpubl. paper, Dept. Psychology, Cornell University, 1967.

Anisfeld, M., and Tucker, R. G. English pluralization rules of six-year-old children. *Child Development,* 1967, **38,** 1202–1217.

Bach, E., and Harms, R. T. (Eds.) *Universals in linguistic theory.* New York: Holt, Rinehart, and Winston, 1968.

Bailey, S. *A review of Berkeley's theory of vision, designed to show the unsoundness of that celebrated speculation.* London: Ridgway, 1842.

Bellugi, Ursula. The emergence of inflections and negation systems in the speech of two children. Paper presented at New England Psychol. Assn., 1964.

Bellugi, Ursula. The development of interrogative structures in children's speech. In K. Riegel (Ed.), *The development of language functions. Univ. Mich. Lang. Develop. Program,* Rept. No. 8, 1965, 103–138.

Bellugi, Ursula. The acquisition of negation. Unpubl. Doctoral Dissertation, Graduate School of Education, Harvard University, 1967.

Bellugi, Ursula, and Brown, R. (Eds.). The acquisition of language. *Monogr. Soc. Res. Child Developm.,* 1964, **29,** No. 92.

Bem, Sandra L. The role of comprehension in self-instruction. Unpubl. paper, Dept. Psychology, University of Michigan, 1967.

Berko, Jean. The child's learning of English morphology. *Word,* 1958, **14,** 150–177.

Bever, T. G. Pre-linguistic behaviour. Unpubl. Honors Thesis, Dept. Linguistics, Harvard University, 1961.

Bever, T. G., Fodor, J. A., and Weksel, W. On the acquisition of syntax: a critique of "contextual generalization." *Psychol. Rev.,* 1965, **72,** 467–482. (a)

Bever, T. G., Fodor, J. A., and Weksel, W. Is linguistics empirical? *Psychol. Rev.,* 1965, **72,** 493–500. (b)

Bever, T. G., Mehler, J., and Valian, V. V. Linguistic capacity of very young children. Lecture at Graduate School of Education, Harvard University, 1967.

Birch, D. Verbal control of nonverbal behavior. *J. exp. Child Psychol.,* 1966, **4,** 266–275.

Bisetzky, A. R. Die Tänze der Bienen nach einem Fussweg zum Futterplatz. *Z. Vergl. Physiol.,* 1957, **40,** 264–288.

Bloom, Luis. Language development: Form and function in emerging grammars. Unpubl. Doctoral Dissertation, Columbia University, 1968.

Bloomfield, L. *Language.* New York: Holt, 1933.

Blount, B. G. *Acquisition of language by Luo children.* Univ. Calif. Berkeley, Lang. Behav. Res. Lab., Paper No. 19, 1969.

Blumenthal, A. L. Prompted recall of sentences. *J. verb. Learn. verb. Behav.,* 1967, **6,** 203–206.

Blumenthal, A. L. *Language and psychology: Historical aspects of psycholinguistics.* New York: John Wiley, 1970.

Bogoyavlenskiy, D. N. *Psikhologiya usvoyeniya orfografii.* Moscow: Akad. Pedag. Nauk RSFSR, 1957.

Bowerman, Melissa. Acquiring Finnish as a native language: Some selected problems. Unpubl. paper, Dept. Social Relations, Harvard University, 1968.

Bowerman, Melissa. The pivot-open class distinction. Unpubl. paper, Dept. Social Relations, Harvard University, 1969.

Braine, M. D. S. The ontogeny of English phrase structure: The first phase. *Language,* 1963, **39,** 1–13. (a)

Braine, M. D. S. On learning the grammatical order of words. *Psychol. Rev.,* 1963, **70,** 323–348. (b)

Braine, M. D. S. On the basis of phrase structure: A reply to Bever, Fodor, and Weksel. *Psychol. Rev.,* 1965, **72,** 483–492.

Braine, M. D. S. The acquisition of language in infant and child. In Carroll Reed (Ed.), *The learning of language: Essays in honor of David H. Russell.* New York: Appleton-Century-Crofts, 1970.

Bristowe, W. S. *The comity of spiders,* Vol. 2. London: Ray Society, 1941.

Brown, R. Linguistic determinism and the part of speech. *J. abnorm. soc. Psychol.,* 1957, **55,** 1–5.

Brown, R. *Words and things.* Glencoe, Ill.: Free Press, 1958.

Brown, R. The dialogue in early childhood. Presidential address, Div. 8, Amer. Psychol. Assn., 1966.

Brown, R. Derivational complexity and the order of acquisition in child speech. Carnegie-Mellon Conference on Cognitive Processes, 1968.

Brown, R., and Bellugi, Ursula. Three processes in the child's acquisition of syntax. *Harvard Educ. Rev.,* 1964, **34,** 133–151.

Brown, R., and Berko, Jean. Word association and the acquisition of grammar. *Child Development,* 1960, **31,** 1–14.

Brown, R., Cazden, Courtney, and Bellugi, Ursula. The child's grammar from I to III. In J. P. Hill (Ed.), *The 1967 Minnesota symposium on child psychology.* Minneapolis: Univ. Minn. Press, 1968. Pp. 28–73.

Brown, R., and Fraser, C. The acquisition of syntax. In C. N. Cofer and Barbara S. Musgrave (Eds.), *Verbal behavior and learning: Problems and processes.* New York: McGraw-Hill, 1963. Pp. 158–197.

Brown, R., and Fraser, C. The acquisition of syntax. In Ursula Bellugi and R. Brown (Eds.), The acquisition of language. *Monogr. Soc. Res. Child Developm.,* 1964, **29** (No. 92), 43–78.

Bruner, J. S., Goodnow, Jacqueline J., and Austin, G. A. *A study of thinking.* New York: Wiley, 1956.

Bruner, J. S., Olver, Rose, and Greenfield, Patricia M. *Studies in cognitive growth.* New York: Wiley, 1966.

Bullowa, Margaret, Jones, L. G., and Bever, T. G. The development from vocal to verbal behavior in children. In Ursula Bellugi and R. Brown (Eds.), The acquisition of language. *Monogr. Soc. Res. Child Developm.,* 1964, **29** (No. 92), 101–107.

Cazden, Courtney. Environmental assistance to the child's acquisition of grammar. Unpubl. Doctoral Dissertation, Graduate School of Education, Harvard University, 1965.

Cazden, Courtney. The acquisition of noun and verb inflections. Unpubl. paper, Dept. Social Relations, Harvard University, 1967.

Chai, D. T. Communication of pronomial referents in ambiguous English sentences for children and adults. Unpubl. Doctoral Dissertation, Dept. Communication Sciences, University of Michigan, 1967.

Chomsky, Carol S. *The acquisition of syntax in children from 5 to 10.* Cambridge, Mass.: M.I.T. Press, 1969.

Chomsky, N. A. *Syntactic structures.* The Hague: Mouton, 1957.

Chomsky, N. A. Review of "Verbal behavior," by B. F. Skinner. *Language,* 1959, **35,** 26–58.

Chomsky, N. A. Some methodological remarks on generative grammar. *Word,* 1961, **17,** 219–239. [Reprinted in J. A. Fodor and J. J. Katz (Eds.), *The structure of language.* Englewood Cliffs, N.J.: Prentice-Hall, 1964.]

Chomsky, N. A. Formal properties of grammars. In R. D. Luce, R. R. Bush, & E. Galanter (Eds.), *Handbook of mathematical psychology,* Vol. 2. New York: Wiley, 1963. Pp. 323–418.

Chomsky, N. A. Current issues in linguistic theory. In J. A. Fodor and J. J. Katz (Eds.), *The structure of language: Readings in the philosophy of language.* Englewood Cliffs, N.J.: Prentice-Hall, 1964. Pp. 50–118. (a)

Chomsky, N. A. Discussion of Miller and Ervin's paper. In Ursula Bellugi and R. Brown (Eds.), The acquisition of language. *Monogr. Soc. Res. Child Developm.,* 1964, **29** (No. 92). Pp. 35–39. (b)

Chomsky, N. A. *Aspects of the theory of syntax.* Cambridge, Mass.: M.I.T. Press, 1965.

Chomsky, N. A. *Cartesian linguistics.* New York: Harper & Row, 1966.

Chomsky, N. A. Remarks on nominalization. Unpubl. paper, M.I.T., 1967.

Chomsky, N. A., and Halle, M. Some controversial questions in phonological theory. *J. Ling.,* 1966, **2,** 97–138.

Chomsky, N. A., and Halle, M. *The sound pattern of English.* New York: Harper & Row, 1968.

Chomsky, N. A., Halle, M., and Lukoff, F. On accent and juncture in English. In M. Halle, H. Lunt, and H. MacLean (Eds.), *For Roman Jakobson.* The Hague: Mouton, 1956.

Chomsky, N. A., and Miller, G. A. Introduction to the formal analysis of natural languages. In R. D. Luce, R. R. Bush, and E. Galanter (Eds.), *Handbook of mathematical psychology,* Vol. 2. New York: Wiley, 1963. Pp. 269–321.

Craig, W. The song of the wood pewee, *Myiochanes virens Linnaeus:* A study of bird music. *N.Y. St. Mus. Bull.,* 1943, **334,** 1–186.

Donaldson, Margaret, and Balfour, G. Less is more: A study of language comprehension in children. *Brit. J. Psychol.,* 1968, **59,** 461–471.

Donaldson, Margaret, and Wales, R. On the acquisition of some relational terms. Unpubl. paper. Dept. Psychol., University of Edinburgh, 1968.

Duncan, S. P. Nonverbal Communication. *Psychol. Bull.,* 1969, **72,** 118–137.

Entwisle, Doris R. *The word associations of young children.* Baltimore, Md.: The Johns Hopkins Press, 1966.

Ervin, Susan. Changes with age in the verbal determinants of word-association. *Amer. J. Psychol.,* 1961, **74,** 361–372.

Ervin, Susan. Imitation and structural change in children's language. In E. H. Lenneberg (Ed.), *New directions in the study of language.* Cambridge, Mass.: M.I.T. Press, 1964.

Feldman, Carol F., and Rodgon, Maris. The effects of various types of adult responses in the syntactic acquisition of two- to three-year-olds. Unpubl. paper. Dept. Psychol., University of Chicago, 1970.

Ferguson, C. A. Baby talk in six languages. *Amer. Anthro.,* 1964, **66,** 103–114.

Fillmore, C. J. The case for case. In E. Bach and R. T. Harms (Eds.), *Universals in linguistic theory.* New York: Holt, Rinehart, and Winston, 1968. Pp. 1–90.

Fodor, J. A. How to learn to talk: Some simple ways. In F. Smith and G. A. Miller (Eds.), *The genesis of language: A psycholinguistic approach.* Cambridge, Mass.: M.I.T. Press, 1966. Pp. 105–123.

Fodor, J. A., and Garrett, M. Some reflections on competence and performance. In J. Lyons and R. Wales (Eds.), *Psycholinguistics papers.* Edinburgh: Edinburgh Univ. Press, 1966. Pp. 135–182.

Fodor, J. A., and Katz, J. J. *The structure of language: Readings in the philosophy of language.* Englewood Cliffs, N.J.: Prentice-Hall, 1964.

Fraser, C., Bellugi, Ursula, and Brown, R. Control of grammar in imitation, comprehension, and production. *J. verb. Learn. verb. Behav.,* 1963, **2,** 121–135.

von Frisch, K. Gelöste und ungelöste Rätsel der Bienensprache. *Naturwissenschaften,* 1948, **35,** 12–23, 38–43.

von Frisch, K. *Bees: Their vision, chemical senses, and language.* Ithaca, N.Y.: Cornell Univ. Press, 1950.

von Frisch, K. *The dance language and orientation of bees.* Cambridge, Mass.: Harvard Univ. Press, 1967.

Gardner, R. A., and Gardner, Beatrice T. Teaching sign language to a chimpanzee. *Science,* 1969, **165,** 664–672.

Gazzaniga, M. S., and Sperry, R. W. Language after section of the cerebral commissures. *Brain,* 1967, **90,** 131–148.

Goldman-Eisler, Frieda. Hesitation and information in speech. In C. Cherry (Ed.), *Information theory.* Fourth London Symposium. London: Butterworths, 1961. Pp. 162–174.

Gough, P. B. Grammatical transformations and speed of understanding. *J. verb. Learn. verb. Behav.,* 1965, **4,** 107–111.

Greenberg, J. H. Some universals of grammar with particular reference to the order of meaningful elements. In J. H. Greenberg (Ed.), *Universals of language.* Cambridge, Mass.: M.I.T. Press, 1962. Pp. 58–90.

Greenberg, J. H. Language universals. In T. Sebeok (Ed.), *Current trends in linguistics,* Vol. 3. The Hague: Mouton, 1966. Pp. 61–111.

Greenfield, Patricia M. Who is "DADA"? Unpubl. paper, Syracuse University, 1967.

Greenfield, Patricia. Development of the holophrase. Unpubl. paper, Harvard University, Center for Cognitive Studies, 1968.

Grégoire, A. *L'apprentissage du langage.* Vol. 1. *Les deux premières annees.* Paris: Droz, 1937.

Gruber, J. Topicalization in child language. *Found. Lang.,* 1967, **3,** 37–65.

Gvozdev, A. N. *Voprosy Izucheniya detskoy rechi.* Moscow: Akad. Pedag. Nauk RSFSR, 1961.

Hall, K. R. L., and De Vore, I. Baboon social behavior. In I. De Vore (Ed.), *Primate behavior. Field studies of monkeys and apes.* New York: Holt, Rinehart and Winston, 1965. Pp. 53–110.

Halle, M. On the basis of phonology. In J. A. Fodor and J. J. Katz (Eds.), *The structure of language.* Englewood Cliffs, N.J.: Prentice-Hall, 1964. Pp. 324–333. (a)

Halle, M. Phonology in generative grammar. In J. J. Fodor and J. A. Katz (Eds.), *The structure of language.* Englewood Cliffs, N.J.: Prentice-Hall, 1964. Pp. 334–352. (b)

Hayes, Catherine. *The ape in our house.* New York: Harper & Row, 1951.

Heran, H., and Wanke, L. Beobachtungen über die Entfernungsmeldung der Sammelbienen. *Z. vergl. Physiol.,* 1952, **34,** 383–393.

Huttenlocher, Janellen, Eisenberg, Karen, and Strauss, Susan. Comprehension: Relation between perceived actor and logical subject. *J. verb. Learn. verb. Behav.,* 1968, **7,** 527–530.

Huttenlocher, Janellen, and Strauss, Susan. Comprehension and a statement's relation to the situation it describes. *J. verb. Learn. verb. Behav.,* 1968, **7,** 300–304.

Irwin, O. C. Infant speech: Variability and the problem of diagnosis. *J. speech hearing Disorders,* 1947, **12,** 287–289. (a)

Irwin, O. C. Infant speech: Consonantal sounds according to place of articulation. *J. speech hearing Disorders,* 1947, **12,** 397–401. (b)

Irwin, O. C. Infant speech: Consonantal sounds according to manner of articulation. *J. speech hearing Disorders,* 1947, **12,** 402–404. (c)

Irwin, O. C. Infant speech: Development of vowel sounds. *J. speech hearing Disorders,* 1948, **13,** 31–34.

Isaac, D., and Marler, P. Ordering of sequences of singing behaviour of mistle thrushes in relationship to timing. *Anim. Behav.,* 1963, **11,** 179–188.

Jakobson, R. *Kindersprache, Aphasie, und allgemeine Lautgesetze.* Uppsala: Almgvist and Wiksell, 1941. (English trans. by A. Keiler, *Child language, aphasia, and general sound laws.* The Hague: Mouton, 1968.)

Jakobson, R. Concluding statement: linguistics and poetics. In T. A. Sebeok (Ed.), *Style in language.* Cambridge, Mass.: M.I.T. Press and New York: Wiley, 1960.

Jakobson, R. The path from infancy to language. Heinz Werner Memorial Lectures. Clark University, 1969.

Jakobson, R., Fant, C. G. M., and Halle, M. *Preliminaries to speech analysis: The distinctive features and their correlates.* Cambridge, Mass.: M.I.T. Press, 1963.

Jakobson, R., and Halle, M. *Fundamentals of language.* The Hague: Mouton, 1956.

James, W. *Psychology, the briefer course.* New York: Holt, 1893.

Jesperson, O. *Language.* New York: Holt, 1925.

Johnson, N. F. Sequential verbal behavior. In T. Dixon and D. Horton (Eds.), *Verbal behavior and general behavior theory.* Englewood Cliffs, N.J.: Prentice-Hall, 1968. Pp. 421–440.

Katz, J. J. Mentalism in linguistics. *Language,* 1964, **40,** 124–137.

Katz, J. J. *The philosophy of language.* New York: Harper & Row, 1966.

Katz, J. J. Recent issues in semantic theory. *Found. Lang.,* 1967, **3,** 124–194.

Katz, J. J., and Fodor, J. A. The structure of semantic theory. *Language,* 1963, **39,** 170–210.

Katz, J. J., and Postal, P. *An integrated theory of linguistic descriptions.* Cambridge, Mass.: M.I.T. Press, 1964.

Kelley, K. L. Early syntactic acquisition. RAND Corporation Rept. No. P-3719, 1967.

Kellogg, W. N., and Kellogg, L. A. *The ape and the child: A study of environmental influence upon early behavior.* New York: McGraw-Hill, 1933.

Kernan, K. T. *The acquisition of language by Samoan children.* Univ. Calif. Berkeley, Lang. Behav. Res. Lab., Paper No. 21, 1969.

Kimura, Dorcen. Cerebral dominance and the perception of verbal stimuli. *Canad. J. Psychol.,* 1961, **15,** 166–171.

Kimura, Doreen. Left-right differences in the perception of melodies. *Quart. J. exptl. Psychol.,* 1964, **14,** 355–358.

Klima, E. S. Negation in English. In J. J. Fodor and J. A. Katz (Eds.), *The structure of language.* Englewood Cliffs, N.J.: Prentice-Hall, 1964. Pp. 246–323.

Klima, E. S. Knowing language and getting to know it. In E. M. Zale (Ed.), *Language and language behavior.* New York: Appleton-Century-Crofts, 1968. Pp. 36–50.

Klima, E. S., and Bellugi, Ursula. Syntactic regularities in the speech of children. In J. Lyons and R. Wales (Eds.), *Psycholinguistics papers.* Edinburgh: Edinburgh Univ. Press, 1966. Pp. 183–207.

Labov, W. Social factors in learning standard English. In R. W. Shuy (Ed.), *Social dialects and language learning.* Champaign, Ill.: Nat. Coun. Teachers Engl., 1964. Pp. 77–103.

de Laguna, Grace, A. *Speech: Its function and development.* New Haven, Conn.: Yale Univ. Press, 1927.

Lakoff, G. On the nature of syntactic irregularity. Computation laboratory of Harvard University, Rept. No. NSF-16, 1965.

Lakoff, G. Instrumental adverbs and the concept of deep structure. *Found. Lang.,* 1968, **4,** 4–29.

Lee, Laura L., and Ando, Kyoko. Language acquisition and language disorder in Japanese. Unpubl. paper, Northwestern University, n.d.

Lees, R. B. *The grammar of English nominalizations.* Indiana Univ. Publ. in Anthro. and Ling., Memoir 12, 1960.

Lees, R. B. Discussion of Brown and Fraser's, and Brown, Fraser, and Bellugi's papers. In Ursula Bellugi and R. Brown (Eds.), The acquisition of language. *Monogr. Soc. Res. Child Developm.,* 1964, **29** (No. 92), 92–97.

Lenneberg, E. H. *Biological foundations of language.* New York: Wiley, 1967.

Lenneberg, E. H., Nichols, Irene A., and Rosenberger, Eleanor F. Primitive stages of language development in mongolism. *Proc. Assoc. Res. nerv. ment. Disease,* 1964, **42,** 119–137.

Leopold, W. F. *Speech development of a bilingual child: A linguist's record.* Vol. 1. *Vocabulary growth in the first two years.* Vol. 2. *Sound learning in the first two years.* Vol. 3. *Grammar and general problems in the first two years.* Vol. 4. *Diary from age 2.* Evanston, Ill.: Northwestern Univ. Press, 1939, 1947, 1949 (a), 1949 (b).

Liberman, A. M., Cooper, F. S., Shankweiler, D. P., and Studdert-Kennedy, M. Perception of the speech code. *Psychol. Rev.,* 1967, **74,** 431–461.

Lindauer, M. *Communication among social bees.* Cambridge, Mass.: Harvard Univ. Press, 1961.

Lissmann, H. W. Continuous electrical signals from the tail of a fish, *Gymnarchns niloticus. Nature,* 1951, **167,** 201–202.

Lissmann, H. W. On the function and evolution of electric organs in fish. *J. exptl. Biol.,* 1958, **35,** 156–141.

Lloyd, J. E. Studies in the flash communication system in Photinus fire-flies. *Misc. publ., Mus. Zool., Univ. Mich.,* No. 130, Ann Arbor, 1966.

Lovell, K. Some recent studies in cognitive and language development. *Merrill-Palmer Quart.,* 1968, **14,** 123–138.

Lovell, K., and Dixon, E. M. The growth of the control of grammar in imitation, comprehension and production. *J. child Psychol. Psychiat.,* 1967, **8,** 31–39.

Luria, A. R. The directive function of speech in development and dissolution. *Word,* 1959, **15,** 341–352. (Reprinted in R. C. Anderson and D. P. Ausubel (Eds.), *Readings in the psychology of cognition.* New York: Holt, Rinehart, and Winston, 1965.)

Luria, A. R. *The role of speech in the regulation of normal and abnormal behavior.* New York: Liveright, 1961.

Marler, P. Developments in the study of animal communication. In P. R. Bell (Ed.), *Darwin's biological work.* Cambridge: Cambridge Univ. Press, 1959. Pp. 150–206.

Marler, P. Communication in monkeys and apes. In I. De Vore (Ed.), *Primate behavior.* New York: Holt, Rinehart, and Winston, 1965. Pp. 544–584.

Marler, P. Animal communication signals. *Science,* 1967, **157,** 769–774.

Marler, P., and Hamilton, W. J. *Mechanisms of animal behavior.* New York: Wiley, 1966.

McCarthy, Dorothea. Language development in children. In L. Carmichael (Ed.), *Manual of child psychology.* New York: Wiley, 1954. Pp. 492–630.

McCawley, J. Concerning the base component of a transformational grammar. *Found. Lang.,* 1968, **4,** 243–269.

McMahon, L. E. Grammatical analysis as part of understanding a sentence. Unpubl. Doctoral Dissertation, Harvard University, 1963.

McNeill, D. The psychology of "you" and "I." Paper read at Amer. Psychol. Assn., 1963.

McNeill, D. Development of the semantic system. Unpubl. paper, Harvard University, Center for Cognitive Studies, 1965.

McNeill, D. Developmental psycholinguistics. In F. Smith and G. A. Miller (Eds.), *The genesis of language: A psycholinguistic approach.* Cambridge, Mass.: M.I.T. Press, 1966. Pp. 15–84. (a).

McNeill, D. The creation of language by children. In J. Lyons and R. Wales (Eds.), *Psycholinguistics papers.* Edinburgh: Edinburgh Univ. Press, 1966. Pp. 99–114. (b)

McNeill, D. Some universals of language acquisition. In H. Lane (Ed.), *Studies of language and language behavior. Centr. Res. Lang. Lang. Behav.,* Rept. No. 2, 1966, Group B. (c)

McNeill, D. A study of word association. *J. verb. Learn. verb. Behav.,* 1966, **5,** 548–557. (d)

McNeill, D. On theories of language acquisition. In T. Dixon and D. Horton (Eds.), *Verbal behavior and general behavior theory.* Englewood Cliffs, N.J.: Prentice-Hall, 1968. Pp. 406–420. (a)

McNeill, D. Two problems for cognitive psychologists. Problem I: Predication. Center for Cognitive Studies Colloquium, Harvard University, 1968. (b)

McNeill, D. Production and perception: The view from language. In D. Olson and Susan M. Pagliuso (Eds.), *From perceiving to performing: An aspect of cognitive growth. Ont. J. Educ. Res.,* 1968, **10,** 181–185. (c)

McNeill, D. Empiricist and nativist theories of Language: George Berkeley and Samuel Bailey in the twentieth century. In A. Koestler and J. R. Smythies (Eds.), *Beyond reductionism.* London: Hutchinson, 1969. Pp. 279–308.

McNeill, D. The capacity for grammatical development in children. In D. I. Slobin (Ed.), *The ontogenesis of grammar in children.* New York: Academic Press, in press.

McNeill, D., and McNeill, Nobuko B. What does a child mean when he says "no"? In E. M. Zale (Ed.), *Language and language behavior.* New York: Appleton-Century-Crofts, 1968. Pp. 51–62.

Mehler, J. Some effects of grammatical transformations on the recall of English sentences. *J. verb. Learn. verb. Behav.,* 1963, **2,** 346–351.

Menyuk, Paula. A preliminary evaluation of grammatical capacity in children. *J. verb. Learn. verb. Behav.,* 1963, **2,** 429–439.

Menyuk, Paula. Alternation of rules in children's grammar. *J. verb. Learn. verb. Behav.,* 1964, **3,** 480–488. (a)

Menyuk, Paula. Syntactic rules used by children from preschool through first grade. *Child Development,* 1964, **35,** 533–546. (b)

Menyuk, Paula. Comparison of grammar of children with functionally deviant and normal speech. *J. speech hearing Disorders,* 1964, **7,** 109–121. (c)

Menyuk, Paula. Children's learning and recall of grammatical and nongrammatical phonological sequences. Paper read at Soc. Res. Child Developm., March, 1967. (a)

Menyuk, Paula. Acquisition of grammar by children. In K. Salzinger and Suzanne Salzinger (Eds.), *Research in verbal behavior and some neurophysiological implications.* New York: Academic Press, 1967. Pp. 101–110. (b)

Menyuk, Paula. Children's grammatical capacity. In T. G. Bever and W. Weksel (Eds.), *The structure and psychology of language.* New York: Holt, Rinehart, and Winston, in press.

Messer, S. Implicit phonology in children. *J. verb. Learn. verb. Behav.,* 1967, **6,** 609–613.

Meumann, E. *Die Sprache des Kindes.* Zurich: Zurcher and Furrer, 1894.

Miller, G. A. Some psychological studies of grammar. *Amer. J. Psychol.,* 1962, **17,** 748–762.

Miller, G. A. Psycholinguistic approaches to the study of communication. In Arm, D. L. (Ed.), *Journeys in science: Small steps—great strides.* Albuquerque: Univ. New Mexico Press, 1967. Pp. 22–73.

Miller, G. A. Personal communication, 1968.

Miller, G. A., and Chomsky, N. A. Finitary models of language users. In R. D. Luce, R. R. Bush, and E. Galanter (Eds.), *Handbook of mathematical psychology.* Vol. 2. New York: Wiley, 1963. Pp. 419–492.

Miller, G. A., and Isard, S. Some perceptual consequences of linguistic rules. *J. verb. Learn. verb. Behav.,* 1963, **2,** 217–228.

Miller, G. A., and Isard, S. Free recall of self-embedded English sentences. *Inform. and control,* 1964, **7,** 292–303.

Miller, G. A., and McKean, Katherine O. A chronometric study of some relations between sentences. *Quart. J. exptl. Psychol.,* 1964, **16,** 297–308.

Miller, G. A., and McNeill, D. Psycholinguistics. In G. Lindzey and E. Aaronson (Eds.), *Handbook of social psychology,* Vol. 3. Reading, Mass.: Addison Wesley, 1968. Pp. 666–794.

Miller, W., and Ervin, Susan. The development of grammar in child language. In Ursula Bellugi and R. Brown (Eds.), The acquisition of language. *Monogr. Soc. Res. Child Developm.,* 1964, **29** (No. 92). Pp. 9–34.

Mitchell-Kernan, Claudia. *Language behavior in a black urban community.* Univ. Calif. Berkeley, Lang. Behav. Res. Lab., Paper No. 23, 1969.

Mowrer, O. H. The psychologist looks at language. *Amer. J. Psychol.,* 1954, **9,** 660–694.

Olson, D., and Pagliuso, Susan M. (Eds.). *From perceiving to performing: An aspect of cognitive growth. Ont. J. Educ. Res.,* 1968, **10** (3).

Osgood, C. E. Towards a wedding of insufficiencies. In T. Dixon and D. Horton (Eds.), *Verbal behavior and general behavior theory,* Englewood Cliffs, N.J.: Prentice-Hall, 1968. Pp. 495–520.

Piaget, J. *The language and thought of the child.* New York: Harcourt, Brace, 1926.

Piaget, J. *The origins of intelligence in children.* New York: International University Press, 1952.

Piaget, J. Review of "Studies in cognitive growth" by J. S. Bruner, Rose Olver, and Patricia M. Greenfield. *Contemp. Psychol.,* 1967, **12,** 532–533.

Piaget, J., and Inhelder, Bärbel. *La psychologie de l'enfant.* Presses Universitaires de France, 1966. (English by H. Weaver, *The psychology of the child.* New York: Basic Books, 1969.)

Pittenger, R. E., Hockett, C. F., and Danehy, J. J. *The first five minutes: A sample of microscopic interview analysis.* Ithaca, N.Y.: Martineau, 1960.

Preston, M. S., Yeni-Komishian, Grace, and Stark, Rachel E. Voicing in initial step consonants produced by children in the prelinguistic period from different language communities. *Annual Report Neurocommunications Laboratory.* The Johns Hopkins Hosp., 1967.

Psotka, J. Computation rate and memory in comprehension and production. Unpubl. paper, Dept. Psychology, Harvard University, 1969.

Quine, W. V. *Word and object.* Cambridge, Mass.: M.I.T. Press, 1960.

Rice, U. M., and di Vesta, F. J. A developmental study of semantic and phonetic generalization in paired-associate learning. *Child Development,* 1965, **36,** 721–730.

Riegel, K. F. The Michigan restricted association norms. *Univ. Mich. Dept. Psychol. Rept.* No. 3, 1965. (a)

Riegel, K. F. Free associative responses to the 200 stimuli of the Michigan restricted association norms. *Univ. Mich. Dept. Psychol. Rept.* No. 8, 1965. (b)

Riegel, K. F., and Feldman, Carol F. The recall of high and low meaningful sentences generated from the Michigan restricted association norms. *Univ. Mich. Lang. Developm. Program Rept.* No. 37, 1967.

Riegel, K. F., and Zivian, W. M. A study of inter- and intra-lingual associations in English and German. *Univ. Mich. Lang. Developm. Program Rept.* No. 15, 1967.

Rosenbaum, P. *The grammar of English predicate complement constructions.* Cambridge, Mass.: M.I.T. Press, 1967.

Ross, J. R. Gapping and the order of constituents. Paper presented at the 10th International Congress of Linguists, Bucharest, 1967.

Rowell, T. E. Agonistic noises of the rhesus monkey (*Macaca mulatta*). *Symp. Zool. Soc. London,* 1962, **8,** 91–96.

Rowell, T. E., and Hinde, R. A. Vocal communication by the rhesus monkey (*Macaca mulatta*). *Proc. Zool. Soc. London,* 1962, **138,** 279–294.

Ruwet, N. La constituent "auxillaire" en française moderne. *Language,* 1966, **4,** 105–122.

de Saussure, F. *Cours de linguistique generale.* Paris: 1916 (English trans. by W. Baskin, *Course in general linguistics.* New York: Phil. Lib., 1959).

Savin, H., and Perchonock, Ellen. Grammatical structure and the immediate recall of English sentences. *J. verb. Learn. verb. Behav.,* 1965, **4,** 348–353.

Schenkel, R. Ausdruckstudien an Wölfen. *Behavior,* 1947, **1,** 81–129.

Schlesinger, I. M. Production of utterance and language acquisition. In D. I. Slobin (Ed.), *The ontogenesis of grammar: Facts and theories.* New York: Academic Press, in press.

Schultz, A. H. Postembryonic age changes. In H. Hoffer, A. H. Schultz, and D. Starck (Eds.), *Primatologia: Handbook of primatology.* Vol. 1. Basel: S. Karger, 1956. Pp. 887–964.

Shankweiler, D. P. Some correlates of performance in dichotic perceptual tasks. Paper presented at a conference on the perception of speech. Univ. Pittsburgh, 1968.

Shankweiler, D. P., and Studdert-Kennedy, M. Lateral differences in perception of dichotically presented synthetic consonant-vowel syllables and steady-state vowels. *J. acoust. Soc. Amer.,* 1966, **39,** 1966.

Shankweiler, D. P., and Studdert-Kennedy, M. Identification of consonants and vowels presented to left and right ears. *Quart. J. exptl. Psychol.,* 1967, **19,** 59–63.

Shipley, Elizabeth Г., Smith, Carlota S., and Gleitman, Lila R. A study in the acquisition of language: Free responses to commands. *Eastern Pennsylvania Psychiatric Institute Tech. Rept.* No. 8, n.d.

Sinclair-de Zwart, Hermine. *Acquisition du langage et development de la pensee.* Paris: Dunod, 1967.

Sinclair-de Zwart, Hermine. Sensorimotor action schemes as a condition of the acquisition of syntax. Unpubl. paper, University of Geneva, 1968.

Slobin, D. I. Grammatical transformations in childhood and adulthood. Unpubl. Doctoral Dissertation, Harvard University, 1963.

Slobin, D. I. Imitation and the acquisition of syntax. Paper presented at Second Research Planning Conference of Project Literacy, 1964.

Slobin, D. I. Grammatical development in Russian-speaking children. In K. Riegel (Ed.), The development of language functions. *Univ. Mich. Lang. Developm. Program Rept.* No. 8, 1965.

Slobin, D. I. Comments on "Developmental psycholinguistics." In F. Smith and G. A. Miller (Eds.), *The genesis of language: A psycholinguistic approach.* Cambridge, Mass.: M.I.T. Press, 1966. Pp. 85–92. (a)

Slobin, D. I. The acquisition of Russian as a native language. In F. Smith and G. A. Miller (Eds.), *The genesis of language: A psycholinguistic approach.* Cambridge, Mass.: M.I.T. Press, 1966. Pp. 129–148. (b)

Slobin, D. I. Grammatical transformations and sentence comprehension in childhood and adulthood. *J. verb. Learn. verb. Behav.,* 1966, **5,** 219–227. (c)

Slobin, D. I. (Ed.). A field manual for cross-cultural study of the acquisition of communicative competence. Unpubl. paper, University Calif. (Berkeley), 1967.

Slobin, D. I. Imitation and grammatical development in children. In N. S. Endler, L. R. Boulter, and H. Osser (Eds.), *Contemporary issues in developmental psychology.* New York: Holt, Rinehart, and Winston, 1968. Pp. 437–443.

Slobin, D. I. Early grammatical development in several languages, with special attention to Soviet research. In T. G. Bever and W. Weksel (Eds.), *The structure and psychology of language.* New York: Holt, Rinehart, and Winston, in press.

Slobin, D. I., and Welsh, C. A. Elicited imitation as a research tool in developmental psycholinguistics. Unpubl. paper, Dept. Psychol., University Calif. (Berkeley), 1967.

Smith, J. The development and structure of holophrases. Unpubl. Honors Thesis, Dept. Linguistics, Harvard University, 1970.

Staats, A. W. Integrated-functional learning theory and language development. In D. I. Slobin (Ed.), *The ontogenesis of grammar: Facts and theories.* New York: Academic Press, in press.

Staats, A. W., and Staats, C. K. *Complex human behavior: A systematic extension of learning principles.* New York: Holt, Rinehart, and Winston, 1963.

Stern, Clara, and Stern, W. *Die Kindersprache.* Leipzig: Barth, 1907.

Stross, B. *Language acquisition by Tenejapa-Tzeltal children.* Univ. Calif. Berkeley, Lang. Behav. Res. Lab., Paper No. 20, 1969.

Thorpe, W. H. *Bird-song: Biology of vocal communication and expression in birds.* Cambridge: Cambridge Univ. Press, 1961.

Tinbergen, N. *The Herring Gull's World.* New York: Basic Books, 1961.

Trager, G. L. Paralanguage: A first approximation. *Studies in Linguistics,* 1958, **13,** 1–12.

Turbayne, C. M. (Ed.). *Works on Vision.* New York: Bobbs-Merrill, 1963.

Turner, Elizabeth A., and Rommetveit, R. The acquisition of sentence voice and reversibility. *Child Development,* 1967, **38,** 649–660.

Velten, H. V. The growth of phonemic and lexical pattern in infant language. *Language,* 1943, **19,** 281–292.

di Vesta, F. J. The distribution of modifiers used by children in a word association task. *J. verb. Learn. verb. Behav.,* 1964, **3,** 421–427. (a)

di Vesta, F. J. A simple analysis of changes with age in response to a restricted word-association task. *J. verb. Learn. verb. Behav.,* 1964, **3,** 505–510. (b)

di Vesta, F. J. Norms for modifiers used by children in a restricted word-association task: grades 2 through 6. *Psychol. Reps.,* 1966, **18,** 65–66. (a)

di Vesta, F. J. A normative study of 220 concepts rated on the semantic differential by children in grades 2 through 7. *J. genet. Psychol.,* 1966, **109,** 205–229. (b)

di Vesta, F. J. A developmental study of the semantic structure of children. *J. verb. Learn. verb. Behav.,* 1966, **5,** 249–259. (c)

di Vesta, F. J., and Dick, W. The test-retest reliability of children's ratings on the semantic differential. *Educ. Psychol. Mass.,* 1966, **26,** 605–616.

De Vore, I. *Primate Behavior: Field studies of monkeys and apes.* New York: Holt, Rinehart, and Winston, 1965.

Vygotsky, L. S. *Thought and language.* Trans. by Eugenia Hanfmann and Gertrude Vakar. Cambridge, Mass.: M.I.T. Press, 1962.

Wanner, H. E. On remembering, forgetting, and understanding sentences: A study of the deep structure hypothesis. Unpubl. Doctoral Dissertation, Harvard University, 1968.

Washburn, S. L., and Hamburg, D. A. The implications of primate research. In I. De Vore (Ed.), *Primate behavior.* New York: Holt, Rinehart, and Winston, 1965. Pp. 607–622.

Wason, P. C. The contexts of plausible denial. *J. verb. Learn. verb. Behav.,* 1965, **4,** 7–11.

Weinreich, U. On the semantic structure of language. In J. H. Greenberg (Ed.), *Universals of Language.* Cambridge, Mass.: M.I.T. Press, 1963. Pp. 114–171.

Weinreich, U. Explorations in semantic theory. In T. A. Sebeok (Ed.), *Current trends in linguistics,* Vol. 3. The Hague: Mouton, 1966. Pp. 395–474.

Weir, Ruth. *Language in the crib.* The Hague: Mouton, 1962.

Weir, Ruth. Some questions on the child's learning of phonology. In F. Smith and G. A. Miller (Eds.), *The genesis of language: A psycholinguistic approach.* Cambridge, Mass.: M.I.T. Press, 1966. Pp. 153–168.

Weksel, W. Review of "The acquisition of language," Ursula Bellugi and R. Brown (Eds.). *Language,* 1965, **41,** 692–709.

Wenner, A. M. Sound communication in honeybees. *Sci. Amer.,* 1964, **210** (4), 116–124.

Whorf, B. L. *Language, thought, and reality.* New York: Wiley, and Cambridge, Mass.: M.I.T. Press, 1956.

White, S. H. Evidence for a hierarchical arrangement of learning processes. In L. P. Lipsitt and C. C. Spiker (Eds.), *Advances in child development and behavior,* Vol. 2. New York: Academic Press, 1965. Pp. 187–216.

Wilson, O. E. Pheromones. *Sci. Amer.,* 1963, **208** (5), 100–114.

Wilson, O. E. Chemical communication in the social insects. *Science,* 1965, **149,** 1064–1071.

Yngve, V. A model and an hypothesis for language structure. *Proc. Amer. Phil. Soc.,* 1960, **104,** 444–466.

Yngve, V. The depth hypothesis. In R. Jakobson (Ed.), *Structure of language and its mathematical aspect: Proc. 12th Symp. in appl. Math.* Providence, R.I.: Am. Math. Soc., 1961. Pp. 130–138.

Zakharova, A. V. Usvoyeniye doshkol'nikami padezhnykh form. *Dolk. Akad. Pedag. Nauk RSFSR,* 1958, **2** (3), 81–84.

INDEX

Abstract ideas, 76
Abstraction, linguistic, 60–69, 151–152, 155–164
    See also Linguistic universals, Transformations
Anagrams, 104–105
Aphasia, 136, 139
Apposition of words, 67, 69
Arbitrariness of meaning, 77–79
Assimilation, *see* Filtering effect of grammar
Autonomy of child language, 93–95
Auxiliary verbs, 90, 92–93, 98, 158–160

Babbling, 130–133
Baby-talk of adults, 131
Bailey, S., 75
Bee communication, 49–51
Bellugi, Ursula, 7, 9, 10, 11, 12, 13, 16, 26, 27, 29, 33, 82, 83, 87, 88, 92, 93, 94, 95, 96, 97, 98, 99, 101, 102, 107, 108, 109, 110, 111
Berkeley, Bishop G., 75–79
Berkeley cross-cultural project, 14
Berko, Jean, 11, 119, 141
Bever, T. G., 7, 12, 68, 123, 130, 132, 133
Bird song, 43–49
Bloom, Lois, 7, 28, 61, 66, 88, 96
Braine, M. D. S., 7, 8, 12, 25, 26, 27, 67, 68, 74
Brown, R., 7, 8, 9, 10, 11, 12, 13, 16, 26, 27, 28, 29, 32, 33, 34, 36, 61, 87, 88, 96, 97, 98, 99, 101, 102, 107, 108, 109, 110, 111, 119
Bruner, J. S., 73, 114

Capacities, linguistic, 2, 58, 69, 72, 104

    See also Hypotheses, linguistic; Linguistic universals
Categorical perception of consonants, 140
Cazden, Courtney, 9, 27, 33, 87, 88, 94, 96, 98, 99, 108, 109, 110, 111
Chaffinch songs, 46–48
Chomsky, Carol S., 99, 104
Chomsky, N. A., 9, 59, 60, 62, 63, 70, 71, 73, 77, 133, 141, 145, 146, 150, 155, 156, 157, 161, 163, 164
Cicada songs, 48–49
Classification of animal communication, 39
Cognition and language, 72–75
Cognitive development, 72–75, 114
Combination of words, 26–28, 61–69
Combinatorial communication systems, 38–39
Competence, 8, 145–148
    See also Capacities, linguistic; Grammars; Grammatical relations; Linguistic universals
Comprehension of speech, methods for studying, 11–14; superior to production, 101–102
Contextual generalization, 68–69
Correct and justified assertion, 76–77
Critical periods, 104, 139–140

Deep structure, 155–164
    See also Linguistic universals; Transformations
Dichotic listening experiments, 139–140
Differentiation of grammatical classes, 58–60, 63
Discourse restrictions, 96–97
Distinctive (phonological) features, 133–136

INDEX OF REPRESENTATIVE EXAMPLES

Designed by Michel Craig
Set in Trade Gothic
Composed, printed and bound by Quinn & Boden Company, Inc.

73   11 10 9 8 7 6 5 4 3